Adventures of a
METALHEAD
Librarian

A Rock n'Roll Memoir

By Anna-Marie O'Brien

Tempe, Arizona
2019

Copyright © 2019 by Anna-Marie O'Brien

All rights reserved. No part of this book may be reproduced or used in any manner without written permission of the copyright owner except for the use of quotations in a book review. For more information, contact me: annamarieobrien@gmail.com.

First paperback edition August 2019

Book Cover design by Blanca Villapudua

Photos © by Anna-Marie O'Brien

ISBN 978-1-7332470-0-9 (paperback)

ISBN 978-1-7332470-1-6 (ebook)

www.annamarieobrien.com

Author's note

This is a true story, and everything happened. To write this book, I relied on my personal journals, ticket stubs and scrapbooks, cards and letters that I sent and received. In addition to my own archives, my mom and my good friends saved much of my correspondence. I consulted with many people to clarify and ask questions. I researched to confirm that my timelines are correct. My own memory serves as my greatest source, but it is not perfect. I have changed the names of some people in order to preserve their anonymity. There are no composite characters or events in the book. I occasionally omitted people and events, but only when that omission had no impact on the truth or the substance of the story.

—AMO

1989

Foreword

Sunday night, October 6, 1991, we found ourselves in the same room witnessing history; a seemingly parallel universe - but we never met that night. Anna-Marie was a bold, barely-20-year-old book-loving metalhead, and I was a thirty-something magazine editor, playing host to a gallery of soon-to-be-legends at THE rock n' roll party of the year.

I was in the eye of a Hollywood hurricane that night. The storied Palladium on Sunset Boulevard was packed to its chandeliered rafters with four-thousand fans, guests, goblins and ghouls, gathered to celebrate the 5th anniversary of *Rip Magazine*, my rag, the era's most-read and respected bible of bang, the monthly pulp non-fiction that parents cringed from while their metal-loving spawn perused the pages of a *Hustler Publications* pet-project.

The party, dubbed in its wake 'The Seattle Soiree" by tongue-wagging insiders and fortunate onlookers, was stuff of music legend. The bill that night included Pearl Jam, Alice in Chains (with GN'R's Duff McKagan joining his northwest neighbors on bass), Soundgarden, Spinal Tap (with axe wizard Joe Satriani taking the leads on their comedic classic, "Big Bottom"), and the only full Temple of the Dog set ever performed live. Say Hello to concert Heaven? Hell yeah.

As the event's emcee, my walkie-talkie was buzzing nonstop. Industry folk were piling up at the back door trying to charm their way in, while the *Rip* staff kept their eyes peeled for special guests like our esteemed, gold-plated publisher Larry Flynt, as well as several cast members from the eccentric hit TV show, *Twin Peaks*. I dated actress Kimmy Robertson - the 'donut girl - in the early '80s. She dumped me for guitarist Bob Mothersbaugh after a Devo concert. Drove home alone that night. But, this isn't about me.

While shooting a quick three-minute on-the-fly interview segment with Eddie, Chris and Layne for my weekly MTV Headbanger's Ball segment, *Friend at Large*, elsewhere in the writhing, grunge-engorged madness, Anna-Marie was having the time of her rapidly changing life. Working at Metal Blade Records, she was a hard-rock loving *Rip* devotee from Columbus, Ohio who showed up in Los Angeles looking for a different life. She'd seen a great deal in her tender, torrid years, bookish and shy, but she had bravely bolted the boring confines of her Midwest 'ville the previous season. She'd wanted to witness the great metallic Mötley myth being writ on streets of tinsel town. And boy, did she ever.

Any memoir worth its salt must bubble in the wounds it opens and expose the lessons it leeches. If you're expecting a one-dimensional heavy-metal journal that glorifies the debauched decade that I faithfully and consciously chronicled from the eye of the leather and fishnet hurricane, think again. Even the deepest Dokken ballad can't touch the depth of soul-mining Anna-Marie undertakes over the next 200 pages. She paints with bold, broad, badass strokes. Take this description of her suburban Buckeyelandia public housing: "My new neighborhood was incredibly diverse; had diabetics, cerebral palsy, drug addicts, giant birthmarks, a cleft-palette, a quadriplegic, the elderly, rampant obesity, a rumored former mobster…" sounds like the Starbucks down the block from my Henderson apartment complex. Ain't no candles in the winds blowing through that joint.

Columbus sucked. She had to get out. Find herself. Get real and righteous, and not to mention, badass. Music was a way for her to release her pent-up frustrations without being too self-destructive. Metal reflected her anger. "You're gonna call my dad and straighten me out!?" she spits to her mom during one epic fight. "Fuck you!!" She almost choked on her venom, she describes - which is far better than choking on your vomit, like Bon Scott or John Bonham, or Mama Cass Elliot, who by the way, died on my 18th birthday. But, this isn't about me. Anna-Marie's story is cinematic. I see Natalie Portman playing the Metalhead Librarian in the film adaptation. And killing it!

In a different universe, Anna-Marie would have written for *Rip Magazine*.

What we have here are the adventures and confessions of a survivor who relocates, reinvents and rediscovers her calling – to work with books and to protect free-speech, and to engagingly pen and chronicle the escapades that informed and influenced this Iron Midwest Maiden's journey. The hook of this book screams off the page like a Halford howl - not only is she a metalhead, she's a fucking librarian! The PMRC's worst nightmare. The metal-muse between the stacks, literate, intelligent, and lovely.

I didn't know her back then, but I sure do know her now.

Instagram united us a year ago. I fired off a series of *Music Man* movie references, email fast talk, Harold Hill style. I called her Marian, the innocent, honest and gorgeous leading lady portrayed in the film by pre-Partridge Family babe, Shirley Jones. In fact, I still call her Marian. While introducing her to a photographer friend of mine in Tempe recently, started to say, "This is Mari – uh, Anna-Marie."

That same day in Tempe, I turned Anna-Marie into a Lana del Rey fan. It wasn't hard because this girl 'gets' great music, regardless of genre. "Life rocked me, like Mötley, pulled me by the ribbons in my hair/Life rocked me, all too softly, like the heavy metal that you wear." The track, "Heroin" resonated intense and immediate with the former-teenager who once longed to be Nikki Sixx's muse. As such, the chapter themes of this book are titles of Crüe songs, in tribute. I've still got the voice mail message Nikki Sixx left me the day his son, Gunner, was born.

Adventures of a Metalhead Librarian is the tale of an *Almost Famous* Band Aid, a savage, sincere stroll up and down Penny Lane. More poetic than prurient, this was not easy material for her to excavate. I've carried the memoir cross twice and am so buried in notes, docs, fatigue and terror, I cannot guarantee there will ever be a third. But like I've said, this isn't about me. It's about Anna-Marie, my Marian, rockin' madame librarian, and her awesome debut.

Did I mention that *Hustler* magazine started in Columbus, Ohio?

Oh yeah, we've also got this crazy synchronicity thing going.

Lonn M. Friend
Henderson, Nevada

Adventures of a METALHEAD Librarian

A Rock n'Roll Memoir

1.0

[In the Beginning]

Day One
June 2, 1990, Los Angeles.

The green gate lurched open, as if by magic, before I could even type in the code. I was standing on the side of the road, deep in Laurel Canyon, as cars whizzed by just a few feet behind me. This was my first Hollywood security gate, and I wasn't sure what the hell was happening.

"Who da fuck are you?" A small, tan man stood on the other side of the opening gate, peering at me with a dark eagle eye. He had a blond ponytail and was wearing tattered shorts with a sweat-stained wife-beater. He clutched a clear tumbler with what looked like orange soda in it. There was also a tall, long haired guy standing there, who seemed to be just leaving; then, I understood why the gate had opened at that very moment.

"I'm Stacy's friend? She gave me the code," I said, looking him directly in the eye.

He grunted and nodded at me to enter.

Just as the tall guy was leaving, Stacy emerged from the garage-top apartment nestled in the trees, and came down the wooden steps. She'd been waiting for me. She had long, silky, light brown hair almost to her butt, sparkling green eyes, and a husky voice. She greeted me warmly and with a hug.

"You made it! So good to see you!" she said.

When we'd talked on the phone a couple of days before, she'd told me that her landlord could be paranoid with who was coming to the house, so we played along like we were friends and really knew each other, but I'd never met her before in my life.

She introduced me to the man, Mario, the landlord. He was friendly enough and pecked around, moving a few things and watering plants. After a few moments, Stacy pulled a joint out of her pocket.

"Do you partake?" she asked in a low voice.

I nodded yes and smiled.

She called over, "Mario, do you mind if we toke?"

"Nah, sweetie, you go ahead."

Right on, I thought to myself.

Mario pulled out some battered green and white lawn chairs for us right under a giant eucalyptus tree. Stacy lit the joint, took a good pull, and passed it to me. I was grateful for this friendly welcome, from strangers, no less.

It was just a happy coincidence that we had hit it off on the phone when I'd called a few days before, trying to track down Kenny, a-friend-of-a friend. Stacy was Kenny's roommate, except that he had moved out a couple of weeks prior.

Stacy was cool, though, and we'd ended up chatting on the phone for a few minutes. I had told her I'd been wanting to come down to LA to find an apartment and a roommate. She didn't hesitate, and graciously invited me to come hang out with her in Los Angeles to see the city for a few days and scope it out. I was stoked at the invite, and we made a plan.

Mario eyeballed me as he pecked, and we smoked. He was kind of cute, but he was older. Maybe older than my dad. It dawned on me that Mario was Italian, and I thought it was good that we had something in common. Stacy and I passed the joint and chatted about our mutual friends-of-friends, Kenny, her former roommate, and my friend Anne, both from Cleveland. Kenny was in a band called Pretty Vacant, and they had just left for a tour.

Within 15 minutes of my arrival in Los Angeles, I was smoking a fatty in beautiful Laurel Canyon, the canyon of myth, legend and lore. In terms of musical importance and history, I knew exactly where I'd landed. It felt like a dream, a green-dappled and breezy canyon fairy tale. Out of time and space, a vortex of déjà vu. I breathed in the California air, thought of Miss Pamela and Frank Zappa and Jim Morrison and Joni Mitchell, enjoying hit after hit of the awesome joint with Stacy.

Right on cue, though, just as my stony kicked in, my stomach started growling loudly. I laughed and mentioned it; Stacy said she hadn't eaten, either, and we decided to go grab some lunch.

"Mario, we're going down to get a bite. Do you want anything?" Stacy called over to him. He had hedge clippers in one hand, the drink still in the other. I assumed *down* meant down the hill, out of the Canyon, back into the city.

Mario walked over, reminding me of a little rooster. "Nah, honey, I'm good. I'm thinking about going down to the club tonight for supper." He looked directly at me. "You girls wanna join me? Your first night in town?"

"Sure, that would be fun," Stacy said, and we looked at each other and nodded. "You want me to drive?"

"Yeah, that's great. How 'bout 8:30?" Mario said. "I'll call ahead so Pops knows we're coming."

"Sounds good, Mario, we'll see you then."

***

Stacy came out with me to my car to grab my bag, and we went up to the tiny garage-top apartment that she rented from Mario. It had a futon, a kitchenette, a lofted bedroom big enough for a queen mattress, and a small bathroom. Maybe 150 square feet. Aside from a tiny slider in the bed area, the only real window in the place was a sliding glass door, overlooking Laurel Canyon Boulevard. It had no screen, so the door was either wide open to the Canyon traffic just below us, with all the noise, smog, and bugs, or it was closed up, making it stuffy in the apartment.

We took a few minutes to get me settled in, then we went back down to the cars. Stacy's ride was an old black Trans-Am with gold stripes. It looked like a proper LA car and had a T-top, much cooler than my plain, rough Corolla. Mario didn't drive much, so Stacy would help him out and give him rides. She explained all this as she pulled a wicked U-turn right in the middle of Laurel Canyon traffic, pointing the car back south and down to Hollywood. I gripped the door handle and held on for my life and said *"Oh my God"* in mock terror as we both laughed out loud. She was fun, and having her do the driving was great. I'd been in the car all day, but now I could gawk at everything without distraction.

We veered left, back onto Hollywood Boulevard.

As we passed a newer apartment building a few blocks down, Stacy mentioned that the London Quireboys had been staying there, and that she knew their singer pretty well. She'd been hanging out with them the last time they were in town.

My skin prickled when she mentioned the band's name, and I decided to tell her about my friend who'd died in a horrible car accident driving home from a Quireboys show.

"…like, no shit, just last week, in Columbus. Tomorrow is his funeral. Kinda spooky, huh?" My eyes opened wide as I explained the connection.

"That is kind of spooky…like, *really* spooky!" Stacy agreed with me. Of all the bands to mention.

I was super bummed that I couldn't be in Ohio for his funeral. He was the last person I'd said goodbye to in Columbus two weeks ago, and he died the day I arrived to my aunt's house in San Jose last week.

If my friend hadn't died after that London Quireboys show, I wouldn't have been compelled to make the phone call looking for Kenny. I'd planned on living with my aunt for the summer, taking my time to figure things out, to reach out to people to make some connections down in LA. But it had all come together so quickly, and here I was, in LA, much quicker than I'd ever thought I'd be when I left Ohio just two weeks ago.

As we made our way out of the Canyon, I wondered if my friend was sending me a sign. He was such a good guy, and he'd wanted to come to LA, too, someday.

Oh David, I'm so sorry you're gone.

***

I was overwhelmed by the beauty, the architecture, the greenery of Hollywood. My childhood had been spent in a gray, flat, Midwestern landscape, with an occasional summer trip to the shores of Lake Erie. I'd never travelled anywhere, really, and Hollywood was resplendent in June, nectar to the eyes. The Roosevelt Hotel, The Chinese Theater, all the old buildings, the iron lamp posts. The hills, the trees, the flowers. It was sensory overload.

We found a parking spot right on Hollywood Boulevard. The balmy air was humid, sparkling, warm, and wonderful. I'd never felt air like this before. The street was teeming with humanity. It was seedy and gritty and old school, and it was all absolutely mind-blowing. It was better in person than I'd ever imagined it.

We didn't have any lunch ideas, figuring we'd find something as we wandered around. As we crossed the street at Highland, Stacy said, "Hey, how about this old place? I forgot this was here. It's a classic."

The Snow White Cafe. It was a little dive of a place, with antique Disney decor and old men drinking at the bar, but it had large open-air windows looking right out onto the Boulevard. It was a great low-key place to sit for a bit and people watch, and it was pretty cheap.

We took a small table back near the bar, with a good view. They offered a simple menu, so I ordered a burger, fries, and a cup of coffee. Stacy ordered the exact same thing.

Stacy and I drank our coffee as we waited for our food and got to know each other. Although we had talked on the phone only once, she felt like an old friend. She was from New Jersey and had been in LA for about a year. She was a singer looking for a bluesy rock band, and knowing a lot of people on the scene, she had some fun stories about the local rockers.

I told her I thought it was nice that Mario, the landlord, had invited us out for dinner later. He seemed like a cool guy. I asked her if she knew where we were going.

"Oh, we're going to The Rainbow. They serve great Italian food," she said.

"That's awesome! My first night in town and I get to go The Rainbow!" I clapped my hands in excitement and sat back in my chair. It couldn't be more perfect. I knew about the storied history of The Rainbow Bar & Grill from all the books and magazine articles I'd read on rock music over the years. Led Zeppelin, John Lennon, Alice Cooper, the guys in Mötley Crüe, Guns N' Roses, and Ratt all hung out there. It was ground zero for the LA music scene, and I was stoked.

Then, Stacy paused and said, "I should probably clue you in about Mario, too." She leaned in closer.

"Here's the deal. Mario is Mario Maglieri, Jr. His family owns The Rainbow."

I blinked at her. *WHAT THE FUCK*, I thought to myself. The sheer luck of it staggered me.

"You're kidding me," I said, my eyes opening wide. My brain could hardly process.

She shook her head. "Nope, his family runs the Whiskey and they have interests in the Roxy, too." she said. I was already familiar with the Maglieri name, knew they were from Chicago. She filled me in some more.

"Wow. All right. Very cool." I let it all sink in. I nodded at her. She grinned and nodded back. "Wow," I said again. I almost wanted to cry. I couldn't fucking believe my luck.

"Yep," she said, smiling.

I thought of Pamela Des Barres and Jimmy Page, John Lennon and George Harrison, Frank Zappa and Jim Morrison and the movie, *The Decline of Western Civilization Part II, The Metal Years*. Mötley Crüe's Nikki Sixx ran through my mind with Ratt, Guns N' Roses, RIP Magazine, and the Sunset Strip, and just…ALL of it. Every last damn thing that had inspired me to move to Los Angeles.

I was eighteen years old, and I'd literally landed right in the middle of it.

All of a sudden, my first day in Los Angeles was turning into quite an adventure.

***

After our lunch at the Snow White, we drove up Highland to Cahuenga, made a sharp left onto Mulholland, and climbed into the Hollywood Hills. She drove up to the lookout and we parked and got out to walk around with a busload of Japanese tourists. The skies were clear of smog, and the city seemed to sparkle in the warm breeze, glittering in the heat. I marveled at all of it, got a real lay of the land.

I wondered at how these houses around here were built, so many tucked and perched on stilts, draping the hills and canyons, like boxes on toothpicks. The Hollywood sign was to my left a mountain over, downtown Los Angeles perfectly centered on the horizon, and the historic Hollywood Bowl was just below us.

It was all so beautiful, this magnificent city. I felt like I was upon the back of a giant, green, undulating beast. It buzzed with energy under my feet. I could almost feel it breathing. It was vast, the expanse of it all. So many people, so alive. I couldn't believe I was actually here. *I am finally here. I'm here. I'm here.*

I thought of Ohio, and the shitty situation I had left behind with my mom. I was so grateful to be away from all the drama and bullshit. I thought back to my first Mötley Crüe show, at an outdoor venue, devotedly enduring the mud and chaos, and my first Guns N' Roses concert just two years ago—the show that changed my life. After that show, I knew for sure I'd be moving to Los Angeles, somehow, some way. I knew it in my gut, in my bones. I was going to make it happen.

I did it. I'm finally here. I really fucking did it.

I called to the Universe in thanks at all the magic that had transpired so far, and I got teary for a minute, facing south into the afternoon sun, Los Angeles at my feet. I closed my eyes. I was overwhelmed with gratitude at how it had all worked out, that I was here. I stood silent for a few minutes, letting the California sunshine soak into my very cells, and I thought of my friend, David. It felt like he was there with me, for that moment, just a flash.

I looked at Stacy with wet eyes and a smile.

"I did the exact same thing when I got here. Isn't this an amazing view?" she asked.

"It's perfect. It's beautiful. I can't believe I'm here. I feel like I'm dreaming."

She smiled back. "Nope, you're really here. And it's *all* for real."

***

After the lookout, we headed west on Mulholland to the top of Laurel Canyon, turned left, and drove down the hill, where she pointed out Frank Zappa's old place that had burnt down and the crumbling remains of the Houdini Mansion near it, perched upon the hill like a gothic Poe character, covered in vines. The canyon walls were steep, and the wild green lushness of it was staggering to the eye. We drove past Mario's house and straight down to the Canyon Country Store, where she pointed out the Jim Morrison house.

Fuck me, there it was! The mythical house of Love Street. It was only a few houses south of the Canyon Country Store. The house wasn't much, though—ramshackle and run down, it looked like it had been burned out beyond habitation, and there was graffiti on the particle board covering the windows. According to Stacy, it was lived in by squatters and hippies.

While some of the books I'd read painted Laurel Canyon as a legendary haven for musicians, artists, and the true center of the peace n' love hippie movement, it had also been home to a lot of shady characters, including members of the Manson family. The Canyon was rustic and dark in the middle of a bright and modern city. It had a troubled past, founded with a "whites only" charter. Mysterious fires broke out. Bootlegger tunnels were dug during Prohibition. There were rumors of a secret government compound, hidden away up near Mulholland. Drugs and overdoses and unexplained deaths were common, and the Wonderland murders in 1981 had changed the hippie culture of the canyon into something darker by the time I got there.

I knew all of this. I'd studied everything I could about Los Angeles and Hollywood, and Laurel Canyon was often mentioned. I'd been most curious about it after reading Miss Pamela Des Barres's memoir, *I'm With the Band,* a few years prior. Now that I was actually here,

I felt like she was sitting on my shoulder like a guardian angel.

Fortunately, the Canyon Country Store was still quaint and psychedelic and homey, like I'd imagined. They were even playing Crosby, Stills & Nash on the radio when we walked in. We grabbed some snacks, ice, and beer for the apartment.

I felt safe, but I was hyper-alert. There was a vibe in the canyon I picked up on right away, a certain darkness. Despite its rustic charm, not everything was as it appeared to be. The energy of the canyon had a heavy, dense patina to it. Patchouli and earth. The hills had many secrets and ghosts. Wild creatures roamed. I felt like I could get sucked up into its vortex and disappear like Snow White herself, into an enchanted forest.

I decided to call my mom in Ohio really quick from the pay phone on the outside deck of the store. I hadn't talked to her in a few days. She answered right away and was so glad to hear from me. The small deck overlooked the intersection at Kirkwood and Laurel Canyon, and as I was telling her about the drive down to LA, my eyes settled on a black convertible Corvette, stopped southbound at the light.

The driver. Huh. Shaggy blonde hair. Long neck. Wait. *Holy shit.* There was no mistaking it.

"Mom, ohmygosh, Duff McKagan is sitting at the stop light in front of me in his Corvette!"

"Who? Who's Duff McKagan?"

Oh, my mother.

"DUFF MCKAGAN!" I yelled into the phone. "From GUNS N' ROSES!" Only the traffic noise kept me from sounding like a crazy person.

Stacy had wandered out of the store and was opening a soda can. I looked at her with the phone still pressed to my ear.

"Oh yeah, he lives here in the Canyon, up off Mulholland. I think Slash does, too." She said all this as if it was just normal life.

My mind boggled. DUFF MCKAGAN.

1.1

After lunch and the quick tour and a stop at the store, we made it back to Mario's. We got ourselves into the apartment and were both suddenly super tired. Stacy crawled into her loft, I splayed on the futon in the living area, and we slept until the sound of rush hour traffic woke us up. We had a beer and started getting ready for our "date" with Mario.

Mario was in the courtyard waiting for us. He was a little more dressed up now, with a collared shirt over a clean undershirt, and pressed slacks. His hair was combed back into a fresh ponytail, and he smelled really good, musky and clean. Fresh-shaven, sharp and moisturized. He was actually good looking, all cleaned up. He definitely had the Italian flair for good grooming.

With Mario's hand, I climbed into the back seat of the Trans Am. Mario sat in front, and Stacy drove. We made our way down Laurel Canyon, flowing with traffic and veering right, past the Coconut Teaszer, and merging onto Sunset Boulevard. It was a warm evening and the city sparkled, diamonds under a sapphire sky. I craned my neck at odd angles to see everything as best I could through the Trans Am windows. Mario pointed things out, naming them for me.

We passed under a giant billboard of a blonde pinup girl: Angelyne. I had seen it on TV somewhere, and I couldn't believe this was it—this was the billboard. Mario told me she was a real person who showed up at the club sometimes.

"She's a real goddess," he said. "She drives a pink Corvette around town, you can't miss her."

She posed above us like a bubblegum saint as we crawled slowly through traffic down Sunset. The Chateau Marmont, the St. James, The Hyatt (Riot) House, past the Whiskey and the old London Fog. From the Whiskey down to The Rainbow there were throngs of people, long haired people, my people, walking from club to club. It was like some kind of rock n' roll street carnival.

The Rainbow itself was smaller than I'd imagined, a little storybook English cottage. The valet in the parking lot recognized Mario right away, and he helped us all out of the car. Mario held my elbow as we greeted his father at the door.

"Mr. Maglieri, so nice to meet you." I shook his hand firmly, smiled, and looked him in the eye. Manners and respect. I was very aware of what my mother had taught me.

When told my name was Anna-Marie, he asked if I was Italian. I smiled and said, "I'm Sicilian, sir."

There is a difference. Italians understand it.

He winked with a knowing look, patted my back and said, "Good girl, good girl." He nodded with approval at Mario Jr. The hostess approached, an old friend of the family who'd worked there for years. She sat down with us for a minute to catch up and take our drink orders. It was just starting to get busy.

When she left, Mario looked at me and paused. "Sicilian, eh?"

I nodded and smiled. I told him my grandparents had emigrated from a village between Corleone and Palermo.

He raised his eyebrows. "Sicilians don't fuck around."

"No, no we don't." I smiled, trying to keep it light. Maybe it gave me a notch of respect.

Pops had saved the table right up front for us, in the booth facing the entrance near the fireplace, and he stopped by after a few minutes to visit with his oldest son, his namesake. Stacy and I sat quietly and let the two men talk. Before he got up, he slid us a dozen more drink tickets across the glass-covered red tablecloth. "Here, girls, use 'em anytime," he said with a wink.

It was busy and crowded on the floor, but once you were in the booth, it was like being in a small womb. Padded red, dark pink lighting, comfortable, and a bit quieter as you nestled in. Lots of pictures to look at. I wanted to stand up and wander around to look at everything, but it was too crowded.

Mario told me that Marilyn Monroe and Joe DiMaggio used to visit the place, before his dad owned it. There was so much history here, like I was literally rubbing elbows with ghosts.

All of Hollywood feels like old ghosts, I thought to myself. The waitress brought my drink, and I gulped a few pulls of it. Cranberry juice and vodka went down easy.

The energy of the room was great. I could see everyone walk in and out, past the giant stone fireplace nearby. A few people nodded at me as they drifted around, and I nodded back, having no idea who they were. Then I started spotting famous people, or at least semi-famous. Blackie Lawless and Chris Holmes were lurking. Some guy from Warrant.

Lemmy Kilmister wandered by, said a rowdy hello to Mario Jr., and slid into the booth beside me, trapping me between the two of them. I shook Lemmy's hand and tried not to be awkward or intrude as he and Mario chatted, leaning across me. I leaned myself back into the plush booth, drink in hand. *Dear God, it's Lemmy!*

My old friend from Ohio, Kevin Amici, had introduced me to Mötorhead when I was 14, as I tagged along to his band practices. There was something about Lemmy that I loved. I'd also had a crush on Kevin when I was 14, which had grown into a friendship. Kevin had moved to LA just a few months prior, but we'd lost touch. I just needed to call his mom to get his number, but I hadn't yet.

As Lemmy leaned across me, I studied him. He had always reminded me of my dad, with his kind eyes and dark hair, moustache and biker vibe. Maybe the red lighting made everyone look good, but I thought he was incredibly handsome.

The night wore on and more people stopped by to say hello to Mario. He held court, it seemed, of old friends and well-wishers. I couldn't believe I was in the middle of all this, so I just sat back and observed and relaxed into it, which is what I usually did at clubs, anyway.

Sam Kinison had been sitting right across from us having dinner, but as the hours wore on and he kept drinking, he became surrounded by an entourage of women and a few rockers. He was being rowdy and loudmouth and bitingly, outrageously funny. From our booth, we had the best seats in the house for a completely improv performance.

This is it, I'm here! I thought to myself. *I am fucking here.* I'd had two cranberry-vodkas already, and Mario ordered another for me. I appreciated the small, warm buzz. The whole day had been a buzz.

Mario, Jr. controlled the pace of the meal, which was slow. The server paid close attention and did exactly as told. This wasn't about turning a table—this was social time for Mario, Jr. Eventually, an abundant dinner salad arrived, drenched in an awesome red-wine vinaigrette.

I've never been a shy eater, so I tucked in to my food, minding my manners as best I could. The salad disappeared in moments and I wanted to lick the plate, I'd been so hungry.

Finally, the cheese raviolis arrived and were just amazing—super creamy, pillowy, with a marinara that was light and fresh, and intensely good.

I was impressed. I finished every bite, sopping up sauce with a piece of bread. Mario seemed pleased at my grunts of pleasure and healthy appetite, and he told me they were all family recipes from his mother's side of the family. I ordered a coffee for desert—their delicious cinnamon coffee—and sat there, sipping it like a queen on a throne, feeling fat and happy and fully content.

As everything swirled around the room, a moment of awareness and wonder washed over me. I was relaxed. I was calm. I was having fun. I felt right at home here, even among strangers.

I had imagined it all to some degree, and I felt like I was in a long moment of déjà vu, almost familiar, like I'd been here before. I'd started my journey at 6am in San Jose, arrived in Los Angeles at noon, and 10 hours later, here I was with Mario Maglieri, Jr. as my host, both at his home, and at The Rainbow having dinner. It had all aligned so perfectly. Stacy and Mario Jr. had welcomed me right into their world, right in the middle of the action.

I knew it was exactly where I was supposed to be.

1.2

We finished our dinner and drinks and socializing, and we made our way out to the parking lot of The Rainbow to get Stacy's Trans Am from the valet. The parking lot was crowded, the atmosphere like a street fair, complete with a man in a purple velvet suit with a cat perched on his shoulder. Mario stood around chatting and visiting with a few people, including a big English man with long curly hair, a rugged face, and tattoos. He asked Mario who I was, and Mario introduced him to me as Steve. Steve was sitting on a huge motorcycle.

After a minute, he looked at me and asked in an English accent, "D'ya wanna go fer a ride on m'bike?"

Buzzed and wired and almost dizzy from fatigue, I thought it sounded like a great idea. I looked at Mario, and he shrugged.

"Sure, sweetie, have fun," he said. "I know Steve."

I hopped on the back of Steve's Harley Davidson with no helmet, and we took off east on Sunset. I thought of the Mötley Crüe video where they're all riding on Harley Davidsons. I tried not to choke on Steve's hair.

Seeing Los Angeles from up on Sunset, the city lights, the night air, the wind in my face—it was intoxicating. Los Angeles was beautiful, a big huge mystery, a wonder. It felt like a dream, or at least like that old Bob Segar song, *Hollywood Nights*.

We pulled up to the Formosa Café. They hadn't carded me, and now I was somehow sipping a Margarita with a mysterious British man almost twice my age in another vintage, historic Hollywood bar. Unfortunately, Steve and I didn't have much in common. He was not real chatty.

In a moment of slight internal panic, I realized that no one in the world knew where I was right now. I could disappear, and no one would figure it out for days. Thank God I had called my mom earlier, at least she knew I was staying in the Canyon with someone named Mario, but still. I might not be able to call her for another few days. She'd have no idea I was even missing until she hadn't heard from me. Stacy and Mario wouldn't know how to get in touch with my mom. I hadn't checked in with my Aunt. Not to mention, I didn't really even know these people. *Maybe it was all a weird set-up.* I didn't think so, but it shadowed my mind for a moment.

I thought about the Black Dahlia. She was alone in the city, too. No one noticed she was missing until her mutilated body, eviscerated and defiled, had been found days later in an empty field. The story of that horrific murder had fascinated me for years. I sat with this thought for a quiet minute near the end of my drink.

"D'yer wanna go outside and fuck?"

He caught my eye and said it with a straight face, and at first, I thought he was joking.

He was not. "I know a dark corner out back, near the dumpster," he nodded toward the exit.

As charming and wild as it sounded—getting fucked out back near the dumpster—I blinked at him and stuttered a polite refusal, trying not to show fear.

"I've just met you, you naughty boy! A drink won't cut it—you'd have to at least buy me dinner first!" I tried to laugh and make light of it, but my alarm bells were going off. *So this is how it goes in Hollywood*, I thought to myself. No romance. No conversation. No connection. Straight to fucking. Out back near the dumpster.

He shrugged his shoulders and wasn't amused, but he didn't seem to take it too personally. He had a hard, dull aura about him, anyway. *Why would I want to fuck this guy? He won't even talk to me.* I wasn't anti-sex, but I was anti-asshole.

After my refusal to have sex behind a dumpster in an alley, he was clearly done with me. He asked me where he could drop me off. I told him I was staying with Mario, Jr., up in Laurel Canyon. As he paid the tab and we made our way out to the dark parking lot, I wondered for a brief minute if Steve was going to try and fuck me anyway. *Good lord, please don't let this guy do anything*, I told myself as I followed him. He gunned the bike, I mounted up behind him, and we sped through Hollywood and up toward Mario's. I hung on to him and hoped for the best.

He knew right where Mario lived. I was grateful for that at least, because in the darkness of the Canyon, I wasn't sure if I'd remember exactly where to pull over. Plus, I was pretty buzzed. But he zoomed up to Mario's gate, I got off the big machine, and he sped away without a glance or a goodbye, doing a U-turn back down to Hollywood. *Eh, whatever. Dickhead.*

My Toyota was still parked there, and so was the Trans Am, so Stacy and Mario were back from the club. I punched in the gate code, feeling kind of weird doing so, since I was a guest. It creaked open into darkness.

They spooked me for a second, but then I saw Mario and Stacy sitting on the two lawn chairs, waiting up for me with an old-fashioned oil lantern on the concrete between them. Mario got up and brought another chair. They were both glad I found my way back.

I was, too.

I sat down, realizing what a stupid thing it was to have sped off in the middle of the night with a complete stranger in a strange city.

Stacy lit another joint. Mario didn't toke, but I was grateful for the smoke and inhaled deeply. I told them all about my experience with Steve. It was kind of funny and weird, just coming out and asking me for sex like that. I told them I had gotten a bit creeped out when I thought about the Black Dahlia

"She was murdered and no one even knew she was missing. It took them a while to identify her!" I took a big puff of the joint.

Mario snickered, and Stacy laughed. They looked at each other.

"What? What is it?" I said. I felt like such a rube, a country mouse.

"Don't you know who Steve is?" Mario asked.

"No...who is he? Someone I should know?"

"Steve Jones!"

"Who the fuck is Steve Jones? Is that the guy from Foreigner?"

"No! No, Steve Jones of the Sex Pistols!" Mario and Stacy said it in unison, laughing.

"Oh, my God, NO WAY! He's a legend!"

I was mortified, but I had to laugh at myself. Stacy and Mario thought I knew who he was as I sped away with him. I didn't have pictures of the Sex Pistols on my walls growing up, and in any pictures I had seen of them, they were pimply, gross, greasy, sometimes bloody.

Nope, not the Sex Pistols. It had been KISS, Mötley Crüe, Ratt, Metallica, Megadeth, and Guns N' Roses on my walls. Plus, Steve had long, curly hair. He looked like a metalhead more than a punk. How would I have known he was a Sex Pistol?

Mario made a remark about me surviving my first test on the Sunset Strip. "Eh, I know Steve, he's a nice guy, but he's had some problems," he said, tapping his arm.

I hadn't noticed anything overtly strange about Steve, but maybe that explained his dull personality and the weird solicitation of sex. Or, maybe he just thought I was an idiot because I had no idea who he was and I didn't kiss his ass or want to fuck him in an alley beside a dumpster.

I felt a little bad, but not too bad. If anything, I was amused.

Apparently, this is how Steve Jones met girls— picking them up in The Rainbow parking lot, like fish on a line. It didn't matter. Even if I had known who he was, I still would've refused the sex. There was no chemistry there. The only thing I felt a little bad about was that Steve Jones had played in a band with Michael Des Barres, Miss Pamela's husband. I was a big fan of Miss Pamela. Maybe we would've had something to talk about, had I recognized him or had a clue. Miss Pamela and her rock n' roll memoir was a huge reason I was in Los Angeles to begin with.

Oh well. It was only my first day in this magical city.

Anything was possible.

Canyon traffic had slowed down and we listened to the crickets and the low roar of the city beyond the canyon. I took a few pulls from the joint and marveled at the entirety of the day. It was past 3am. I had been awake for almost 24 hours. My last shower had been in San Jose, and it felt like a distant memory, a lifetime ago. I couldn't believe all that had happened since I'd left my aunt's house the previous morning.

I was also ready to pass out from exhaustion.

There are no more doubts about anything, I thought. I was completely at peace. Everything I had dreamed and imagined had crashed right into me—a cosmic alignment of circumstance and luck and timing. I had just had the most amazing day of my life. All my fear, hope, anxiety, pain, wonder, sacrifice—all of it was answered immediately upon my arrival in Los Angeles. It wasn't just great.

It was fucking magnificent.

I fell into a deep sleep on Stacy's futon and woke to a beautiful, sunny Laurel Canyon morning. I got up and opened the sliding door to let the breezes in.

I was still here. It was all for real. It hadn't been a dream.

Los Angeles.

Good morning.

Thank you. Thank you. Thank you.

Stacy and I stirred up some instant coffee and blazed another joint. We packed towels and supplies, and headed to the beach.

2.0

[Bastard]

Truth is, I'd been dreaming of California since I was a small child, dreaming of a place far away from everything I knew. I'd always felt a little different, a little set apart from the world around me.

I was born in Ashland, Ohio, located about halfway between Columbus and Cleveland, not too far off the interstate. A mixture of old Victorian charm with a cute downtown, Ashland also had a couple of factories, and plenty of farms. Sitting right on the edge of Amish country, buggies and horses and bonnets were a common sight all throughout town.

We were 50 miles directly south of the wide, gentle beaches of Lake Erie's shore. My mom and I would visit on weekends during the summers of my early childhood, sometimes with my cousins, sometimes just the two of us. I loved the beach, the smell of the water, the sand on my feet, the feel of a mild sunburn after only having my mom's Hawaiian Tropic Deep Tanning Oil to use for the day. We'd lay on the beach and listen to a small radio tuned into the local top-40 station while we baked ourselves brown, swam, and played. On long walks with my mom, we'd collect jars of small seashells and colorful sea glass, plucked from the sugar-soft sand with my small fingers like magnificent jewels from a pirate's treasure chest.

Shallow, warm, and gentle, Lake Erie was a perfect place for a kid to swim and explore. Driftwood stood like fine sculptures in an art gallery dotted along the beach. An ancient stone fishing pier jutted straight out into the lake near our small beach cabin, and I'd go hike the pier alone, hopping the giant limestone rocks to get all the way out to the lighthouse, where I could watch the cargo freighters cruise by and feel the fresh breezes of this giant, inland ocean.

***

Papa, my mother's father, was born in 1892 and emigrated from Sicily as a young teenager, following his three older brothers to Lorain, Ohio. He waited tables in a restaurant and trained as a body builder and boxer; he was a small man at 5'3", and scrappy.

Eventually, Papa ended up in Ashland, hoping to remove himself from family ties that would bind him to La Cosa Nostra, and yet, at his family's request, he returned to Sicily in 1930 for an arranged marriage to my grandmother, Mama, who's family was deeply involved.

After the birth of my oldest uncle 9 months later, they returned to Ashland and built a life together, never seeing the old country again. Although he only had a 7th grade education, Papa knew five languages fluently and wrote a multitude of short stories, in English, hoping to get published. Papa was a trained stone mason and, with that skill learned in the ancient stone quarries of Sicily, he started a brick factory in Ashland, supplying the town's stone and brick building needs for decades and providing a comfortable living for his family.

After having three boys, and with my oldest uncle a senior in high school, my mom was an unplanned surprise in 1947, born when Mama was 42 and Papa was 56. They named her after both of their mothers: *Caterina Mariana*. Catherine Mary Ann, as it said on her birth certificate, always going by Mary Ann, her middle name. She was an airy Gemini child; small, dark, and pretty, with glossy black hair and sparkling dark brown eyes. She was loved and doted upon as their only girl, the child of their old age, raised in a house built with Papa's bricks and labor, on a small family compound on the corner of Park Street and College Avenue.

This small compound included the original farmhouse on the corner, built in the 1880's and bought by them in the early 40's. Behind the farmhouse, Papa built the family bungalow. And in between the two was a small rental apartment on top of a one-car garage and utility room. With Ashland College nearby, he was able to rent out the front properties to students, and eventually, one of my uncles bought the farmhouse and raised his family there. My mom and I moved to the garage-top apartment when I was a toddler.

My mom had loved music and been a talented child, taking quickly to the piano and mastering it by the time she was a teenager. She endured Catholic school for many years but switched to Ashland High School as a freshman, where she was a cheerleader and a majorette and an all-around social butterfly. After graduation, she moved to Pittsburgh to attend cosmetology school with the plan of being a hairdresser.

My mom and dad met in this small town where they both grew up, right after she returned from Pittsburgh with her cosmetology degree, and directly after he served in combat in Vietnam with the Marines.

Born in 1950 and raised on a farm on a county road outside of town, my dad roamed the woods and swamps of Mohican country in his childhood, hunting, fishing, and trapping. He was a patriotic country boy with a drinking problem. With rumors of a draft heating up, he visited the Marine recruiting station the summer after his graduation in 1968, and off to Vietnam he went.

He served, and survived, one brutal tour in the 1st Marines Medical Battalion as an ambulance driver. He came home with only minor injuries, but he had a lifetime of complications. After his tour ended, he spent a couple of months travelling and doing drugs in Asia. He made his way back to Ashland in late 1970.

He was still shell shocked from Vietnam, from all of it, and was terrorized by his own dreams. Years later, he'd say he felt like a raw, wounded animal, that he shouldn't have been put back into society right away. He'd always been a partier and drinker. Vietnam pushed him into full blown alcoholism quickly.

My parents met at the bar where she waited tables as her second job. She got pregnant on New Year's Eve, they were married on March 12, and I was born September 14, 1971, 13 months after he saw his last combat in Vietnam. He was 21 years old, alcoholic, newly married with a baby girl, and suffering extreme PTSD.

Our little family unit was all over with pretty quickly. I have no memories of my dad and mom ever together, and I wouldn't see them in the same room until I was teenager. My dad left when I was 10 months old, and they were divorced soon after, by late 1972. He was drinking and abusive and running around with a motorcycle gang out of Cleveland.

He left us with the rent and electric due on a single-wide trailer in a muddy trailer park on the outskirts of town, while he went out and bought a new motorcycle and started road-tripping around the country, refusing to pay child support. Apparently, it was the scandal of Ashland, his family was embarrassed by his behavior. It sounds like a bad country-western song.

Despite this, his parents, my other grandparents, Bea and Herb, would watch me for an occasional night or weekend out on the farm, and sometimes, my dad would sneak into the county to see me, even though he had a few outstanding arrest warrants. My grandparents were decent and kind people to me, but not overly affectionate. It was fun for me to be around the farm animals and pets, though, and I was always happy to see my dad.

My earliest memories of him are shadowy and sometimes arrive in snippets: him pulling up to the farmhouse on his big motorcycle and reaching me up to sit in front of him, his strong arms hugging me close as I cuddled in, sniffing his leather vest; riding his shoulders and playing with his long hair as I clutched his forehead; snuggling up and reading a book; picking strawberries with him in a wide field, with friendly cows lowing just beyond the fence; walking down to the crick with the beagles and a calico cat following along as I poked cow patties with a long stick.

***

During a Christmas visit in 1976, my grandmother, Bea, handed me a small, wrapped package to open up.

"It's from your Dad!" she'd said.

It was the last gift of the day, and I'd be going home soon to celebrate Christmas with my mom. I had already received a new doll and crib from my grandparents, plus a really cool doll-head that I could put makeup on.

My Dad! I thought. I hadn't seen him since my birthday, when I turned four. It had been more than a year since I'd seen or heard from him.

I hurried and ripped into the festive package. Inside, wrapped in tissue paper, was a green photo album with a little pink cartoon on the front. There was a small pearlescent shell necklace carved into the shape of an 'A' for my initial, which was taped into the front cover of the album, a small pretty trinket, bought on a trip to the ocean, the card said.

The album itself was full of pictures of my dad and a strange woman with long hair like Cher's. Tammy, my dad's new wife. They were holding a tiny, black-haired alien baby. My grandmother explained that my dad had moved away for good, and that I had a new half-brother in California. His name was Zachary.

"Isn't that exciting? A new baby brother?" she asked.

I wondered if she was teasing me. I didn't want a brother. I studied the pictures of my dad's handsome face and long brown hair, and he reminded me Jesus. I wondered why he loved this new baby boy, and why he didn't love me.

As I looked at the pictures of my dad and his new family, I spotted a few palm trees. They reminded me of trees I had seen in the illustrated Holy Bible that I had been looking at. I wondered about California, and how long it would take to walk there. I knew it was far away.

"Across the whole country!" my grandmother told me when I asked. She showed me, on a giant old map of the United States that they had framed in the wood-paneled dining room of their farmhouse. "We are near this big lake here, Lake Erie, and your dad is near the ocean, all the way over here." She pointed.

"Do they have a lot of beaches in California?" I asked her, eyeballing the long coastline, and then eyeballing the giant space between Lake Erie and California. She told me yes, there were lots of beautiful beaches all along the Pacific Ocean.

"Can you walk there?" I asked her.

"No, you'd have to drive, or go in an airplane. It takes three or four days to drive there." She looked surprised that I wasn't happy with the news of the move and the new baby.

And then, I realized the truth: I knew that I'd not see my dad again. Not for a very long time. He had another life, in California.

Saigon fell in spring of 1975, when my dad was 25. I'd turn four a few months after that, blowing out candles on a cake my grandmother had made, sitting with my dad right beside me, both of us looking happy and having fun. I had no idea what he'd been through, or how much pain he was in. I had no idea that there was another wife and a new baby. I'd get this green photo album for Christmas a year later that told me the truth of the situation as plain as day: He was gone. The green photo album would be the last I'd hear from him for 10 years.

As he grew into a myth in my mind and he faded into the haze of early childhood, I always kept this one thought central: He looked like Jesus. He was in California. He was starting his life over—and he must be happy in California. Maybe I could find him there, someday.

It turns out, I went there to find myself.

2.1

My mom and I never had a good working TV. We bought a few at garage sales, and sometimes they'd last a few months, usually black and white and 13". Most of the time, though, I just watched TV at other peoples' houses—my uncle's, my grandparents', my babysitter's. I started seeing images of California on shows like Three's Company and the The Brady Bunch, looking at the carefree and sunny life full of laughter and fun. I also loved CHiPs and Erik Estrada, so exotic and manly, riding a big motorcycle like my dad.

During a phase in which we had a working TV, of my favorite shows to watch was called *In Search Of*, hosted and narrated by Lenard Nimoy (Mr. Spock). The show had great, creepy music, and compelling, mysterious topics. The show examined and offered theories about the paranormal, unexplained mysteries, lost civilizations, UFO's, psychic powers, and Bigfoot— all topics that fascinated me.

There seemed to be a Bigfoot craze during this time in the late 70's, and Mama told me very certainly that Bigfoots were real. She'd tell me of the strange, hairy people who would come down from the hillsides and caves in Sicily to gather food and supplies during the full moons. She'd seen them during her childhood, believing them to be what we knew as Bigfoots.

She talked of the *malocchio*, the evil eye, and did strange rituals with oil and water to cast it away. She tossed salt over her shoulder. She knocked wood. Cast away bad spirits by making the "devil horns". Yet she was a good Catholic, attending mass every week, a rosary always in her apron pocket. Mama had her statue of St.

Francis out near the garden, and the Virgin Mary in the front flower bed. She talked with them as she tended to her vegetables and flowers.

She had a terrific green thumb and grew a wonderful garden, complete with a verdant pear tree, grape vines, abundant tomatoes and an asparagus patch. I'd help her weed and pull ripe things, and she'd sprinkle on her fertilizer, calling it Magic Fairy Dust in her broken English.

In the kitchen, she had a sewing corner set up—right under the portrait of a long-haired, pretty, blue-eyed Jesus. She'd sew leather scraps into women's purses, which she'd sell to the ladies at church and around town. Obtaining leather scraps by the pound from the local leather-coat factory, the purses she made were beautiful, with pretty patterns stitched with an old-fashioned iron sewing machine, and with her awl and needle, by hand. They smelled so good, rich and leathery. Leather and long hair—a positive association I made early.

She baked her Sicilian chewy cookies, and let me frost them. She let me play with her bingo markers, and I helped her with her canning and preserving projects in the basement kitchen. She saved wishbones for me, and we each held a side and made a wish. She always let me win.

And even though they lived right next door to us and we shared a driveway and we saw her just about every day, she called my mom on the phone every Sunday morning before her walk to church, just to check in.

There was always soup or pasta on the stove, and always a treat for me at her house. She loved birds, and kept a small parakeet near a shady window, right beside her sewing machine. Perry, the Parakeet, named after

Perry Como. Sometimes, she'd tell me to go hide and come back, and then she'd call out the kitchen window and tell me she had been visited by Mr. Cardinal, or that the Blue Jay had stopped by, and she'd hand me a mini Hershey's chocolate bar. For a while, I really believed this happened because cardinals and blue jays and fat red-breasted robins often perched on her windowsill feeders, and Perry the parakeet would sing at her command.

Every trash day, Mama wrapped her white hair in a scarf, babushka style, and set off down the street pulling an old red wagon, holding a thermos of strong black coffee. She picked the rubbish, looking for treasure, and many of my childhood toys were plucked straight from the trash heaps of Ashland.

When I was five, she brought home an old stereo and turntable with a bad needle. I borrowed a few records, and an older cousin donated a new needle to the cause. Soon, I was listening to borrowed albums like KISS, The Beatles, Boston, Queen, and the Bee Gees. When I was alone up in my attic room, I was always playing music, singing, and settling in with my books. Listening to music made me feel things that I didn't know existed. Sometimes songs made me feel colors, sometimes they made me cry. Mama made it possible with that dust-bin turntable.

All through my childhood, I thought Mama had magical powers, like seeing Bigfoots and talking to birds, and getting magic chocolate, and being superstitious at signs, and throwing salt, and kneeling before saints, and finding treasure in trash heaps and having a beautiful singing voice. She seemed to understand that maybe I was a little different, too.

And then, one day, I found the small paper bag of Hershey's chocolate in the bottom drawer near the sink in her kitchen. I understood then that Mama didn't really have magical powers. At least not when it came to chocolate. I decided not to say anything, instead letting her continue to call for the birds and give me the magical chocolate in a grand and loving manner. It was our special thing, me and Mama. She was my grandma, like my second mom. I didn't want the magic to be over.

2.2

It was a cold and gray day, with a dusting of snow that crunched under my boots. As I walked over to Mama and Papa's house across the gravel driveways that we shared, I tongued my lower front tooth, which had been loose for weeks. The gap kept getting bigger, and I probed mercilessly. It was my first loose tooth, and I couldn't seem to stop bothering it.

Pausing on the gravel, and with my wool-gloved fingers that gave me good purchase, I yanked hard. Suddenly, I had a small, white, bloody tooth pinched between my fingers like a small pebble, and my gum throbbed, almost like an itch I couldn't scratch.

I couldn't believe it. I couldn't believe I had just yanked a tooth straight out my head. I stood there for a minute, under a big pine tree, mouth open, feeling elated and scared, inspecting the tooth. I tongued the hole in my bottom row of teeth and tasted something funny. My nose started running, dripping in the chilly air, and I wiped my cold face on a sleeve. I went on into the house, treasure in hand, having gone through this little rite of passage all by myself. I was excited to tell someone.

I showed Mama my tooth and handed it to her; she laughed with raised eyebrows as she looked at my face.

She shooed me into the bathroom to wash it, handing me a thin washcloth. Under the florescent light and the blue-green tile, I paused and leaned into the mirror to look at my face and inspect my mouth.

The mirror told a tale of gore and savagery that looked much worse than just a lost tooth.

There was dried blood and spit running down my chin from the corners of my mouth, and my runny nose had shellacked some of it to my upper lip. I had a blood-snot goatee. Some of it was smeared on my cheek, and I had drips of blood on the bib of my pink corduroy overalls.

I was a mess. I smiled at myself. I stuck out my tongue, fascinated. I thought I looked like Gene Simmons, and I stared, daydreaming. Imagining possibilities. He was big and scary and made me feel safe for some reason. I pictured him being my dad.

Someone knocked on the door and startled me out of my daze, so I ran the water and rubbed the washcloth against a bar of Zest soap and reluctantly started wiping my face. I didn't want to clean it off. I wanted to wear it all day, like a badge, a nametag. It felt like I was wiping away proof that I had a dad.

What if Gene Simmons didn't recognize me if we happened to come upon each other in Ashland, Ohio?

It's hard to say why I was so fascinated with Gene Simmons, but he represented something to me that even today, I can't quite explain. Power, freedom, imagination, facing fear. A big, brave, fearsome man in a ridiculous costume—it was mind blowing to a kid. He was a superhero. Maybe he'd rescue me somehow. The music and images I saw of KISS resonated in my mind.

For a while, my entire childhood was devoted to KISS. I wrote away and sent money—precious dollars to a poor girl—to become a member of the KISS Army. I had their posters on my wall, and I went in a homemade demon costume for Halloween.

I loved the song *Do You Love Me? Yes, I do*, too young to understand all the sexual innuendos. I loved *Detroit Rock City*. On yet another shitty TV, black and white with a paperclip for an antenna, my mom let me stay up and watch *KISS Meets the Phantom of the Park*—a terribly cheesy movie, but there he was, Gene Simmons himself, walking around and talking with a Brooklyn-Israeli accent.

The blood spewing and fire breathing didn't scare me like it did my little girly girlfriends. Although my mom was bothered by it because of her Catholic upbringing, it didn't really scare her, and remarkably, she didn't ban it. She knew how much I loved it. I was drawn to that hyper-masculine, primal force. The guitars, the hairy chests, the bloody tongue, the bulging and spiked codpieces, the lipstick, the fantasy of it all. It absolutely delighted me.

Truth be told, it still does.

2.3

I started reading well in kindergarten, and by first grade, I was far past my grade level. I read anything I could, including my mom's college textbooks, her girlie romance novels, her Cosmo magazine. I inhaled books anywhere I could find them, and browsed encyclopedias for fun when my mom would take me to the college library so she could meet with study groups.

We'd go to the Ashland Public Library every few weeks, and I'd haul books home and sleep in bed with my treasures. As an only child, I spent vast amounts of time alone. If I wasn't at a babysitter's house, I was home—supervised, but alone—there was a grandparent or an older cousin in the next house over. I roamed freely between the houses, but just as often could be found curled up with a book in my attic room.

It was during this time that I started dreaming about an imaginary friend. For a while, Thomas seemed very real to me. He was tall and dark, with a beard and kind eyes. I told him I didn't have a dad, and he told me he didn't have a mom, and we became good friends. He'd lay in bed with me and listen and hold my hand as I chatted about my day.

We had deep and meaningful conversations, me and my imaginary Thomas. I'd offer him candy whenever I had any, he knew all my secrets. I imagined him hugging me and protecting me, like an older brother. Thomas loved me. Thomas was my playmate and friend, and with him around I felt safe and not so alone.

For my 6th birthday, my mom took me out to a friend's house, a friend that lived in the country on a farm. There were lots of animals, and lots of kids, and I spent the whole day there with her having fun and roaming and helping with projects. Near the end of the day, after I blew out birthday candles, a basket of fresh kittens was brought to me—six weeks old and ready to go home. I picked out a silvery kitten with Siamese markings and named him Frisky. It was a great birthday.

Not long after my birthday, Mama was diagnosed with colon cancer. In addition to working, attending classes, and shuffling me around to different babysitter's houses, my mom was also driving Mama to all her doctor appointments at the hospital in Mansfield, and eventually, to radiation and chemotherapy. Mama was placed in hospice on a morphine drip just as I started second grade. For a while, I hardly saw my mom at all.

It was going to be a long year. At least I had my books, my kitty cat, my friend Thomas, and my music.

2.4

Built in 1890, and one of the oldest school buildings in Ohio, Grant Street Elementary School was located an easy block away from our apartment, and sat just across the street from the Ashland College campus. Grant was a big, dank, gothic, red brick building with wooden floors, proper slate blackboards, and high Victorian ceilings.

My first two years at Grant were fairly normal, with nice teachers who played piano and would lead the class during music lessons. They were fun and they liked me. However, my second-grade teacher, Miss Strong, did not like me at all.

She was an ugly woman, with a black bouffant, cat-eye bifocals, and the shadow of a downy black moustache just above her thin, chapped lips and overbite. She also had a dark, black heart under her cheap polyester dresses. Miss Strong harassed me on a regular basis, including a few occasions that left me with physical bruises.

After teaching for 25 years, she was a humorless bully. Her annoyance with me seemed to grow throughout the year, and as she continued picking on me, I withdrew into my own world even further. I was already a quiet kid, daydreaming, thinking about my books, imagining new worlds set to rock n' roll soundtracks, and just generally not paying attention in class. I had a messy, overflowing desk, and I had trouble following directions.

I always felt lost, even when I *was* paying attention. I was busy in my own head, figuring out answers before everyone else, or being the last one to understand an easy concept. It annoyed Miss Strong to no end.

I was also distracted with worry about Mama, and I missed my mom a lot. I had real trouble keeping up in class, partly because I was nearsighted and couldn't see the blackboard, but they wouldn't figure this out for another year or so. She just thought I was lazy and dumb. Maybe even retarded, as she called the class of "special" kids.

"Are you stupid?" Miss Strong would ask me when I didn't know an answer in class, spitting in my face from her lispy overbite. She tried to trick me with questions about our assigned readings, which I had done and mastered, and it only seemed to piss her off more.

One morning, a book we were reading mentioned the word *bastard* and Miss Strong explained to the entire class that the definition of a bastard was someone who didn't know who their father was, or if you were born and your parents weren't married. She was looking directly at me, and asked if my parents were married.

I didn't know what to say or how to respond. I didn't know. I wondered, *AM I a bastard? Is she calling me a bastard? Is that what I am? Is this why I feel so different? Is this why she doesn't like me?* Although I remembered my dad, by this time it had been three years since I had seen him. I wasn't sure if my parents had for sure actually been married, even though my mom and I both used his last name. I'd never even seen them standing in the same room together. There weren't any pictures of them from a wedding, and no one in my family talked about it.

School was boring and made me sad. I dreaded going every day, but I didn't want my mom to worry, so I didn't say anything. I kept to myself and read books and listened to my music and endured the abuse. I was sick a lot that year with strep throat and sinus infections, and my mom started to figure it out.

Finally, after discovering another set of bruises on my arms, my mom went to the school, and had a meeting with the principal where she told Miss Strong to keep her hands off me. Miss Strong had grabbed me so hard, her fingers had left four distinct dark purple marks on the underside of my skinny, milk-tender arm flesh.

My mom told the principle that she could practically see fingerprints, the bruises were so deep.

It helped for about a week, but then Miss Strong just picked on me more and made fun of me in front of the other students. I daydreamed and imagined Gene Simmons breathing fire all over her, or vomiting blood in her face and her melting away into a heap of goo. I imagined the entire gothic brick building that was Grant Street School falling from the sky and landing on her, squishing her, like the Wicked Witch, with her feet sticking out from under it.

Miss Strong was awful.

Instead, it was Mama who was vanishing before our eyes. I'd visit her every few days in the nursing home. She showed me her colostomy bag. She had lost 80 pounds and was a shell of the Mama I knew.

When I turned seven in September, I took her a big piece of my chocolate birthday cake. She smiled so sweetly, and said in her broken English that she was going to save it for later. I understood suddenly that she probably couldn't eat it without terrible pain. I felt bad for making her lie to me. She touched me gently on the face and forehead with her bony hands, and I knew she suffered. Death was upon her, and I could smell it. I could feel it. I hugged her gently, my bony, sick, magical Sicilian Mama.

2.5

Mama died in November of 1978.

Miss Strong told me in front of the class with an icy sternness, "Your grandmother has died. You need to get your things together and go wait for your mother."

I felt entirely numb with everyone looking at me, and I didn't want to cry, especially not in front of Miss Strong. I held back a sob that made my stomach hurt, stumbling out of the classroom alone to lean on a wall near the water fountain for a minute, blinking, breathing. *Mama is dead. Mama is dead*, I repeated to myself. *I'm never going to see Mama again.*

I took a drink of cold water and put my fingers in it and held them to my hot eyes. I waited for my mom on the steps of the school, alone and quiet, the trees barren of leaves, the sky thick with clouds. My mom's car pulled up. She got out and ran up the steps to me. We caught each other and both started sobbing.

The entire family was in an uproar over Mama's death—and they blamed my mom for it, mysteries of blood that even Sicilians can't explain. *She was the daughter! She should have known earlier! She should have done more!* Even though my mom was half-dead with grief and exhaustion already, the family didn't speak to her for a while. My mom made it through the funeral and her finals in college. And then she collapsed and had the flu for three weeks. I came down with strep throat again, and we both just stayed home, together, grieving.

I dreamed of Mama every night and knew that she had been greeted by angels in Heaven—I dreamed the whole thing and it comforted me. I told my mom all about it, about the conversations I had with Mama in my dreams, that she was at peace. My mom always listened and took my visions seriously. I had seen Heaven in my dreams, beautiful things. I knew Mama was OK. I knew we were going to be OK.

2.6

On the one-month anniversary of Mama's death, the phone in our apartment rang on a sunny Sunday morning, just as it had done for years, with Mama calling to check in before her walk to church. Only this time, on this Sunday morning, Mama wasn't there. No one was. The line was dead when my mom answered it.

My mom and I looked at each other and she said to me with wide eyes: "I wonder if that was Mama calling to check in?"

We both started laughing, and then we both started crying.

Mama's pear tree died that winter and never bloomed again. All the flower bulbs she had planted went dormant. The garden was barren, and choked with weeds, her saints covered in the dirt of neglect, her basement kitchen coated with dust. Papa wandered the house, lonely and sad, lost without his mate of 48 years. All her clothes and things stayed in place, her overcoat and garden shoes still sat by the back door. They would stay there until he died, five years later.

We all missed her very much. She was the glue that had held the family together. Nothing was ever the same after she died, but I looked for signs from her: A red cardinal flitting by, a Beatles song on the radio, or the smell of peonies. These things felt like a little bit of magic, a soft nudge from Mama.

For many, many years after her death, even after we moved away, our phone would ring on random Sunday mornings with no one on the line.

I felt her presence on the other side, as if it were only a thin veil between us. It was Mama who taught us about magical thinking, through her superstitions and religion and playful ways. It was Mama who showed me that magic was a part of everyday life, and that signs and symbols were everywhere, if you looked.

After Mama died, my mom managed to finish her college degree, and on a beautiful spring day in May 1979, I walked over to the grand lawn of Ashland College in my nice clothes with my aunt, uncle, cousins, and Papa to watch my mom receive her diploma. She was turning 32 years old that month. I understood very clearly what a huge accomplishment it was for her. I was proud of her. We wished Mama had been with us, but I knew she was close by.

2.7

My other set of grandparents—my dad's folks, Bea and Herb—sold their farm and moved away to northern Michigan. They never said goodbye to me, and I never heard from them or saw them again. They were just gone, like my dad, a vapor. When Mama died, at least I understood what had happened to her and where she had gone. At least I knew that she had loved me.

With them, I never knew, and I wondered about it for years. I still do.

I survived second grade and was looking forward to a long summer. It was during this time that I started reading the *Little House on the Prairie* books. Any hardships and sadness that I had were small when compared to the hardships that the Ingalls family endured. I wished I had sisters, and a Pa. I wished for an adventure where I could go west in a wagon and camp under the stars. West was California. West was escape. West was hope. I thought that if I were Laura Ingalls, I would've kept going until I got to the ocean. The California Ocean. That's where my dad was.

That summer, I also read *A Little Princess*, by Francis Hodgson Burnett. A quiet, lonely little girl is sent to a gothic boarding school and is then orphaned and banished to an attic room and abused by a mean woman teacher. This book, and the main character, Sara Crewe, touched my heart deeply.

I felt like the book was written just for me. I felt like an orphan and my dad was gone. Dead? I had no idea. My mom worked all the time, and we were poor. Both of my grandmas were gone. I spent vast amounts of time alone in my own attic room, listening to whatever music I could borrow from my older cousins. And I had just survived Miss Strong, who seemed to be the modern-day Miss Minchin.

I had known that type of heartless cruelty and unfairness from an adult, just like Sara Crewe, and things turned out really good for her. I knew I would have to endure, and I knew I'd have to survive.

The books I enjoyed gave me an example to aspire to: bravery, dignity, kindness, hope, and most of all, the power of coincidence, the kindness of strangers, and magic. Dreams *could* come true, and goodness *does* prevail.

I still believe it to this day.

2.8

With her new shiny and mostly useless college degree in business administration, my mom was now an assistant manager at a small clothing store in Ashland, and in the fall of 1979, she went on a buying trip to New York City with the owner of the store, a friend of hers. I stayed with my aunt and uncle for a week. I was close with their daughters, my cousins, who were like older sisters to me.

When she got back, she took me out to dinner to celebrate her big adventure. We drove to the Red Lobster in Mansfield, my first time in a nicer restaurant. We ordered King Crab legs and it was all very fancy, it seemed.

My mom had never been to New York City, and as we cracked open the crab legs and dipped our pickings into melted butter, she told me all about what she did and what she saw—the horror of being chased by a giant cockroach in the hotel and getting stopped at airport security for her pair of huge earrings. She handed me a wrapped package and I tore into it: a soft yellow t-shirt with KISS vinyl lettering across the chest with each of their faces on one letter, outlined with glitter—which was a very popular look in 1979, disco chic and Xanadu. It was my first band t-shirt, bought right in New York City. I loved it.

And then she mentioned that she'd had a job interview while away. It had gone well. She paused for a long moment and looked at me hard.

She broke the news as matter-of-factly as she could: She'd been offered a job with Casual Corner, a chain store with potential for growth. They were opening a new store, and she'd accepted an assistant manager position. It was more money. We were moving to Columbus, 80 miles or so south of Ashland, straight down I-71. It had been decided, and we were moving in January.

The news hit me hard, and I was paralyzed with fear for a minute as she told me all this. I didn't want to move anywhere. We knew no one in Columbus. I had never even been to Columbus. What about school? What about my kitty cats? It meant that I had to leave third grade in the middle of the year. I hated it.

And most of all, I was stricken—just staggered— by the thought that my dad wouldn't know where I was, and there was nothing I could do about it. He was gone. Mama was gone. My other grandparents were gone. My entire family had fractured. And now I was moving to a strange city.

I picked at my crab meat in silence and tried not to cry.

She bought me a Shirley Temple and we splurged on a piece of strawberry cheesecake. She broke down and we both shed a few tears and she said she was sorry and she knew it was going to be hard for me. But it was a chance for us to get ahead, to escape our small town and limited opportunities. It was a chance for my mom to move into her first "big" management job after college. It was retail, long hours, but we could make it work. She begged me to understand.

And I did. I understood. We were always going to struggle in Ashland.

I still hated it, but I quietly accepted it over the next few days for my mom's sake. I knew she felt bad, but in the big scheme of things, my anxiety didn't matter. There was hope for a better future, and she had to take the opportunity. An adventure. A gamble.

Alone with my fears and worry over moving away, I prayed that night, at home under my KISS posters, that Gene Simmons would find me and rescue me, just like Mr. Carrisford finds and rescues Sara Crewe in *A Little Princess*. That he'd swoop in and gather me off to a different, easier life.

And although it never came to pass, and we did move to Columbus, and everything was mostly OK, this fantasy of a father-demon-lover-superhero rescuing me never really went away.

It wasn't Gene Simmons himself who saved me—but the music. His music, and the hard, fast, sexy, obnoxious, rebellious music that my love of KISS would lead me to—hard rock and heavy metal—it was the music that taught me, comforted me, saved me, became my parent.

I was imprinted early with biblical visions of apocalypse, demons, and magic, strange creatures and mystical visions. I was drawn to this music by forces unseen. It made sense to me, on a gut level. This love of heavy, masculine music would serve me well in the future.

It would help me rescue myself.

3.0

[Knock 'em Dead, Kid]

Ohio to California 1989-1990

I graduated high school in June 1989, somehow managing to squeak by with an embarrassingly low 1.8 cumulative GPA. My legacy of being a poor student, starting with Miss Strong in the second grade, had carried all the way through my public school career.

For my 18th birthday in September, while I was busy working two jobs and going out to see my favorite bands with some new friends, my Aunt Linda invited me to come visit her in San Jose. She even sent a free plane ticket for the trip. It was the best graduation and birthday gift I'd received, by far.

So, I flew by myself to see her, and we spent the week sightseeing, going to the ocean, and eating our way through the Bay Area. She was a great tour guide and companion. We had a fabulous time. I loved the vibe, the freedom, and the geography of mountains and ocean.

As we walked on a cold beach in Santa Cruz, I told her that I wanted to move to California. To Los Angeles, specifically. I told her all about my plans, my jobs, my hopes and dreams, the drama with my mom. I left California refreshed and hopeful, ready to start adulthood and get on with my life.

When I got back to Ohio, my only goal was to work and save as much as possible so I could get the hell out.

I started working at the Victoria's Secret Catalog call center, taking orders from 6:30 at night until 3am, which was a great time slot for me. Plus, I was able to catch some really good deals—when I let myself indulge. To stay on track, I also started working in the office of a furniture store on the weekends, inputting orders, taking payments, and arranging deliveries. And I had a little gig on the side, helping a wedding photographer. I was tired, but I knew it would all be worth it.

3.1

I had a lot of fun my last in year in Ohio, and despite working so much, I went out to see bands and hang with my friends. I dated a few guys, including one bad one that I called my boyfriend for a while. Through him, I kept bumping into a guy named JJ, a local musician and production guy.

JJ had lived in LA for a while, done sound at a club on the Sunset Strip, and had some connections. He was also friends with my friend Kevin Amici from high school. Everyone knew him and I thought he was really nice.

In early February, and knowing I was a KISS fan, JJ invited me on a road trip to deliver some drum equipment to a studio in Fishkill, New York, where Ace Frehley was working on some solo stuff. I arranged a couple of days off and agreed to go out of curiosity. I loved road trips. I wasn't at all attracted to JJ, and I'd always had a lot of guy friends, so it didn't seem like it would be a big deal. He felt like an older cousin or something. He talked all about living in Los Angeles, what it was like, the difference between living in the Valley and the City. He was a great source of information, and he appreciated the company for the drive.

He already had all the equipment loaded into the 26-foot box truck that I'd be riding shotgun in for the trip, so I packed up my small duffle bag, and we set out from Columbus. He drove us all the way to New Jersey, choosing to bypass New York City by driving around it.

Driving north along the beautiful Hudson River for another hour or so, we found the studio in Fishkill. We dropped the equipment off, collected the payment, and met a couple of production guys handling the delivery and equipment. At their invitation, we toured the studio and saw some of Ace's guitars. They were nice guys and easy to talk to, old road dogs who had worked with KISS for years.

Afterwards, JJ and I drove up to Poughkeepsie to see the historic town. We looked around for a bit, then grabbed some Wendy's and checked into a hotel near the highway to spend the night before driving the 11 hours back to Ohio the next day.

I was bummed that I didn't get to meet Ace, but, whatever. Poughkeepsie was a cute little town, and I had enjoyed myself on the road trip. It was a good day and I'd be home tomorrow night, so I was happy.

JJ had brought a bottle of Jack Daniels, and mixed with ice and a few Coke's from the hotel machines, he started pounding drinks as we laid on our separate queen beds, watching cable TV.

After an hour and nearly finishing the bottle, he suddenly pounced over to my bed in his tighty-whiteys and tried to pin me down, lunging in, trying to kiss me. I was shocked at first, then pissed. He pawed at me and started grabbing for my crotch. Thankfully, I still had my blue jeans on, acting as a good barrier.

"Get the fuck off of me, dude!" I scolded him. I didn't want to scream. Not yet, at least.

We struggled for a moment, his bloodshot blue eyes bulging from his drunken exertion, wild in a frenzy. He relaxed for just a moment and I used my feet to help heave him off of me. To my astonishment, it worked. He landed over on his bed with the thud of a corpse. He curled up, and fell asleep in moments, mumbling to himself.

I was frozen in place on my bed for a few minutes as I wondered if he would come back to life like Michael Myers. He had settled on his side, with his head on a pillow. *At least he won't choke on his vomit,* I thought, thinking of John Bonham.

JJ was a fucking putz and a raging alcoholic, but I didn't want him to die.

Not sure what to do, I put on my shoes and grabbed my bag and purse, the truck keys, and both room keys. I left him there in his underwear, hoping he'd stay passed out.

I went down to the hotel coffee shop, hoping to settle down. By some sweet magic, I ran into the same two roadies I'd met at the studio earlier that day, Dan and Steve. They were both older, in their 40's, and super friendly with a fatherly vibe. Steve said that I reminded him of his daughter, who was 16. I pulled up a chair and joined them at their table.

After telling them what had happened with JJ, and my plan to wait it out in the coffee shop and possibly sleep in the truck, they immediately offered me one of their rooms. They were concerned for my safety and were in agreement—I should not be sleeping in the same room as JJ, nor pull an all-nighter in a coffee shop or the cab of a truck. It was cold and unsafe.

Dan told me that he had gotten a weird vibe from JJ earlier in the day. He was glad that I ran into them.

"Something about that guy bothered me," he said.

"Yeah, well, maybe this is it," I said. "He's a drunk alcoholic and just tried to assault me."

Dan gave me his room key and his home phone number in Jersey, and told me to check out whenever I needed to the next day. I told him I hoped to get JJ up early to drive the truck back to Ohio. He asked which route we had taken and made me promise to call him when I got home to Ohio so that he'd know I was safe.

I gave him my phone number in Columbus and told him to call my mom if he didn't hear from me tomorrow evening. It felt kind of silly, but the episode with JJ was so out of character and freaky, that it seemed I should take the precaution in case any shit went down on the way home. Dan told me it would be no problem to call her.

I had really misjudged JJ.

But for some reason, I trusted these guys, and I was not disappointed. There was no hook or angle. They were genuinely concerned and genuinely chivalrous.

I slept in the borrowed room and went to wake JJ at 6am. We had to get on the road. He bumbled around and reeked of vomit; unfortunately, he was still pretty drunk. Squinty-eyed, slurry drunk. I got him wiped off and dressed and out to the truck. I went back into the hotel to check out and to grab some coffee and pastries from the breakfast spread, hoping maybe he'd sober up. I walked back out to the truck with my hands full, and saw JJ's pasty, smeared face on the foggy glass of the passenger side door as I approached.

I eyeballed the big white box truck. I had to accept that the only way I was getting home that day was if I drove it home myself. I'd never even driven a van, much less a 26 foot truck.

I mounted up, settled in, looked at the map for a general sense of where I was, and started driving. Thank God the heater worked, as the weather had turned bitterly cold with flurries and blowing snow. JJ was barely coherent, napping on and off and curled up on the far corner of the bench seat. While driving, I managed to check the map myself for the round about route we'd taken on the way to Fishkill. There was no way I wanted to drive a big box truck through New York City.

Somehow, through the winding roads and forested hills, I found my way. I drove the truck for 14 hours straight. Just outside of Allentown, we met a full snowstorm head on, and I drove us all the way across the turnpike and through the tunnels of Pennsylvania, slowly, trying not to slide off the road. The truck swayed around since it had no cargo, and my hands cramped from clutching the steering wheel so goddamned tight.

I was scared the whole way and bitterly pissed at JJ for being such a jackass. He was more awake and apologetic as the day went on, but still unable to drive due to the massive migraine that was just "killing him." I kinda wanted to punch him for that comment. I'm pretty sure he had no clue that he tried to assault me. And if he did, well, fuck him.

We arrived safely in Columbus in the evening. I drove myself to where I had parked my car and left JJ to fend for himself with the stupid truck.

I finally got home and called Dan the roadie. He was glad to hear from me. I thanked him again for the kindness and told him how much I appreciated his help. He was great. He told me he was going on the road with KISS next month for a while, and to make sure to keep his number so I could call him if I needed tickets. It was so very kind of him.

Despite the weirdness with JJ, I'd gotten myself home in one piece and now there was a KISS show somewhere in my future, thanks to Dan the awesome roadie.

Little did I know that the show would be on my 19th birthday, eight months later, in Los Angeles.

3.2

Shortly after my trip with JJ, my Aunt Linda in California called me with an idea.

She was newly divorced and her ex had finally moved and she had an extra bedroom. She asked if I wanted to come stay with her for a few months, rent free. I could use it as a launch pad, get a job, start college—do whatever I needed to do to start a life in California. My skin tingled as we talked on the phone, my heart racing as she explained the proposition to me.

I said YES immediately, knowing I'd have a lot of details to work out. This was it! I had a place to stay in California. I didn't expect my mom and step-dad to be supportive. We'd had some major trouble the past few years. I deeply resented all of them, all of the adults in my life.

Except my Aunt Linda. She was cool.

And yet, mom and step-dad decided to help. They'd been letting me live with them for a year for cheap while I worked and saved money, which I really appreciated. I knew my mom was going to be sad that I was moving away, but she couldn't have been surprised—I'd been obsessed with California for years.

I'd be leaving for California in eight weeks—two short months. My mom and step-dad arranged to take a week off of work to caravan with me across country to my aunt's house near the end of May. Aunt Linda was my step-dad's sister, so it would be a quick family vacation, too.

I had about $1200 saved up, and an old blue Toyota with a tricky clutch. Two months. This gave me time to save a bit more and get the car fixed up. I could downsize my stuff and pack up my room so my folks could use it for something else.

I went to a bunch of shows with different friends—like my friend Anne from Cleveland, whom I'd struck up a good friendship with after meeting her at the Alrosa Villa—the best rock and metal live-music venue in Columbus. My last time going up to visit her in Cleveland, just before moving away, we partied with Salty Dog and I ended up with the worst hangover of my life, almost stranded in downtown Cleveland.

These last few shows were a lot of fun. I let loose and partied more than usual, saying my goodbyes to all of my friends. I was as ready as I would ever be. The days were counting down, and I was going to California.

With a full heart and an open mind, my fate pointed West.

3.3

I've always had a lot of guy friends, and one of my close friends during my last year in Ohio was David. I'd known his younger brother and sister, who went to Westerville South, but I didn't know him until after I'd graduated. David was gorgeous—dark, curly hair down to his shoulders and beautiful green eyes, dusky tan skin, and a smile that would light up a room—one of the handsomest men I'd ever meet. He was so funny and genuine, and we shared a deep love of The Doors and Queensrÿche.

We had many mutual friends between us, and he had a girlfriend, so when he'd see me at the Alrosa and would hug and kiss on me, I knew it was more brotherly. He was an affectionate dude, and funny. We would shoot the shit and do shots together. He didn't have a car for a while, so sometimes I picked him up and we'd go out to a club or a party as a twosome, sometimes in a group, and sometimes I gave him a ride home or to his job at the Record and Tape Outlet. We never ever had any sexual chemistry or awkwardness; he really was like an older, goofy and affectionate brother.

One night, we drove out to a party together on the east side while listening to *Operation Mindcrime* and singing at the top of our lungs. We found ourselves out in a small enclave of split-level homes down a country road, surrounded by rolling farm land in eastern Franklin County.

When we got inside, we realized that we didn't know anyone. Not one person looked familiar and we were both like, *Are we even in the right place?* We had no clue. So, David kidnapped a shrimp tray and I grabbed a six-pack of beer from the party spread; we found a spare bathroom in the lower level and locked ourselves in.

With him sitting on the toilet seat and me on the edge of the bathtub, we balanced the tray of shrimp on our knees and gorged ourselves, fighting our shrimps over the last of the cocktail sauce. When we came out of the bathroom, the party was all but dead, and we were buzzed and stuffed. In addition to the horror of eating in a stranger's bathroom, we braved a snowstorm, our drunkenness, and my shitty brakes to get home that night.

David was always fun to hang out with, and we always talked about California. He wasn't quite ready to move out there yet, but I told him he'd have a place to stay if he ever wanted to come visit and check it out.

In the few years before that, there seemed to be a mass migration of Ohio musicians to California. Joey C. Jones, the new lead singer for Shock Tu, had almost found success in Los Angeles with his band Sweet Savage—losing the record deal to Poison, I'd heard. Mad Moxie had moved out there. Mike Hannon had moved out there and gotten signed to Geffen with Salty Dog. A local band called Lollipop Factory was out there, playing around LA. My friend from high school, Kevin Amici, and his singer, Sam, had moved with their band, Bad Reputation. Deron from Nasty Action was going to the Guitar Institute in Hollywood, and his singer, Doug, was moving out there, too. A few Cleveland guys were there, like Spoyld and Pretty Vacant, which I knew of through my friend, Anne.

I figured I'd just run into everyone out there at some point. Somehow, I knew it would work out, and I counted down the days until my departure. I planned, I packed, I gave stuff away, I turned in my notice at my jobs, and saved every last scrap of money that I could.

3.4

May 18, 1990.

My time approached. I was leaving for California in a week. I'd already said goodbye to most of my friends, and I decided to go out one last time to see a good band and to bid farewell to my favorite music club, The Alrosa Villa.

The Alrosa Villa had been around for decades as a bar and live venue, but it got really popular in the 1980s when Rick Cautella (aka "The Rock and Roll Reverend") started booking hard rock and metal bands.

It was a low-slung beige building, sitting in the middle of an overgrown gravel parking lot that backed up to the train tracks and I-71, near an industrial park on the north end of Columbus. It became the epicenter of the Columbus metal scene in the 80s. No other place in the area had a Thursday-Sunday lineup of local and regional hard rock and metal acts. Most shows were all ages. They'd just put a big black X on the back of your hands if you weren't old enough to drink, but it was pretty easy to get older long-haired guys to buy you drinks to sip in dark corners of the club.

It was a balmy evening, and people were out and in a good mood. A band called Shanghai was playing and they had an amazing guitar player, Bryon Sheppard, whom I'd taken guitar lessons from for a while. It was always fun to watch him play.

The Godz, a Columbus legend, were playing that night down at the Newport on campus, and when they finished their show, the crowd migrated north to the Alrosa Villa for more music and drinking. In addition to the rocking guitar licks by Mark Chatfield, Eric Moore of the Godz was the Midwestern version of Lemmy Kilmister. The crowd in attendance at the Alrosa this night were rough and tumble bikers and ne'er-do-wells. They mixed with the prettier, hair-metal crowd, which made for an interesting stew.

Headline bands didn't usually go on until midnight, at least, and Shanghai always played to a full house. The Alrosa had opened a new patio area, which made it feel a bit more festive. It was a perfect night to celebrate and bid farewell to the last of anyone I might have missed before I moved away.

I made my rounds and gave out hugs and my Aunt Linda's phone number in San Jose. It was surreal feeling, knowing that I wouldn't be around at the Alrosa anymore. It was like my home away from home. I'd cut my musical teeth listening to live bands on their stage for the last few years.

The very last person I talked to that night was David. I was so glad to run into him. We embraced in a big hug. I ran down my plans with him, again, and he listened, nodding.

"You be careful out there, sweetie. I know you're gonna do great. Call me when you get settled in." He looked into my eyes with genuine affection and concern.

"I will, Dave, don't worry."

We hung together a few more minutes near the pool tables and finished our beers. As the bar shut down and the crowd broke up after the show, I knew it was time.

"All right, this is it," I said. They had turned on the overhead house lights, making me squint a little against the blue florescent glare.

David and I exited the club together out the side door. He walked me to my car as I held his arm over the gravel parking lot, and then he turned to me, gave me a quick peck on the lips for good luck, and one last bear hug.

"Knock 'em dead, Kid," he said, holding my shoulders, his warm eyes sparkling in the amber glow of the parking lot lights. I appreciated the Mötley Crüe reference. I got in my car and rolled down the window.

"I'll try man, I'll try. Be good, OK? I'll call you soon." I put the Toyota in reverse.

He tapped the hood of the car as I pulled out and blew me one last kiss. The gravel crunched as I pulled out onto Sinclair Road, tears in my eyes.

Goodbye, David. Goodbye, Alrosa. Goodbye, Columbus.

3.5

A few days later, on a bright, May morning, we started out for California. My stepdad had decided to bring his kids along, and we filled up two cars with our stuff—their big maroon Oldsmobile Cutlass and my little blue Toyota Corolla. I'd just had the clutch replaced on the Toyota, and the whole thing was serviced and road-trip ready. I'd even wired up my Walkman to the car speakers so I'd have a tape deck for the trip.

My stepsister was 13, so I invited her to ride with me. I knew that whatever crap I had been through with my folks she was now dealing with, too. She had her own parental issues, and I felt a bad for her. So, while my mom, step-dad, and my stepbrother were in the other car, I had a teenage shotgun companion with me for most of the trip. She gladly endured all the heavy metal in turn for not having to ride in the other car.

We left Columbus at 6am and my excitement grew as we clicked through the states, heading west on I-70. I'd really not travelled much—one time to California on an airplane, one time to Michigan, and up and down I-71 in Ohio and that one fateful trip to New York with JJ—so this was my first time really seeing the vastness of the country, rolling across fertile farmlands and prairie. We spent the first night in Salina, KS.

I was a flea on top of a giant haystack. I thought of Laura Ingalls and her covered wagon and how vast it must have seemed to the early settlers who'd traversed these trails west, across the open plains, with nothing but what they could carry in their wagons. Not unlike what I was doing now—pursuing a better life west, with only what I could carry in the car.

Setting out on the second day, my anticipation grew as we drove toward Colorado. As the road gently undulated, I could start to see the peaks of the Front Range shimmering in the distance. The sight of them overwhelmed my eyes. I'd never seen mountains like this in person. We finally made it to Denver and stopped for lunch at a local steakhouse.

We climbed into the Rockies just west of Denver, and I rolled down the window to breathe in the clear mountain air. It smelled so delicious, the coolness and earth and mineral and pine and freedom and the golden sunshine. Nothing like the low gray skies of Ohio. It was a crispness and clarity I'd never experienced before.

Despite my own enchantment and easy daydreams, the little Toyota labored at the altitude. I kept it floored and managed to keep speed. My stepsister and I were quiet and enjoying the scenery. It was her first time really seeing the West, too. Growing up in the green, muddy flatlands of Ohio, nothing quite prepares you for the splendor of the Rocky Mountains. It was like being in a postcard, it was so beautiful, and we both felt it.

Just as we were rounding a corner to another splendid vista, the Toyota wobbled and blew a tire. I struggled for a second to keep the car straight, and I steered quickly toward a notch, a gravel pull-out etched into the mountainside with enough space for me to feel safe getting out of the car along the interstate. It had appeared just in time. My folks were ahead of us, and oblivious for the moment. My stepsister and I unloaded all my stuff from the trunk, and I wrestled the spare tire out. I eyeballed the flat and the lug nuts and the weird little jack in the tire kit.

All right. I had a vague idea of how to change a tire. I knew I had been shown, but did I remember? *Shit.* It was time to learn, for real. *I am a tinkerer, I can handle this*, I thought. I started to read the instructions on the jack but my eyes were distracted by a large plume of dust up ahead.

It was my parents' Oldsmobile, flying down the berm of the highway in reverse, hugging the mountain wall along the bend against traffic. *Holy shit!* When my folks had noticed that I wasn't behind them, they pulled over and waited for a minute. Then, my stepdad put the Oldsmobile in reverse and backed it all the way up until they found me. There was no way and nowhere to turn around otherwise; had they used the next exit, it would've taken them more than an hour to backtrack to reach me. Exits along this stretch of I-70 were far and few between.

We got the tire changed and the car loaded back up, and we made it to Glenwood Springs for the night. We had the Toyota checked out at a local repair shop, and in addition to a new tire, there was some bracket that needed to be fixed and a part to be ordered. We spent Thursday waiting for the Toyota repair, and thankfully, my folks paid for it.

We were back on the road Friday, making our way across western Colorado and through Utah, the salt flats, and the vast nothingness of northern Nevada. We passed Winnemucca at dusk, pushing through to Reno for the night to stay at a Best Western hotel and casino.

I'd never been in a casino before, and I wasn't old enough to gamble. Instead, I completely enjoyed and took full advantage of the gluttonous dinner and breakfast buffets. I've always had a thing for a good buffet.

We got on the road at 10am, and as we crossed into California moments later, I made sure we were listening to Mötley Crüe's *Too Fast for Love*. I wept tears of gratitude and joy and said a few times out loud:

"I can't believe I'm actually moving here. I'm moving to California!"

3.6

We made it to my Aunt Linda's house in Cupertino in mid-afternoon on Saturday, May 26, rolling through the endless suburbia that led us there, it seemed. As we pulled up, Aunt Linda came out through the garage to meet us.

She gave me a quick hug and said, "You've got a phone call."

I looked at her in confusion for a second.

"Do I need to make a phone call?" I asked, thinking I'd misheard her.

"No, no. Your friend Barb is on the phone, I told her you'd just pulled up. She's on long distance, on the kitchen phone."

What? Now I was really confused. I'd told Barb and all my other friends I wasn't sure when I was arriving in California. They knew I'd be on the road all week.

It was weird. I hurried in and took the call.

"Barb, are you OK? What's going on?" I asked her. I could hear her sniffling.

"David is dead." She rasped to me.

My heart went cold. No no no. "What? What do you mean?"

"There was an accident last night. He was coming home from the London Quireboys show at the Newport. He lost control of the car in the rain on the exit of 71 south/70 east." She sniffled loudly, her raspy voice cracking with emotion.

"Oh my God." I sat down on the floor, maneuvering the cord around me. *Sweet Baby Jesus, no.* I was crying as my parents entered the house with some of our luggage. Barb and I talked for a few minutes and then hung up.

The phone rang almost in my hand, so I answered it. It was my other friend, Laura, calling to tell me the same news. Poor David had been thrown from the car and had hit a tree. He died a few hours later, after heroic efforts to save him.

Holy shit. My sweet David. I'd literally just seen him a week ago, felt his warm hug, his humanity. Now he was gone.

Knock 'em dead Kid, he'd said. It felt like a punch in the gut.

Dear God. I thought of his brother and sister, both former classmates of mine. I knew I wouldn't be able to go back to Ohio to attend his funeral. I had just arrived in California. I couldn't turn around now. I was on my own out here, away from all my friends. I sobbed for the first two hours of my arrival, with my parents trying to be helpful, trying to console me as we unpacked the cars. Fuck. David was dead, and there was nothing I could do about it.

Finally, I accepted the situation as it was. I was in California, my friend was dead, and I was going to miss his funeral.

3.7

There were advantages to staying with my aunt, and I was prepared to settle for a bit in the South Bay. There was a nice community college nearby, and the Apple headquarters just two miles up the street. Tech was just starting to boom in Silicon Valley, and opportunity was everywhere. Santa Cruz was a cool town and only 30 miles away, with San Francisco an hour north.

I opened a bank account at Wells Fargo because they had horses and a cool western theme as their logo, very different than my conservative and sterile bank in Ohio. I wanted to establish my California status as soon as possible. I'd dreamed of it for years.

I went to the Valley Fair mall and collected a few applications for retail jobs, although my choices were pretty dismal. After a brief chat with the manager, it was looking like Payless Shoe Source would have the pleasure of paying me $5.50 an hour.

I drove around that week, and I tried to get familiar with the area, but my natural sense of direction felt way off. I was always getting lost in San Jose, making right turns when I should've gone left. North went south. I felt disoriented and off-kilter.

I drove to Santa Cruz one afternoon and sat on the beach alone for a few hours, just taking in the powerful ocean energy and thinking of David, of Ohio, of why I had come to California.

I realized very quickly that San Jose didn't feel right to me. It had no magic to it. I couldn't imagine my future here, in this location. I *wanted* it to feel right, but it just didn't. I didn't have any friends here, and rock n' roll was non-existent, without having to drive up to San Francisco or Oakland. San Jose really didn't have much going on, it seemed. It was a techie town. I didn't even know where to start meeting people, much less people who liked my kind of music.

I thought of David and his family and all our friends, and the timing of his death—and I wondered if I had made a huge mistake. What was the meaning of it? Why now? The irony and sadness weighed heavy on my heart.

After an afternoon of wrong turns, I went to the Walgreens near my aunt's house to pick up a few things. I walked by the magazines, and a display of books and maps. I paused and browsed. I should have bought a map to help me around the San Jose and Bay Area, but when my eyes fell upon a brand-new Thomas Guide for Los Angeles, my heart did a flip. I knew I had to buy it, practicality be damned. I tore the plastic off the pristine new book when I got home, sniffing the smooth, clean pages, and flipping through, looking at the keys and the master index. I loved reading maps.

3.8

I studied that Thomas Guide all night, and the very the next day, I made the fortuitous phone call, trying to get in contact with Kenny. That's when I made a plan with his old roommate, Stacy, instead.

It all sounded crazy, driving so far to a strange city to meet a strange girl, but I was doing it, anyway. I'd bought a map, and within 24 hours, I had an invite to Los Angeles. It was meant to be, it felt like. I hadn't come this far to not follow the path that opened before me, and life was too short not to take the chance. Whatever happened, I was pretty sure I could handle it.

I borrowed a small cooler from my Aunt and packed snacks and water for the drive to LA. It was a place I had thought about for years, missing my dad and dreaming rock n' roll dreams. I was headed to Hollywood on a wing and a prayer, driving six hours down into a new, huge city to meet a stranger who used to be roommates with a friend of my friend from Ohio.

Los Angeles was like a magnet, an overwhelming force. I could feel the energy of it, like a giant heartbeat throbbing for me at the end of the road. It was a pull I had never felt before.

But it was familiar, too, like I was somehow remembering it. As I pointed my nose south and drove toward whatever lay ahead, I marveled at the geography of California. The mountains, the pastures, it was so vast and beautiful. I teared up at times, thinking of my mom, of my best friend Kathy, and of David. His life had been too short, and it was profoundly unfair.

I blasted Mötley Crüe as I made the final descent over the mountains into Los Angeles, sad, and happy and excited and scared. Starry Eyes played, reminding me of Kathy.

She should be here with me. I can't believe I'm doing this alone.

I finally crossed over into LA County, excited and curious about this Laurel Canyon address, not sure what was ahead of me as I merged into city traffic from the 5 to the 170 to the 101 straight into the belly of the beast: Hollywood. It was so foreign, so beautiful, so familiar all at once.

I was certain it was all good, though.

I came up on the exit and down Highland, took my time driving, and tried to get into the vibe of the place. I didn't mind the traffic as I crawled toward the boulevard. Hollywood traffic. Through the grittiness, it all sparkled with historic charm. It was all so old-school elegant, historic. I rolled down the windows to breathe it in. I turned right on to Hollywood Boulevard, alive with humanity, traffic, signs, stores, all tucked along these magnificent hills and mountains that oozed lush green. It really looked like a wonderland to me, a Cinderella in her ball gown.

This is it. This is Hollywood. Nikki Sixx is here, somewhere.

I wanted to rub it into my skin, it felt so good being there.

I made my way toward Laurel Canyon, confident that I was heading in the right direction. I didn't need to look at the map to verify or double-check. I knew exactly where I was and where I was supposed to be.

This was it. I was in Los Angeles.
I was finally, really home.

4.0

[Home Sweet Home]

Ohio 1980-1989

The first time I ever moved away from home was when my mom and I moved from Ashland to Westerville on January 17, 1980. I sat stoically in the front seat beside her as we drove down I-71 with only a tear or two escaping my eyes as we rolled through forests and farmland, away from my small life as I had known it. I was eight years old and in the middle of third grade.

My mom had scouted the Columbus area for a nice place to settle, and she chose the small suburb of Westerville on the north side, fairly close to the mall where she would be working. Home to Otterbein College, Westerville had the same brick-street Victorian flair as Ashland, complete with a walkable downtown, historic homes, and a grand old college campus with beautiful old trees.

In the 1920s, Westerville had been the center of the Prohibition movement, home of the Women's Christian Temperance Union, and it was still a dry town. Lots of parks and woods and safe neighborhoods to roam, and excellent schools. Westerville felt like home, immediately.

My mom found us a HUD apartment in a complex off Schrock Road, called Season's Four, right past the Honda Dealership and the Roller Chalet. Even with her new management job at the mall, we still qualified for public assistance. The complex itself was fine, made up of one, two, three, and four-bedroom apartments nestled up against the railroad tracks, a mile south of old-town Westerville.

Our apartment, at 38 Scott Ct, was a two-bedroom townhouse end unit with linoleum tile everywhere, including the bedrooms. But it had a full bathroom upstairs with a shower between two bedrooms, and a full, unfinished basement. It also had a half bath on the first floor in the hallway that led to the back door. Two toilets and a real shower? I'd never even taken a real shower because we'd never had one—just an ancient, plain, porcelain tub in the one bathroom we had, where I'd take my baths and wash my hair with a rubber showerhead hose that attached to the bathtub faucet. The new townhouse was 800 square feet of luxury compared to our much smaller apartment in Ashland.

But the Season's Four complex itself was not luxurious, and neither were the people. As I settled in and started hanging out with other kids, this didn't matter. We were all in the same boat. We were all poor. There were only a few kids in the complex that had a dad, and those dads usually worked two jobs and were hardly around. Most all of us were latchkey kids with single, working moms. We were like refugees on the Island of Misfit Toys, all of us different somehow, surrounded by a sea of working-class midwestern families.

There were packs of us. Our ages ranged from five up to about 14, with the older kids acting as chaperones and co-conspirators on various projects and adventures. Two doors down lived the Ward family, a family with four kids: Amy, Patty, Karen, and Jimmy. They had a cable box and HBO, which I had never seen before.

We'd never really had anything more than a used 13-inch black and white, which had broken a year prior. We'd be without a TV for three more years, but it didn't matter. Everyone around us had large color TVs to watch stuff on.

Next door to us were the Boorman twins, Randy and Ron, obsessed with Star Wars, Playboy, and Dungeons & Dragons. Their mom was Jeanette, a widowed, Virginia Slim-smoking cake decorator that worked at the new Kroger Sav-on across the street. A few doors down in the other direction were Holly and Kim and their divorced mom, Darla. Their dad was in Florida. Holly was two years older than me, and Kim was a teenager. They also had cable and HBO, and I hung out with Holly quite a bit. Across the street were the Gourley boys, three of them, running wild in the neighborhood, and in the courtyard behind me were Heather and Matt, who lived with their mom.

The moms in our neighborhood had a loose tribe of their own, too, and often relied upon each other to help with general and loose supervision. Parenting decisions weren't really questioned. Sometimes, certain kids went hungry, and sometimes certain kids were smacked around and we all knew it. But every one of these moms sheltered me after school and fed me at one point or another when my mom was working, and my mom did the same when she was home and could help.

My new neighborhood was rampant with various disadvantages. We had diabetics, cerebral palsy, drug addicts, giant birthmarks, a facial deformity, a quadriplegic, the elderly, rampant obesity, a rumored former mobster, and a number of African-American families. I never saw racism or unkindness here, though. We were all scraping by or struggling somehow. Poverty, divorce, and disability were not easy on us, but it bound us all together and gave us a lot of freedom. We were all the same, but with different crosses to bear. Expectations from our parents were not high. We accepted each other, and our circumstances, without question. We shared what we had, if we could.

We roamed our neighborhood and little 'ville for miles, we played in the crick, we put pennies on the railroad tracks to squish them under the wheels of the afternoon train that would rumble by, and we'd wonder if a derailment would take out our apartment buildings. We'd walk over to the Kroger Sav-on and play Asteroids, if we had a couple of quarters to spare. We captured caterpillars and lightning bugs and kept pet rats. We built obstacle courses, played hide and seek, had water balloon fights, and played kickball in the courtyard. We rubbed marigolds on ourselves to keep away mosquitos, and we collected wild strawberries and raspberries from the woods and ravine nearby, coated them in sugar and froze them. Sometimes I pretended that I was Laura Ingalls tromping through the forest, being self-sufficient and living off the land.

I settled in to my new school, Longfellow Elementary, and tried to make the best of it in my new third-grade class, feeling painfully shy and awkward. I finally got glasses through the Lion's Club and could see the blackboard, although I was still daydreaming. I had a very nice teacher who was gentle with me as I settled in, and made me feel welcome. I made new friends and walked the mile to school and back every day, through a beautiful old neighborhood lush with giant maple and oak trees, brick streets, and huge historic houses that I could imagine living in.

It was the older kids who introduced me to all kinds of new things, including new music.

I still loved KISS, but my mom always listened to top 40, Motown, with a little bit of rock thrown in. Now there was Foreigner and Journey and Pink Floyd and Black Sabbath and Rush and Queen and AC/DC and Led Zeppelin and Heart and Styx.

I loved all of it. I felt powerful and free after my experiences with Miss Strong, singing at the top of my lungs—*We don't need no education! We don't need no thought control!* It was powerful stuff to an eight-year old, this rebellion, this music. We had a great rock station in Columbus, QFM 96, that fed us a steady diet of it all, and I would listen to it on my mom's old Panasonic FM radio.

But then my friend Holly got a new stereo for Christmas, along with a bunch of Led Zeppelin albums. We were soon both totally obsessed.

4.1

Holly had pictures of Robert Plant on her wall, with his magnificent mane of hair and bulging trousers. There is one picture of him holding a cigarette and a bottle of beer in one hand, and a resting white dove on the other, standing onstage in front of an audience.

Everything about this photo captivated me. He was in command, but things were not in his control. He was a bad boy on one hand with the vices, and holding peace in the other. He has wild lion hair, and is wearing a woman's blouse, yet he is very clearly masculine. He looks amused at the absurdity of this bird, daring to perch upon him as he performed.

I contemplated all these things, but mostly, I wondered about the bulge in his pants because I had only seen the bulge of a Ken Doll, and the studded codpiece of Gene Simmons, which in my mind was just a fancied-up Ken Doll bulge.

I knew the word *penis*, but I had never actually seen one or had any idea of what a penis was. The actual outline of one through Robert Plant's skin-tight jeans made me curious. He was so magnificent. He wore a bead necklace and puffy sleeves. His bulge was lumpy and on one side of the seam, and went down his leg. I didn't understand. *What was that thing?* I wondered. It kind of made me tingle.

And then one day, when my 14-year-old neighbor, Randy, was showing me his latest Star Wars collectables and new Dungeons & Dragons set, his penis fell out of his gym shorts and I saw the whole hairy, pinkish package. I was surprised, and I said *gross, put it away*. I wasn't sure if it fell out on purpose—if he was trying to molest me, pull a joke on me, or just doing it to generally fuck with me—or maybe it was an accident. I didn't know.

I told Holly about it later, and she told me, "Oh, beware, he always flashes his thing at the girls."

How creepy. "Gee, thanks for warning me," I said, rolling my eyes.

"Did he have a boner?" She raised her eyebrow, curious.

"What's a boner?" I had no idea what she meant. "It just kind of flopped there, on his thigh," I told her.

"No, it swells up and gets hard and sticks up, like a bone. It has to be hard so they can put it inside of you," she explained.

"OH! Wow. I had no idea." I was both horrified, and intrigued.

It finally started making sense. All the rock n' roll innuendo's that I'd missed, all the romance books that alluded to the act. I hadn't understood fully, but now I did. Sex was penetration. *I'm going to be penetrated. Good grief.* I felt a little anxious over it and wondered, *would it hurt?*

Holly said that it hurt at first, but got better, according to her older sister, Kim, who was having sex with her first boyfriend. Holly explained everything to me as best as a sixth grader can explain these things to a fourth grader.

She even showed me a real condom and described ejaculation.

FINALLY, I understood how a penis functioned, and sort-of, how my vagina would function. I started reading the articles in Cosmo with a new knowing, indoctrinating myself into a culture of glamorous, independent womanhood. I studied my mom's box of Tampax for anatomical reference, even though I wasn't bleeding, yet.

How else was I supposed to gain this knowledge of my body, of sex, of boys and men? My mom hadn't really told me much, and I didn't know what to ask, anyway. I had no relationships with any males—no brothers, my uncles were in another city, and my grandfather was 90. My mom didn't date or go out. There was no "guy" humor or boner talk in my house. I wasn't sure how men were supposed to behave, or even how I was supposed to behave. So I learned from my neighbors, my friends, romance novels, Judy Blume, Cosmo, and Led Zeppelin.

If you listen to enough Led Zeppelin lyrics, you start to get to know how men function. Now that I had more of the information I needed, it started to all make sense. *The Lemon Song* wasn't about fruit, after all.

4.2

My mom always had books around the house, and we could walk to the Westerville Public Library from the apartment, which I did once or twice a week on my way home from school. I didn't even bother going to the youth area. I stayed in the adult fiction section, and worked my way through authors. Sometimes, I'd jump over to non-fiction, especially after seeing the movie *Mommy Dearest* and wanting to read the book and learn more about Joan Crawford and Hollywood.

My teacher in the 4th grade was a nice lady who knew I loved to read, and she started a book report contest for the class. The smartest, most popular girl in the class, Tanya, turned in 5 book reports over the course of the contest. I turned in over 30, and most of them weren't kid books. It was the only time I ever excelled at something in school.

By then, I had started reading Stephen King. My mom was working, and I could hole myself up in the apartment for the whole day and lay in bed and read. I finished *Salem's Lot* in less than 24 hours. I read *Carrie*, *The Shining*, *Cujo*, *Pet Semetary*, and the *Dead Zone* in the same way—in vast inhales. I was totally absorbed by his writing, his stories. I would read for hours and lose entire days to his books about strange happenings and magical forces.

I also loved reading historical romances. My very favorite author was Kathleen E. Woodiwiss. She wrote these truly epic, suspenseful, terribly romantic books, *The Flame and the Flower, Shana, The Wolf and the Dove*, and many others. I was fascinated by the history, the depictions of life in various time periods, especially *in The Wolf and the Dove*, set in medieval times, at the time of the Norman Invasion. Reading those books taught me a lot about sex, romance, men, relationships, and history. Reading them all while listening to Led Zeppelin with their talk of ancient lands and mythical things—it was almost like learning about history in a three-dimensional way.

I was in the early stages of puberty, and started having strong romantic feelings toward Robert Plant. He seemed to me some ancient warrior, mounted on a stallion, conquering foreign lands in a plate-armor suit. Like Wulfgar, the main character in the *Wolf and the Dove*. Regal and Arthurian. Jimmy Page seemed like his wicked personal magician, his Lancelot, his dark foil, compelling and mysterious, with magic symbols on his velvet pants. It furthered my love for all things medieval and esoteric.

Led Zeppelin were like gods to me that summer. Holly and I watched *The Song Remains the Same* whenever it was scheduled on her cable TV, and we'd lay in her room and listen to every album, in order. I worshipped them. *Houses of the Holy* became scripture, *Led Zeppelin IV* my chapbook of happiness. "Going to California" and "The Ocean" both reminded me of my dad. I started fourth grade with a good working knowledge of Led Zeppelin's entire catalog of music, and I had made my way through a good stack of reading, too.

4.3

In late September 1980, we got news on a Friday that John Bonham, the drummer of Led Zeppelin, had died. Holly came down to my apartment and knocked on the door, red-eyed and sniffling on my doorstep, and broke the news. I felt terrible.

"Choked on his own vomit!" she said. She held a newspaper clipping out for me to read.

How awful. We looked at each other, wide-eyed, trying to fathom it. And then we started giggling in a fit of black humor. How stupid and gross and weird. We didn't even know that someone could die that way. We were still young and oblivious to the fact that many other rock stars had, indeed, choked on their own barf

"The Who's Keith Moon died that way," her sister Kim had told us, and we were like, *Who's Keith Moon?* She just looked at us and blinked. "No, *The Who's* Keith Moon," Kim stated, more emphatically. Our response was, *who's Keith Moon?* and it drove her a little crazy.

"Keith Moon is another drummer, in a band called The Who," she explained. "He died by choking on his own vomit."

Oohhhhh! We finally got it. "So did Jimi Hendrix, and Bon Scott, the guy from AC/DC," Kim informed us, smirking.

In honor of Bonham, Kim propped her giant stereo speakers in the front bedroom windows of their apartment and started blasting Led Zeppelin, which echoed throughout our little court as dusk fell. We roamed the neighborhood until all the moms came out to sit on the front stoops to enjoy the fresh September night air and visit. Someone fired up an old charcoal grill so we could stop by and toast up some marshmallows. We started a game of hide and seek, playing until way after bedtime to the beautiful noises of Robert Plant, Jimmy Page, John Paul Jones, and our dearly departed and ever-eternal John Bonham.

We raised our toasted marshmallows to him around our little fire, and we played on into the night.

A few months later, John Lennon was shot dead, and then, we just cried.

4.4

My mom lost her job at Casual Corner, and she collected unemployment for a while, and we visited the food pantry for a few months for rice and cheese, just like most of our neighbors did.

Then, she found a job as an assistant manager at RAX Roast Beef—a fast food chain, similar to Arby's. They had great sandwiches and a nice salad bar. I ate really well for a while, my mom bringing home leftovers after her shift every night. I'd get cold roast beef sandwiches and potato salad in my lunches for school the next day.

Our old, shitty car died a smoky, engine-blown death, finally, after driving it for years with cardboard under the rubber mats to cover the spots that were rusted through to the pavement below. We were both glad to see the junker go.

My mom bought a 1971 Chevy Impala coupe from a coworker at RAX, a ridiculously huge car with a huge front seat that she had to scooch all the way up to fit her 5'1" self. The Impala had an enormous trunk that could fit our garage sale hauls, and it came with an eight-track tape deck, with two cassettes tucked into the glove box: *The Beach Boys Greatest Hits*, and *Kenny Rogers Greatest Hits*. We listened to the two cassettes a lot, and those songs etched a deep hole into my heart.

She closed the restaurant four or five nights a week, which meant I would come home from school to an empty apartment, or have days alone, on the weekend. I'd call her from our yellow rotary wall phone to check in. She usually had a dinner plan for me—a fresh bowl of tuna salad, or a few TV dinners to choose from in the freezer, a couple of Faygo's in the fridge. We had a neighbor with a one-year old and a new baby, and some days I'd go to her house for a few hours to help her fold diapers and hang out, and she'd feed me, too. There was always a bologna sandwich to be had at the Wards' place. Holly always had chocolate treats—her mom kept Snickers bars on hand all the time, it seemed.

But mostly for these years, I was left to my own devices. I'd go knocking on my neighbors' doors, or they'd come knocking on mine to hang out. Music and HBO down at Holly's, playing Barbies over at Heather's, board games at the Wards' with Karen. And then I'd make my way home after playing, eat my dinner, and settle in to read a book. I'd call my mom again, before I went to bed, and she always came in to say goodnight after she got home, usually around 10:30pm.

One night, I startled awake at midnight and realized that my mom wasn't home. I got up to look and see if she was in her bed, and then I looked out the front window for her car. Not there. The street was quiet, her parking spot empty under the orange glow of the street light. I checked the clock. I went downstairs and got something to drink. I tried calling the restaurant, but the phone just rang and rang.

I went back to my bed, worried. She always came straight home after work.

Finally, at 3:30am, I heard the lock turn and the door open. I sat up, and she immediately ran up the staircase to my room. She gathered me in a hug and began to cry. She sobbed and sobbed and I started crying, too, not knowing why, only that my mom was scared, shaken, and that she was home, finally home. We hugged for a few minutes and she told me what happened.

The RAX store had been robbed. She'd had a gun in her face, and one of her employees was beaten. They were all locked in the walk-in refrigerator for a few hours until the Columbus Police Department had noticed the employees' cars and the lights still on in the restaurant at such a late hour, and stopped to check, and ended up rescuing them. An ambulance was involved. Employees all had to stay and give their statements. My mom stayed the longest, as the person in charge of the restaurant during the robbery. She was not injured, just scared shitless. She'd had to remain calm throughout the entire thing, knowing that I was at home, alone. She couldn't panic and get herself killed.

She also couldn't let the police know that she had a little girl at home waiting for her, either. It would be bad if they found out, she said. She sobbed the whole thing out, and as we sat up and talked about it all, I realized how very alone I was in the world. *If something happened to her, what would become of me?* I wondered. *Who would I call?*

Maybe I could lie and just live here, like Jodi Foster did in *The Little Girl Who Lives Down the Lane*. Maybe no one would notice that my mom was gone and I could just live in the apartment by myself for a while.

I didn't want to go back to Ashland. *Maybe one of the neighborhood families would take me in*, I thought. They were like my family, kind of. Otherwise, I would be an orphan in the world. Truly an orphan. A ward of the state.

I remembered the old orphanage in Ashland, a dank, gothic, scary building on the edge of town that stood in a desolate field. My Aunt Merk had told me it was an awful place. I was pretty sure bad things happened there. It had a creepy, black vibe every time I drove by, like people had suffered and died there.

Most likely, though, I'd have to go back to Ashland and live with my aunt, uncle, and cousins.

I could hardly bear the thought of it. I liked Westerville, my new home. I was actually happy here. We were poor, but we were together, and I had friends.

Maybe I could find my dad? Maybe he'd take me. I still had no idea where he was. California? It tickled the back of my brain—was he still there? I didn't know. I was 11 now and hadn't seen him since I was four. I didn't know where my grandparents were, either—somewhere in Michigan, I thought. I hadn't heard from them at all. Were they still alive? How would I find them? Would they even care?

I worried about it for years afterward and it lurked in the back of my mind that my life would change forever if anything were to happen to my mom. It was just us, we only had each other. Without her, it would just be me, alone. Surviving this world.

I had crawled in bed with her after she got home, and we slept in, *snuggled like two bugs in a rug*, she'd say. My mom kept me home from school the day after the robbery, and she stayed home from work. We went over to the Westerville Mall to see an early showing of *Rocky*

III. After the movie, we walked hand in hand down the mall to Mr. C's Diner to get a hamburger and a malt.

Soon after the robbery, she picked up a second job, in the seafood department at the Kroger Sav-On across the street. She came home stinking of fish and rot and chlorine, but she did it with humor and as much grace as she could muster while wearing a paper hat and a bloody apron to serve my richer schoolmates' parents their piles of shrimp, crab legs, and salmon filets.

She had a plastic trash bag in the front hall closet for her stinking work clothes and we doused it with baking soda until she could do a load of laundry—but the smell of rotting fish still wafted through the apartment if you were near the closet. That closet never smelled the same, even years later.

4.5

Eventually, she was able to quit both RAX and the stinky fish job at Kroger when she found a job managing a small gift shop at an outdoor shopping mall nearby. The Giftique was at The Continent, an open-air mall loosely modeled after a European city market, with retail stores at the street level, and apartments above. Everything you could need to live there was within walking distance, a faux-European village. The Giftique was still a retail job with bad hours, but the store was pretty, with small collections of handcrafted and unique gifts.

While she worked there, I'd go with her every Saturday and Sunday, and soon, I was working the register and ringing up sales. I loved helping my mom and being with her all day. If it was slow, I could read my books in the back room, and I could wander the whole mall when I went out to pick up our lunch or to the bank to get change.

During the weekdays of summer, I started going to a sitter's house. She was an older lady named Sarah that had a big old brick Victorian-style house near Otterbein College in Westerville. Sarah was smart like a fox: she had us kids clean the house, do her yardwork, and fix our own meals.

My mom had always been lenient on chores—she didn't teach me how to do much, probably because it was just easier to do it herself, and my room was always a mess. So, it was at Sarah's house that I learned how to do laundry properly, wash dishes and windows, dust and vacuum, all the household ironing. Sarah supervised everything and taught us the "right" way, and then she'd sit back and watch her soap operas for two hours while the kids did the whole house.

Every day for months, I'd change this woman's bed sheets. She insisted on fresh, line-dried sheets, EVERY DAY. I hosed off her screens, I washed her car, I scrubbed her toilets, and I weeded her garden. Although I resented it for a while, I was also secretly grateful. I liked "keeping house," and there was something soothing about the routine of chores. She had a small handheld radio that she'd let me borrow so I could do chores while listening to music. It was something, at least.

If we did the house quickly, she'd let us watch cable for the last hour of the day, and she had MTV. So we'd squabble over the channel we'd watch, but I was usually able to convince others, so I did get to watch MTV a few hours a week. This was the era of Michael Jackson, Culture Club, and Duran Duran, and I loved their music videos. I begged my mom to get a real TV and cable so that I could watch MTV. It took her two more years, and only after Papa died, until she was finally able to buy a brand-new color TV, and a year after that before she splurged and got cable.

My mom was a hard worker, but it was almost impossible for her to save for the future. Whatever money she earned, was spent—not only on the basics, but also to decorate and make our apartment comfortable and pretty and tidy, unlike many of the other homes in our neighborhood. Sometimes, I was shocked at how dirty, cluttered, and gross their homes were. My mom had scented candles and dried flower arrangements and glue-gunned toss pillows. She'd bitch at me for leaving messes, even though I was hardly aware that I did.

My mom usually didn't have a lot of free time, but when she did, we were together and we tried to have fun and go do things. When we could, we'd go try a restaurant, or to the movies, or go on a Saturday morning garage sale adventure in search of treasure. She'd throw me a few of her hard-earned dollars every week so I could roam around and take care of myself, too. Some weeks we had to cut back, some weeks we lived larger.

Either way, I knew I was loved.

She told me so every single day that I was loved, that I was good, that we'd be OK, that my life was up to me, and to work hard. *No one owes you anything*, she'd say if she ever sensed entitlement or an attitude from me. I tried not to give her too much shit.

She was also tired, critical a lot, and she was emotive the way that Sicilians can be, and a yeller—you always knew where you stood with her, and she would call you out on your BS, too, with a bite. When I'd leave the kitchen a mess, I heard all about it. No silent treatment, ever, in our house, and, once in a while, she threw a few swear words out of frustration and fatigue, which always seemed to shock her more than it did me. It offended her good-girl Catholic core. She'd say "fuck" in a tirade and I'd laugh, and then she'd laugh, and then she'd be fine, and tell me she loved me.

My mom had a fiery, generous nature and an unfailing work ethic and a silly sense of humor. She was both up in my shit all the time, and a grantor of my autonomy. She never let me go out of the house looking sloppy or unkempt. Good grooming was everything. She insisted I use manners and show respect to my elders. She taught me proper eating etiquette, and praised my neat handwriting.

But most of all, she never, ever gave up. She always tried to better our circumstances, always hustled. It was just the two of us against the world, and my mom didn't waver in her love, or her responsibility to provide for me, no matter what the sacrifice.

For a long time, my mom's fierceness and love made up for not having a dad. She was a great single parent, by any set of measures. She didn't drink or do drugs, she didn't date men at all. I once asked her why, and she told me it was because she still loved my Dad— which shocked me into silence. It was one of the only times she ever talked about him, or her feelings about him, and it startled me. He was not a topic of regular conversation because he just didn't come up much in our daily life. She'd answer questions I had, when I had them, but guardedly. She didn't talk badly about my dad, just…carefully. So I'd had no idea how she really felt.

Her answers sheltered me from the cold, ugly truth: he was a deeply troubled man who ran from his responsibilities. He'd not only left me and my mom, but he'd also left his second wife and the baby brother I'd never met. He left both his children vulnerable, in poverty, and without a father because he was still fighting demons from Vietnam.

It's still hard to know what is forgivable, and what is not.

4.6

Even though I was alone, and sometimes lonely, I wasn't ever abused. Just the opposite, I now think. I was sheltered. I was sheltered by my mother's ethics. Her basic morality and dignity. I was sheltered by the neighborhood of poor people who looked out for me.

Our biggest troubles were economic, but I was lucky—we had our basic needs met, and we more than made up for it with love. She also drove me a bit crazy, like mothers do to their strong-willed daughters.

I had many freedoms simply not available to children today—the freedom to set my own course over the days and weeks that I was home alone, the freedom to read whatever I wanted, to do what I wanted with my time, to listen to music that I liked—to create, read, play, listen, explore, eat, sleep—all of it my own choice on my own timeline, with minimal input from my mom. My mom trusted me. She trusted my judgement.

She would never, ever question a book I was reading, even if it was a semi-pornographic, loins-thrusting bodice-ripper that I loved. She was proud of the fact that I was an advanced reader, and we'd talk about the stories, the history, the plot. We talked about adult books like I was an adult. She let me read whatever the hell I wanted, and would answer my questions if I had them. I was reading books about Jack the Ripper, the Black Dahlia murder, and paranormal stuff. I loved ghost stories, Edgar Allen Poe, and mythology, past lives. Danger, drama, history, smut. Whatever I could get my hands on.

I became a big fan of Jackie Collins. I loved the book, *Chances*, with the character of Lucky Santangelo. I wanted to be Lucky Santangelo. I moved on to the *Hollywood Wives* series. With many of her books set in Los Angeles, I started to really envision California, the people, the culture, the game. I learned a lot about sex, drugs, and rock n' roll from reading Jackie Collins' books. That woman told a great, rocking story. I also loved Sidney Sheldon, Michael Crichton, Elmore Leonard. I learned how to research at the Library, looking for tidbits of information about Los Angeles.

My mom and I went to see R-rated movies all the time: *The Amityville Horror* when I was seven, *Creepshow* when I was nine, *Friday the 13th part 3*, *The Best Little Whorehouse in Texas*, *Footloose*, and *Purple Rain* when I was a young teen.

She was even awesome enough to keep me out of school to go the Northland Mall for the first screenings of *The Empire Strikes Back* and then *Return of the Jedi* a couple of years later.

"This is historic," she'd said as we walked down the mall to queue up in line with hundreds of other people. I was almost taller than her, but we'd still hold hands sometimes as we strolled. We both loved the Star Wars stories and the concept of The Force.

The Force felt very right. The thing that connects us all together. The energy of vibrations, of intention, of dreams, of magic.

I understood it. I'd felt it all my life.

4.7

By 1984, My mom had taken a job with an insurance company, selling policies.

Insurance was tough in the early-to-mid 1980s, and not too many men would buy policies from her. So, she focused on making connections with women. Through her friendliness and word of mouth, she had gained a number of African-American women business owners who opened their doors to her and became her clients.

My mom had always had black friends, from the time I was a small toddler. One of those friends, a hairdresser named Aquanetta, had twin baby boys my age. We played well together and all napped in the same bed when she would watch me. When my mom was in college, she hosted an exchange student from Kenya, who lived with us for three months. My mom loved Motown music, and I grew up thinking Lando Calrissian and Apollo Creed were as handsome as Han Solo and Rocky Balboa—it made no difference to me that they were black. My mom never made a big deal about race. She treated everyone with kindness and humor.

One of her clients, Earlene, owned a shoe store at the Westerville Mall, and they became friends. Earlene offered me a little side gig after school and on weekends, organizing the back room, helping with inventory, and doing chores, like dusting the displays. The work wasn't difficult, so I agreed immediately. Plus, Earlene was fun to hang out with.

Earlene also had steady summer work for me, and every August for seven years, I'd help her sell Minnetonka Moccasins at her vendor booth at the Ohio State Fair. My summer job with Earlene was the equivalent to summer camp, or an exotic vacation. I looked forward to it every year. The booth was in a big open-air barn, right in the middle of everything. My mom would drop me off, or Earlene would pick me up in her sporty Subaru, and I would be at the fairgrounds from 8am until 10pm on some days, and on my feet for most of them.

The Ohio State fair is huge, the largest in the country. Earlene's booth was in an agricultural building with a hundred other booths, selling everything from crystals and jewelry to baseball cards, antiques and art work, fabric paint to roach clips, chef's knives, popcorn poppers, and pool tables. It was crazy how much stuff you could buy at the fair.

The next building over was the poultry and rabbit barn, and the variety of different chickens just fascinated me. I could wander the fair on my breaks and eat awesome food and go visit the horses and cows and the butter statue, go down the giant slide on a burlap sack just for the heck of it. There was a horse show every day, and I could wander the barns and say hello to these beautiful creatures. I could go hold a baby pig, which was awesome, and I often stopped to pet the cows, too, which reminded me of being on the farm with my dad and grandparents. I knew the layout of the fair like the back of my hand, and my vendor badge let me in a lot of places.

Earlene's moccasin booth was close enough to the music stadium that we could hear the live music all the time, and sometimes I could go see a show. Dolly Parton, Kenny Rogers, The Beach Boys. It was fun knowing all the songs and seeing them performed live. One time, Earlene and I walked over together on a balmy evening to see Gladys Knight and the Pips, and we both had a great time dancing and moving to the music. It was a great job for a kid—it was hard work, but balanced with freedom and fun.

I made three bucks an hour, plus a dollar per pair of shoes I sold. Except for the first hour of the fair, we were busy all the time, it seemed. Everyone loved moccasins, and we sold a lot of them. Older folks with bunions. Hunters. Invalids. College co-eds. Rednecks. Hippies. I wore them, too—it was the only way to survive standing on the asphalt and the miles of walking I had to do. Plus, it helped me sell more shoes.

Earlene had been in business and at the fair for years and was well-loved by her customers. If they were coming from a distance—and people drive from all over the Midwest to attend the biggest state fair in the country—they'd make it a point to come by to see Earlene and buy four or five pairs of shoes every year. After counting the register, she paid me out in cash every night.

By the end of the fair, 17 full days plus set up and teardown, I could clear six or seven hundred tax-free dollars, after the couple of hundred I'd blow at the fair itself, feeding myself and having fun. Earlene would let me pick out a couple of pairs of moccasins, too, as a bonus, before we did inventory. The money I earned by working for Earlene is how I bought school clothes and books and other luxuries from the time I was 11 until I was 17. Even with other part time jobs over the years, I always cleared my schedule to work the fair for her.

Earlene was like a second mom to me, and always gave me hugs and kisses. She worked me hard, but was kind and generous. We had fun and were always kidding and making jokes, a sort of odd-couple: an older, glamorous black boss-lady and her young white, awkward protégé.

I loved her very much.

4.8

Blendon Middle School sat right next to the high school I'd eventually graduate from, a low brick building with a few open concept classrooms, pods, as they were called. It was all new and overwhelming, but at least I had a locker in the blue section, just steps away from my homeroom. I started noticing boys a bit more, and they started noticing me, even with the bad hair, plastic mauve glasses, and crooked teeth. Top that off with legwarmers, prairie skirts, rubber bracelets, and blue Maybelline mascara, I fit right in with every other awkward seventh grader.

This was the golden age of MTV—Duran Duran, Madonna, Michael Jackson, and Cyndi Lauper, with a bit of Prince and Billy Idol and Joan Jett thrown in. It was hard not to like some of it. I was a big fan of Duran Duran and Prince. Both were sexy, yet effeminate. But that music just didn't quite get to me like KISS or Led Zeppelin had; I liked melodic music, but I liked it much heavier, and there was no denying my love of the long-haired guys in their denim and leather.

But for a while, Duran Duran were a great distraction, and I loved John Taylor. Along with Gene Simmons, it was always the bass players that I loved the most: Nikki Sixx, Duff McKagan, Lemmy.

Walkman cassette players were a new thing, and a kid named Scott let me share his headphones to listen to the new Van Halen album (with keyboards!) when we rode the bus to school.

I eventually bought my own Walkman with my fair money, and Scott let me borrow all kinds of new music during our bus rides—the Scorpions' *Love Drive*, Dokken's *Tooth and Nail*, Def Leppard's *Pyromania*, and RATT's *Out of the Cellar*.

Still Lovin' You, by the Scorpions, and *Alone Again*, by Dokken were two songs I was obsessed with for a while, because they were in my vocal range—those power ballads were addictive to me because I could sing them. I could sing my heart out to them.

I became friends with a Ukrainian girl named Julia Kogan, who lived not far away from us. Julia and I bonded during seventh and eighth grade Girl's Glee club, where we were both second sopranos. Julia had a beautiful singing voice and always encouraged my own abilities. She tolerated my rock and pop stuff, and I learned about her classical opera and show tunes, and we spent hours together listening to music and talking about books. Her family was happy, warm, and inviting, grateful to be in America, and they treated me like a daughter. It was with Julia that I first felt the comfort and joy of singing, and I discovered that I actually had a half-decent singing voice.

Julia would go on to become a world-class and award-winning coloratura opera singer in Europe.

Performing in front of people, however, gave me a lot of anxiety.

4.9

My eighth grade English teacher, Mrs. Furniss, was a known hard-ass and stickler, but I was curious about these rumors. How bad could she be? Nothing could ever be as bad as Miss Strong, I was sure of that. I was a mediocre student, but I always had hope that I'd get decent teachers. Most of the time, I did.

Mrs. Furniss turned out to be wonderful. With her help, I was the only student in the school to write and publish three pieces in the annual school magazine. She took a shine to me, and wrote me encouraging notes on the work I turned in.

It was in this class that I met Kathy. We were seated next to each other, alphabetically by last name, and we both had short, brown hair. She had the braces and I had the glasses. She was quiet and polite, but all over her book covers were drawn pentagrams and band logos, and I was curious about her immediately. We also had gym class together, and soon after starting the school year, we were best, best friends.

She was the middle child in a middle-class family that owned a nice house in the nice subdivision not too far from our condo. Her dad was an Air Force reservist and an engineer, her mom a nurse-turned full-time stay-at-home parent. Kathy had devilish green eyes and a mischievous streak, and we spent every free moment together from eighth grade all the way through our senior year. Unlike me, she was pretty much a straight-A student, and yet she taught me how to shoplift from the drug store just down the street. The only thing we ever stole was makeup, but we were both scared straight and stopped our sticky-fingered ways when our mutual friend, Jeni, was busted at the same store for shoplifting a single Cover Girl Cheekers blush.

Kathy introduced me to Mötley Crüe and a lot of other music she liked—Bon Jovi, Aerosmith, Ozzy, Dio. Soon, we were both completely obsessed with Mötley. Everything about The Crüe, I loved. I read the liner notes on their albums, memorized names and lyrics and absorbed anything about them I could find.

I felt a strong connection to Nikki Sixx through his lyrics, and so much of the pain and uncertainty I had felt as a child was reflected in the music. Plus, it was sexy and dirty and totally rebellious and dark. Mötley Crüe pushed boundaries that no one else was doing at that time. They were dangerous and punk and a bit Mad Max. I was always intrigued by anything with the Devil or supernatural thrown in.

And sex. *Watch her scream, watch her suck you clean.* This was beyond what I had read in Cosmo, or the Woodiwiss romance novels, or Judy Blume. This was down and dirty and raunchy. Subversive, even. I was attracted to it all, immediately. These nasty boys with their makeup and spandex and devil talk had hooked me right in. Danger and androgyny, an intoxicating duo.

Nikki was handsome, rebellious, and wrote great songs. He was a little scary, too, but you could hear tenderness in some songs—the pain. Soon, he was plastered all over my bedroom walls. I loved the guy, I really loved him. A kindred spirit, or maybe my spirit animal. Nikki was my inspiration, the one I wanted to run away with. Kathy was obsessed with Vince, and I loved Nikki. We both agreed that Tommy was our second choice.

4.10

Mötley Crüe's third album, *Theater of Pain*, was released the summer before we started our freshmen year, and it was a fun change after two dark and raw albums. *Theater of Pain* was lighter and glam. Some good songs, like *City Boy Blues* and *Raise Your Hands to Rock*, but the songs weren't as meaty or angry as the first two albums. Of course, then there was *Home Sweet Home*—the ballad of all rock ballads. My favorite guitar solo of all time, I think.

That summer, Kathy and I would sit in front of MTV and call in to request the *Home Sweet Home* video over and over again, which stayed in the number one slot for something like three months until they changed the rules. It didn't stop their rising popularity, though. With the help of MTV, bands like RATT, Ozzy Osborne, Poison, and Def Leppard were getting hugely popular, and heavy metal was going mainstream.

With Kathy, I now had a partner in petty crimes and rock n' roll adventures as we made our way through middle and high school, listening to every rock and metal band that we could, and plotting our escape from Ohio.

***

One morning, I came down to breakfast and my mom had saved a newspaper article for me to read. It mentioned Mötley Crüe and Prince, and she knew I liked both of them. *Cool*, I thought. *Mötley Crüe is mentioned in the Columbus Dispatch!* But then, I was shocked at what I read.

A senator's wife, and our future second lady, Tipper Gore, was heading up a committee called the

Parent's Music Resource Center—PMRC—that was exploring the concept of labeling albums with warnings and ratings, kind of like the movies. These labels and ratings would inform parents if the music contained within the package was indeed appropriate for their children.

The PMRC released a list of the "Filthy 15"—fifteen songs that they were specifically concerned about—like Prince's *Darling Nikki* for describing masturbation, and Mötley Crüe's *Knock 'em Dead, Kid*, for advocating violence. Other songs were targeted for promoting drug use or sado-masochism or cop-killing.

The whole idea of the music I loved being subject to censorship by these uptight Stepford Wives was galling to me. I was willing to lock arms with my fellow music fans—black, white, metal, rock, rap—whatever—to stand together in the face of government censorship.

The whole thing escalated to the point of congressional hearings in Washington, DC. I watched the testimony of Frank Zappa, Dee Snider, and John Denver with rapt amazement. While Dee Snider was quite the spectacle with his wild hair and bulging trousers, I paid the most attention to Mr. Zappa, mostly because he was Italian.

The things that were said that day by Zappa, Snider, and Denver really opened my eyes. Up until their testimony, I had never thought of heavy metal as "art" or that musicians were "artists." I was a fan purely for the entertainment factor.

Not only was Frank Zappa a musician, he was eloquent and funny, and loved to challenge assumptions and push the envelope. He was a smart man. Best of all, he was a parent of four children—just like Tipper and Al Gore. In other words, he was no less concerned for the well-being of his own children—but he had a completely different viewpoint about what to be concerned with. Government censorship? Hell yes. A few sexy lyrics? Absolutely not. *How awesome would it be to have a dad like Frank Zappa?* I wondered to myself.

I tended to see the whole debate in terms of generations. The PMRC seemed like a bunch of post-Vietnam Baby-Boomer guilt about the loss of control over their own children, my generation, which wasn't named yet, but who were loving the music and artists that the PMRC were so upset about. We went on to be called Generation X. The latchkey kids, an entire generation lost to divorce, hopeless slackers, born to mediocrity.

That's the common narrative, at least, and it's mostly true for me, although I know I'm making a lot of sweeping generalizations. Vietnam was a Boomer war, and it affected us in a second wave, a ripple through our generation that dealt with parental instability, divorce, addiction. Probably more than is acknowledged. Many guys, like my Dad, came back from Vietnam, barely able to function. The kids in my generation, we knew we were going to have a harder time of it than our parents, and it came out in the rebellious, heavy music.

Of course, everything sounded like "heavy metal" to our parents—Bon Jovi was heavy metal, as was Slayer. They didn't care for any of it, and didn't understand the differences or subtleties of each "type" of metal. It was all bad to them. Long hair was bad. Tattoos were bad. It seemed like our parents couldn't handle the truth that the music revealed, the sexual freedom, rebelliousness, the anger, and the darkness. It was our form of self-medicating due to the unstable world they created for us.

At least it was, for me.

And now they were trying to censor it.

More than any history or government class, the testimony of Zappa and the others during that time taught me what the First Amendment actually was about: not only free speech, but the concept of Freedom of Information, Freedom of Self-Expression, Freedom of the Press, Intellectual Freedom, Artistic Intent and Vision, all of these things.

I credit Frank Zappa with that paradigm shift. It's the shift that left me clearly seeing the connections between books, music, and art. The shift that made me understand that no one had the right to tell me what I could read, write, listen to, support, or believe. This was powerful to me. It gave me confidence. I had rights as an American citizen, and the freedom to think as I wanted, to inform myself, to speak freely—the beauty of the First Amendment.

It's First for a reason, I read somewhere. It was freedom of mind, an "inalienable right" granted from the Creator, and protected by our Constitution. Our entire Republic stemmed from it. It made a lot of sense to me now.

While attempting to inform parents about what their kids were listening to, the PMRC episode actually served a much greater purpose—to teach kids like me about our rights as American citizens. It was a giant civics lesson.

It sparked more rebellion in me than if we had just been left alone to enjoy our favorite artists.

Fuck them. Fuck Tipper Gore. Fuck the PMRC. *Fuck censorship.*

Luckily, my mom let me listen to anything, anyway. Just like letting me have KISS posters on my wall as a child, or letting me read sexy books and seeing 'R' rated movies, she could not have cared less about these PMRC ratings and what they meant. She gave me gift certificates to Record & Tape outlet for birthdays and Christmas so I could buy whatever I wanted. I had some of those targeted albums in my own collection. My mom didn't care.

"I raised you right and I'm not worried about music lyrics," she said to me. "People have a right to make the music they want to make, and to buy the music they want to listen to. Same for books. A few sexy words? Big deal. There are worse things to worry about in this world."

4.11

My mom was still selling insurance when she met a guy at her office named Dick. They fell in love. Trouble was, he had a wife and two small children. His marriage had been on the rocks for years, he'd said.

So, he left his wife and two weeks after I met him, he moved straight into our condo with us. I was pretty surprised it all happened so quickly. She'd never even dated a guy since I'd known her.

My mom was happy, and he was a nice person, but it was hard having a man in the house. With another adult around, my mom started placing a few limitations on me and acting more like a parent. I started to chafe under their expectations for a clean room and regular chores and good grades. It had never been required before. And I never felt capable of sustaining any of it for very long. I was always in my own little world.

Dick's ex-wife fought everything, and he proceeded through his divorce and custody arrangements, going to lawyer appointments and court dates. It all became a big drama, and soon it began to feel ridiculous. All they did was talk about it, speculate, plan, worry, pay. It was an ugly divorce, and when his kids would come over, I'd have to deal with them, too. The ex-wife was nasty and scary, saying awful things, sending vile letters calling us names, and making threats against me and my mom.

I'd lay in my room and listen to music as loud as I could. Scorpions, Dokken, Def Leppard, Motley Crüe, Ratt. *Shout at the Devil* and *Invasion of your Privacy* were the perfect albums for what I was going through. Sexy, loud rebellion. Vince Neil and Stephen Pearcy sang to me and soothed my frayed emotions.

4.12

One afternoon, when no one was home, I was in my bedroom putting on makeup and getting ready to walk over to Kathy's house. I had *Shout at the Devil* turned up pretty loud, and was putting on my eyeliner. The door to my bedroom opened suddenly, startling me into a near eye-poke.

It was Dick's ex-wife, standing there in a beige trench coat. I must've left the front door unlocked, because she'd let herself into our condo and had been poking around downstairs while I was upstairs, unaware. She was a thick potato of a woman, with a hard, Slavic face and dark hair. Dick had described her as spiteful, and now I understood why. The Devil herself, it seemed.

Oh my God, she reminds me of Miss Strong. Mean. I knew the type. I recognized the energy. My stomach clenched up.

"Turn down the music," she ordered me.

"NO. Get out of my house," I told her, pointing to the door.

She paused there, glaring at me, fists clenched. I wondered if she was going to hit me.

"Where is Dick?" she asked, sneering.

I stood up and moved toward her.

"Get the fuck out of our house!" She looked shocked. I lunged at the phone and told her I was calling the police.

"Get OUT!!!" I shouted at her again, pointing to the door with the handset. I was ready to throw the whole phone at her if I needed to.

Instead, the Devil turned on her heel and left. I turned the music up louder to help her out the door.

Fuck you, fuck you, fuck you for making me feel unsafe in my own home.

My heart was pounding, and I was pissed. When my mom got home, we filed a report with the Westerville Police department.

The whole thing left me angry and shaken. My mom was living with a man who had a crazy ex-wife. Who knew where else she might pop up? We lived in the same town.

My mom was right—there were much worse things to worry about in the world than music lyrics.

It wouldn't be the last time the ex-wife made me feel unsafe. She continued to send nasty-grams, and started rumors about me, spread from her friends to their kids. She even had me followed by a creepy football player from the other school.

Dealing with all of this changed me. It didn't feel fair, and it wasn't right.

I felt more grown up than the adults in my life.

5.0

[She Needs Rock N' Roll]

Westerville South High School was one of the largest high schools in the central Ohio area, with about 2,500 students during the years I attended. There were so many kids that they had to break the day into nine periods over three shifts to process us through the building every day.

Westerville wasn't rich or poor—we straddled the line of affluence. We had a few rich kids, and a few really poor kids, but most of us were right in between—middle class kids with working parents. It wasn't the type of high school that *Ferris Bueller* went to, nor was it quite like the *Breakfast Club*. Only years later did I see it represented in a movie, and that movie was *Dazed and Confused*.

Everything seemed to revolve around football and partying, set to a 1980s rock and metal soundtrack. Teachers were blasé and ambivalent. It was fairly easy to buy pot, acid, and 'shrooms, and anyone could slide under the radar if they wanted to.

Despite being an average student, but because of a recommendation from Mrs. Furniss, I was selected for a gifted English class, where we debated culture and literature and wrote papers about it. It was a great class, my teacher Mr. Hiser, was engaging, and I had a lot of fun with my classmates. I also started a typing class, and was looking forward to moving past the hunt n' peck.

My mom was always pushing me to try new things, so I cut off all my hair my freshman year, and I instantly regretted it.

She also convinced me to try out for the cheerleading squad. Somehow, I made it on the team, which I also instantly regretted.

One of my cheer mates, Beth, had an older, long-haired brother named Chad who played guitar, and I started hanging out with her a bit so I could meet him and his cute friend Kevin Amici, who was in his band. Kathy lived right near Beth and Chad, so this made it even more convenient to bug them. Chad and Kevin were seniors, and they both had cars and guitars, and I had a huge crush on Kevin.

But this was never to be, and Kevin and Chad became more like older brothers.

Kevin was super cute with long, thick, black hair, an impish smile, and an easy, patient attitude. He played bass. His mom was an English teacher, and he was a reader, too, so we talked about books and music a lot. He let me tag along with him to a recording studio where he and his band practiced, and he was always urging me to listen to harder, heavier music.

He was a huge Metallica fan, and had just seen them with Armored Saint at the Newport Music Hall, and he also loved Motorhead. He turned me on to both. When I saw the video for *Ace of Spades*, I was completely intrigued by Lemmy. I loved the pretty hairspray boys, for sure, but I was absolutely enthralled by the "ugly" ones, too.

I thought Lemmy was quite handsome.
In fact, he looked just like my dad.

5.1

During my freshman year, a rumor was started by Dick's ex-wife through her network of friends that I was performing sex acts in the locker room with the football team. Members of the Westerville South High School football team were privy to this rumor, and I spent the entire year wondering why I was being pestered by the jock seniors who snickered and pinched me when I walked by.

Many of them were in my typing class, and I hated going to it, even though I really wanted to learn to type. With the teasing and anxiety, I almost failed the class, but squeaked by with a D.

Finally, another friend's older brother who was on the football team clued me in to what was going on, and why, and I suddenly felt very vulnerable at school. I had no idea what "pulling a train" even meant until my mom explained it to me, in tears. I was stunned when I found out.

I was still a virgin, after all. I hadn't ever had a boyfriend, just a few crushes. The jock boys scared me with their teasing, pinching, and casual chauvinism. I felt much more comfortable with the long-haired guys like Kevin Amici, who accepted me, talked to me, laughed with me, and shared music, which made school a bit more bearable. The long-hairs didn't touch me or harass me. I felt safe amongst these guys, the rockers, metalheads and punks.

School was still hard for me, as it always had been. I was placed in a gifted program based on my writing ability, but otherwise, my grades had never been great. With everything going on at home, and the sex rumors, now my grades were almost hopeless. I failed two classes that year and took mostly C's and D's in the other ones. No one seemed to notice or care. My mom was caught up in her own drama.

Like my teachers always said, I just needed to "apply myself," and I'd somehow do better in school. I never really knew what that meant, though. I hated school. Just like when I was in Miss Strong's class all those years ago, I still had trouble paying attention and keeping up. I would read and daydream at the back of the class, I would write long short stories to my good friends and fantasize about rock star adventures, and I'd show up every day to my algebra class, completely and hopelessly confused.

Then, because my GPA was so low, I lost the spot in the gifted program.

5.2

I started my sophomore year during the fall of 1986, and Mom and Dick got married at the Franklin County Courthouse on September 26. While they were getting married, I was at school listening to Metallica's *Master of Puppets* with a nice kid named Matthew. He had a fuzzy blond mullet and kind blue eyes, and would share his Walkman earphone with me. We sat at the back of the class, near the casement windows, and would watch as other kids took puffs of pot from a small one-hitter to blow out the windows. The teacher, a senile old lady with armpit hair and body odor, never said a word.

Within a few days of my folks getting married we found out that Cliff Burton, Metallica's bass player, had died in a horrible bus crash somewhere in Europe. I was just starting to get into Metallica. No one knew for sure if they would even stay together.

I eventually brought my own Walkman to school, and had it with me all the time now as I attended classes. That was the thing about Westerville South, we had huge classes and the teachers didn't really connect with the students—especially the marginal ones, like me, who showed up but didn't do much work or understand the material. Although I pretended things were normal and I scraped by, I didn't really feel normal at all. I always felt like an oddball, a misfit, an outsider.

In addition to the rumors around my high school, Dick's ex-wife continued to send my mom and me nasty letters and notes. She called my mom a fat pig, a dirty whore. I had never been exposed directly to hate like that, and I couldn't believe my mom had married this guy. The baggage he came with was too much to bear. I wanted to drown it all out with my music, and the louder it was, the better I felt. Rock and metal were like therapy to me.

But really, just about any music could make me happy, and to get out of the house, I started going to concerts with an older friend named Debbie. Our moms had worked together at RAX and become good friends, so Debbie and I started hanging out. She was 10 years older than me, a lot of fun, recently divorced, and a big girl, over 300 lbs.

None of that bothered me a bit and we got along famously. She was like an older, trusted sister. We went dozens of times together to see the Rocky Horror Picture Show and to other various movies, and sometimes she'd let me drink a wine cooler. Debbie and I saw the Thompson Twins, Howard Jones, and Paul Young—she was into more new-wave and pop music stuff, but that was fine with me. I liked hanging out with her and getting away from my house and all the drama with my family.

She drove us to Cincinnati to see The Power Station, a group that included the object of my brief obsession, John Taylor of Duran Duran. Instead of Robert Palmer handling vocals for this tour, a guy named Michael Des Barres was filling in. I'd never heard of him, but it was a fun show watching them play some groovy music in the dusk of a midwestern summer evening, right on the banks of the mighty Ohio River. John Taylor was dreamy.

Debbie came over to our apartment to watch *Miami Vice* with me when The Power Station was featured on an episode of the show. She was totally in love with Don Johnson. I always swooned a little, too, but not over Crockett or Tubbs—it was Lt. Castillo. I loved his seriousness, his pocked face, the steamy handsomeness and authoritative demeanor. Edward James Olmos absolutely intrigued me.

Debbie also took me to see Fleetwood Mac down in Cincinnati at the Coliseum in late 1987, and I realized how much I absolutely loved them. I had heard them on the radio for most of my childhood, and I found out they had formed in Los Angeles, part of the California soft-rock sound of the 1970s, along with the Eagles, and Crosby, Stills and Nash, and many others. I loved all those bands, and started to read about them.

I continued to read anything I could find about Los Angeles: Helter Skelter by Bugliosi, all about movie stars and Hollywood history, the Black Dahlia murder, Hollywood Babylon. I devoured biographies of Marilyn Monroe and Joan Crawford. I read more Jackie Collins and Jonathan Kellerman. The more books I read, the more enthralled I became with Los Angeles and its history, especially the music scene.

A few books crossed my path that really sparked my imagination, mostly books on the Doors, Elvis, The Beatles, and, of course, Led Zeppelin's *Hammer of the Gods*. I was enthralled by Led Zeppelin, learning about each of the band members and how the music was recorded, the decadence, the women, the adventures, their antics in Los Angeles. It was all quite fantastic.

But really, no other book excited me as much as *I'm With The Band: Confessions of a Groupie*, by Pamela Des Barres. Michael Des Barres' wife, Miss Pamela, published a book about her life on the Los Angeles music scene as a muse and a groupie, and it changed my life forever. Her descriptions and stories captivated me. She was free and open and loving and funny and hung out with and loved the men of rock and roll. She'd lived in Laurel Canyon with the Zappa family, it turned out. The music moved her, too—and she admired the men who made it. In my mind, she was a bigger Rock Star than her husband ever would be. I adored her from afar and would try and catch any interview or tidbit about her that I could.

She was a Virgo soul sister—a muse and very much an inspiration. Not because I wanted to sleep with rock stars, but because I wanted to be moved by the music and witness history and maybe write books about it all, someday, too.

I wanted to see the places she described. I wanted to see Laurel Canyon and Zappa's little hideaway. I wanted to go to shows at the Whiskey and party at The Rainbow.

I wanted to feel that hopeful, magical California sunshine on my skin.

5.3

Kathy and I started hanging out with a group of friends our freshman and sophomore years—Vince and Kate and Tall Tim. Kate was an earth mother hippie chick who loved Heart, and Vince was a rocker and a Doors fanatic, and Tall Tim was a 6'3" metalhead with a white Mustang.

Tim could buy beer because he looked about 30 years old with his auburn moustache and frizzy mullet and dark brown eyes that could stare you down. He was a pro at conning gas-station clerks—he just acted 30 and it always worked. It was like a Jedi mind-trick, he'd say. He was 17, and he never got carded.

It was in the back of Tall Tim's Mustang that I smoked pot for the first time, as we cruised down State Street right past the police station, jammed in the back seat with Kathy and Kate, Vince up front rolling a joint, and Tall Tim driving carefully with an open beer tucked up against his balls in his tight white jeans.

With the girls coaching me, I learned how to inhale and hold it and not make myself sick. Kathy held my beer as I tried. Ozzy Osborne's *Bark at the Moon* played on the tape deck. It was relaxing and fun and I rolled down the window to air out the car. The crisp autumn night and the laughter of friends and good music. We hung out together like this for months. I was finding my tribe, finally starting to feel a bit normal.

Kate lived in a big old Victorian house on a brick street near Otterbein College, complete with leaded and stained-glass windows, a huge porch, and a foyer with a grand staircase. Built in bookcases throughout the whole house, 12-foot ceilings. Fireplaces in every bedroom.

Pink carpeting and cabbage roses and hand painted tiles and houseplants everywhere and four friendly cats roaming around. It was a grand and beautiful house—much different than our little 800 square foot condo with a galley kitchen. I felt like Alice in Wonderland in this house, it was so beautiful.

When her parents were out of town while her older brother was home from college, we all had a sleepover at her house. It wasn't a huge party—there were seven of us. We ordered pizza and there were plenty of wine coolers, beer and pot, and the older brother brought hits of acid and two Queensrÿche albums. He explained that they were from Seattle, and that there were some really good bands coming out of the Pacific northwest. I was already obsessed with Heart. Soon, I was obsessed with Queensrÿche, and just about every other hard rock and metal band that passed my ears. Old music, new music––I wanted to hear all of it.

5.4

February 11, 1987. The Ohio Center, Columbus, Ohio.

"What? What do you mean Andy Taylor isn't playing?"

Kathy and I got this news as we made our way to our 11th row seats to see David Lee Roth, who had recently left Van Halen. I was 15, Kathy had just turned 16. We were at the concert with my friend Debbie, and her mom Brenda. I'd always tagged along to Debbie's concerts, but this was the first concert that I really wanted to go to, and I asked my mom a couple of times before she agreed. My mom even stood in line to get us the tickets, and she scored four of them, 11th row seats. We were so stoked.

One of the big stories in music in the mid-1980s was that David Lee Roth left Van Halen (or had been fired) in an acrimonious split. Each of them went on to record hit albums—Van Halen's *5150*, with Sammy Hagar singing, and David Lee Roth's album, *Eat 'em and Smile*, with Steve Vai, a former Zappa guy, playing guitar. I loved both albums when they came out.

Debbie handed me the show flyer. Some band named Tesla was listed as the opening act, not Andy Taylor, as we expected.

Who the hell was Tesla? What a weird name. *Ok, well, whatever*, I thought to myself. There was nothing to be done. We'd have to sit through a band we didn't know. I was sorely disappointed—Andy Taylor was the guitar player from Duran Duran and, well...I was still a Duranie at heart. Seeing him open up for Roth would have been awesome, but apparently, he was off the tour and this band, Tesla, was in his place as the opener. The flyer said the name of their album was *Mechanical Resonance*.

We got there early, and the house lights were still on. We marveled at how close we were to the stage and settled in for a few minutes before the lights dimmed and the emcee from the local radio station made a few announcements and introduced the opener. The Ohio Center held about 6,000 people and probably wasn't even half full when the show started.

Tesla roared onto the stage and we were on our feet immediately. I didn't know the names of the songs, but every one of them was just fucking great, fierce and energetic. The band members were all in tight jeans and t-shirts, except the lead singer, who was shirtless with a jean jacket vest. None of them wore spandex. They all had long hair, but no hairspray. No eyeliner. High top tennis shoes. They looked like the long-haired guys I went to school with—normal, cute, earnest.

The music was heavy and melodic, and the dual guitarists were smoking hot. Kathy and I looked at each other and just said "WOW." They were impressive. I told myself theirs would be the next album I'd be buying, for sure. I was immediately glad that I had missed Andy Taylor. There was just no way he would've been as good as Tesla, I was convinced. They rocked.

We were amped for Roth to hit the stage. As his set was about to start, Kathy and I looked at each other and had the same thought. Acting on pure instinct, we darted out of the 11th row, abandoning Debbie and Brenda to the fates. We grasped fingers, weaving quickly through the crowd as we slipped right up to the metal security barrier in front of the first row.

Just as David Lee Roth and the band hit the stage, a swarthy looking guy on the other side of the barrier looked at us and said *hello* as he passed in front of us. He had a lanyard around his neck with laminated passes. A crew guy.

"Hello!" we said back to him, smiling. He wandered on.

We were standing directly in front of Steve Vai, and it was a great show, with Roth prancing and doing his classic Roth thing—part Liberace, part porn star, part surfer. After seeing the raw energy of Tesla, Roth seemed a little too contrived. But Steve Vai was amazing to watch, right up close. His hands were huge and he was so animated when he played. His facial expressions and body contortions matched the notes, and his fingers were a blur. His solo was long and indulgent and amazing. That, and he was staggeringly handsome with those cheekbones and dark eyes.

Billy Sheehan was on the other side of the stage, playing bass, and he also had a solo, which was equally as mind-boggling. I'd never seen a bass played like that, with chords and harmonics. He was a master of his instrument, and really fun to watch.

As the show was ending, that swarthy-looking crew guy walked back up to us and introduced himself as Sal, and he asked how old we were.

I looked at him square in the eye. "I'm eighteen," I lied. I knew it was the magic number, though.

"I'm nineteen!" Kathy said right behind me.

Sal nodded and smiled and took two rectangular patches out of his back pocket. He pulled the backing off and pressed it firmly to my tender left breast, lingering a little too long. I was a little surprised, but I didn't flinch. He then did the same thing to Kathy.

"Dave and the boys would like to meet you after the show. Just go sit on those bleachers," he pointed stage left, "and wait for me to find you." We said OK, and he walked away.

Kathy and I looked at each other, a bit stunned. *It was that easy to get a backstage pass?* Right on! *We are going to meet the band!* We squeezed hands and silently screamed at each other in excitement.

Moments later, as the show ended, Kathy and I didn't try to find our chaperones, and we certainly didn't want to be found. I stopped to make one quick phone call to my mom, telling her we couldn't find Debbie and Brenda, and we had these passes to meet the band, and that we'd just take a cab home—which was ridiculous, because growing up in the midwestern suburbs of Columbus, I'd never even been in a cab and wouldn't know how to get one. Columbus isn't New York City, or even Chicago. The area around downtown was dead at night. But it's what I pitched to my mom: *We'll be fine! We'll be home in an hour or so!* Then, I hung up the phone just as my mom started to yell at me.

Fuck it, I thought. *I'm going to go meet David Lee Roth.*

Keeping our heads low, we made our way back to the bleachers that Sal had pointed to, only to find that there were 30 other women sitting there with the same passes pressed onto their left breasts. The cold, fluorescent light reflected off the harsh, ashy, hot pink makeup of a mass of women who were all much older than Kathy and me. The smell of Aqua Net hung heavy and low. There was a buzz of excitement as we all sized each other up. There was quite a herd of us.

We sat there for a few minutes, marveling at how quickly the place transformed from a seething, energetic rock concert to an empty concrete box with a crew loading out like a swarm of ants. It took no more than 15 minutes total for us to lose Debbie and Brenda, call my mom, and find our way to the bleachers. It felt like hours.

Then, we spotted Sal, and said hello again. He put one arm around each of us as we followed the whole crowd of women into the backstage area, down a long hall, and into the dressing room. There was a party already going on with purple strobe lights, a disco ball, and loud music.

We made our way into the darkness, found a cooler of beer, and tried not to look obviously underage as our inexperienced fingers cracked open cans of Budweiser. Our eyes adjusted to the dim light, and then I spotted Billy Sheehan in the corner, surrounded by a small mob of half-naked women cooing over him. A whole group of them disappeared into the bathroom. I saw a flash of boobies as the door closed behind them and looked at Kathy, wide-eyed. *Groupies!*

Roth made his way through the crowd, and he brushed right past us—handsome, no doubt, smiling his Cheshire smile, and much shorter than we expected. We didn't get to meet him, but it was close enough. I saw his full face, in person, walking toward me, and his perky spandex buns as he walked past. He kind of reminded me of Richard Simmons as he bopped through the crowd. Oh well. It was good enough for me.

And then, as I turned around, Steve Vai was standing there, smiling.

"Hello, I'm Steve," he said, extending one of his huge, magical hands toward me. I reached out and shook it, hoping that the small weird wart that had appeared on my ring finger a few weeks before wouldn't be evident to his sensitive, elegant paw.

I about died at the thought that my wart was touching Steve Vai. He didn't seem to notice. He was even more handsome in person. *And he knows Frank Zappa! How cool,* I thought. Kathy and I introduced ourselves by name, and then he moved on, saying hello to other people and working the crowd in a gracious manner. As he walked away, I leaned toward Kathy and said *"Steve Vai just touched my wart!"* and we both cracked up laughing.

Just two minutes later, a very tall and large black man with a walkie-talkie in his hand came up to us with a friendly smile and said, "Hi ladies, are you Kathy and Anna-Marie?"

"Yes! Yes we are." We looked at each other and nodded.

"Someone wants to see you," he said. "Follow me."

Curious, we followed this very large man, thinking that maybe Steve Vai wanted to talk to us alone, or wanted us to star in the next video—who knew? My mind ran wild with possibilities.

Someone famous had remembered our names! We were being summoned by a rock star! For a few brief seconds, I was imagining myself as Lucky Santangelo, from the Jackie Collins novels. Glamorous, mysterious, jetting off with famous people.

But no. No, no, no.

It was not like that at all. As we made our way down the dark hallway and out into the harsh light of the loading dock, both of our moms were standing there, clenching their purses, sharing a look of grim disbelief and fury.

Holy shit. It was the very last thing we expected. The man with the walkie-talkie turned to us and said, "Sorry I had to do that, girls. Good luck."

Apparently, my tiny mom had waved a quarter at him and threatened to call the Columbus Police Department and shut down the party if he did not get our underage asses out of there right a-fucking-way. He had moved quickly and found us after getting our names and descriptions.

And indeed, within an hour, unmolested and with only one beer ingested, Kathy and I were on our way home, all thanks to my mom springing to action after that stupid phone call. I did feel bad for Debbie and Brenda and making them worry, and I apologized to them for the whole thing. But I was not one bit sorry that I'd gone backstage and met Steve Vai.

Kathy and I were both grounded for six weeks and forbidden to hang out after school for that time period. It didn't matter, though. We shared a locker and were in classes together at school, anyway. The next day, we were un-showered and bleary from being up so late having "difficult conversations" with our parents about our behavior. There was no way our folks were letting us skip school because we were tired.

We grinned at each other when we met at the locker that morning, a few hours after our awesome adventure. Too bad we were both grounded.

Whatever. It was worth it, we decided. We skipped math class that day and walked to Taco Bell for lunch under a sullen February sky. We smoked a cigarette on our way back and marveled at the night we'd had. We pressed our colorful backstage passes onto notebook paper and carried them around in our notebooks for months, like a lucky charm, touching them for inspiration, dreaming of escape, remembering our brief time in the same room as greatness. I stroked my wart thinking, *Steve Vai touched my hand, my fingers, and my magical wart.*

That wart eventually disappeared, but the magic of meeting him never did.

6.0

[All In the Name of…]

In support of their *Girls Girls Girls* album, Mötley Crüe announced a show in July 1987, at Buckeye Lake Music Center, out near Newark, Ohio. It was an outdoor venue, located in the middle of cornfields and rolling hills of the Ohio countryside.

On the bill that day was Mötley Crüe, Whitesnake, and Anthrax. This was our first concert together after the David Lee Roth incident, so Kathy and I had to be on our best behavior. Our moms were skeptical of letting us attend after our antics at the Roth show, but Kathy's older, more responsible sister and a few of her friends would be with us. They were "good kids."

The thing about these outdoor concerts was that you showed up the night before to get good parking, and then you camped out overnight and partied. Somehow, we talked our moms into allowing us to do this. We swore not to do anything stupid. We knew it was a test, and we had to pass if we wanted to keep going to concerts in the future.

The show was on Sunday. We packed a small cooler with ice and soda and a couple of sandwiches, and set out on a Saturday afternoon. We had a few other things with us, but nothing practical, really. Lip gloss. Eye drops. A bottle of water. I was wearing cut-off shorts, a pair of slip-on Keds sneakers, a white tank top, and I had a button-down flannel to tie around my waist.

We thought we were set. We crammed into the Dodge Dart with three other older teenagers and drove the hour out to the venue in the country. *We are going to see Mötley fucking Crüe! Nikki is right here in the middle of BFE Ohio!*

There were hundreds of cars already there, parked row after row, wide enough apart for people to pull out their grills, lawn chairs, and tents. We hadn't thought to do any of that. We didn't even have a blanket with us. So, we wandered up and down the rows of cars, and as the sun set, we made friends with all kinds of people around campfires and barbeques. We got drunk on free beer, ate other people's hot dogs and chips and potato salad, and fell asleep in a tent after smoking a joint with a 16-year-old long-haired kid named Gary who was parked a few cars down from us.

The whole thing was like some weird hillbilly heaven.

The next morning, I woke, bleary-eyed and dehydrated. Kathy and I both walked to the edge of the field and vomited onto different trees, then made our way to the Porta-Potties. We bought some water from a guy who was selling bottles of it, and asked around until we found someone who had aspirin.

We had to walk about a mile down a gravel road to get into the venue. It felt like a death march, but we made it, and then all 10,000 people descended upon the food vendors. Kathy and I shared a big order of nachos, draped in bright orange cheese and jalapeños, and we licked our filthy fingers clean as it started to rain.

If you've ever spent time near a midwestern cornfield in summer, you know that it doesn't take much rain to create a lot of mud. The squall lasted 10 or 15 minutes, and we all huddled where we could, or just stood out in the rain, like turkeys. It was going to be 90 degrees that day. The steam from the herd of muddy people started to rise as soon as the sun came back out. And then, we all started to stink. Pigs in mud, it felt like.

Anthrax took the stage and stomped around. A massive mosh pit started whirling up near the stage, and Kathy and I hovered near the edges of the field to stay out of it. The band was great, energetic and fun.

Whitesnake came on an hour later, and the heat was almost as unbearable as watching David Coverdale preen about. It was intense sunshine, followed by quick showers and stinking humidity.

The mud got thicker, almost like cake batter, coating our ankles and lower legs as we slopped around in it. People were drunk and vomiting. It was literally a cesspool.

We were hungry and hungover and filthy. I was getting a wicked sunburn, as was everyone else. I craved a Big Mac and a Coke and a shower, followed by my clean, cool sheets and a long dark sleep.

That wouldn't happen for many more hours.

We endured what the day served us.

It was Mötley fucking Crüe.

We made our way to the left front of the stage, near where the tour buses were parked. I started trying to make eye contact with anyone who had a pass around their neck, but no one paid any attention. We just wanted to meet the band. We still had the magic of the David Lee Roth concert on us. Maybe it could happen again? I wanted to shake Nikki's hand and tell him how much I loved his music. Then, I wanted him to fall in love with me and have him rescue me away from my life. I wanted to be his muse.

But mostly, I wanted to see if it was possible to just meet him.

Thank God I didn't.

Instead, I got to watch a fun show under a temperamental sky. Nikki looked tanned, handsome, and a bit bloated, squeezed into tight leather pants. *He looks hot and miserable. I bet he stinks, too,* I thought, standing ankle deep in muddy filth and watching my idol thump it out on his bass. Nikki fucking Sixx, live in the flesh. My god, how I loved him. I was fifteen, he was 28. It was possible, wasn't it? Someday, maybe?

She's only fifteen, she's the reason I can't sleep....

Kathy managed to get up on some cute guy's shoulders, so she could see the stage better. Vince danced around with a tambourine. There were back-up singers, which didn't seem right at Mötley Crüe show, but Mick's guitar sounded great. And Tommy, I really loved Tommy, too. He seemed like such a big, goofy sweetheart. Every song was a song we knew, but we really just wished they'd play every song on every one of their albums right straight through, in order. Wouldn't that be something? A dream come true.

They ended the show with pyrotechnics, which were loud and smoky, but the effects were lost in the hazy, humid afternoon. As much as I didn't want the show to be over, I was also relieved. I was starving, and I had a wicked headache.

The giant crowd turned to scatter and walk back to the parking lot. I realized that my feet were stuck in the thick mud, and I walked right out of my shoes as I pitched forward and almost fell down. I grabbed onto Kathy to keep my balance, and looked back in horror as my trusty white Keds disappeared forever, trampled by others, sucked down into a vortex of filth.

There they were! But then...they were gone, swallowed by the mud. Impossible to rescue.

Kathy and I laughed in shock. There was nothing to do but to keep moving forward, shoeless, with a boot of mud now coating my feet and lower legs, and a gravel road to conquer to get back and find her sister's car.

As we made our way off the field and out of the venue amongst the crowd, I felt like I was being chased by a herd of wild bison on an open plain, as the shoed, sure-footed people barreled along and outpaced us back to the parking area. Kathy and I held hands and hobbled toward the gravel road and tried not to get run over. Kathy also lost a shoe at some point and the other one was barely hanging on and was slowing her down to a lurch. It was full of mud and squishing, useless. She took it off and flung it into a field in solidarity.

Both of us were now barefoot with our elbows locked, and we continued down the gravel road toward the car. Two steps into this, my foot found a hidden post-hole in the grass and I felt my ankle pop as I fell into it.

Fuck! I sat there and moaned for a minute in disbelief.

Holy shit, I had a wicked sprain. It throbbed as Kathy helped me to my feet and we staggered down the side of the road, trying to avoid rocks and glass and other debris.

We got 10 steps into our hobbled, old-lady walk of hell when two huge, studded-leather vest-wearing, tattooed, biker-looking guys came up and asked if we needed help. They were both about 6'4" with bandanas around their heads. One was older. Father and son.

The dad had grizzled mutton chops and kind, crinkly blue eyes. He reminded me of Hulk Hogan, with Willie Nelson braids. One patch on his vest said *United*

States Marine Corps. Another said *Vietnam Veteran, U.S. Marines.*

I trusted them instantly. I was sure we'd be safe with these guys, and I was grateful for the help. We said *yes, please.* They crouched low and I climbed on this older man's back, piggyback style. I felt like a little girl again, playing horse with my dad, bouncing around. Kathy and I looked over at each other as she mounted the younger one, the son.

As we both lifted our arms to put them around their sunburned necks, we caught a whiff of ourselves and made a face in mock horror at each other at what we smelled like. I took another good sniff and gagged. *Good lord.* I had hoped it wasn't that bad, but it was. Worse than anything I've ever smelled like before. We started giggling as we were jostled around like little kids, muddy and stinking to high heaven. My ankle throbbed with every step.

We navigated them in the direction we thought the car was, and they carried us right up to it and dropped us off, like boy scouts doing a public service. Our angels of mercy showing up as scary looking bikers, right when we needed them. We thanked them over and over. *Happy to help!* They said, smiling and waving goodbye.

We didn't get to meet Mötley Crüe, but I still felt damn lucky. I was grateful not to meet them in the middle of a humid Ohio cornfield while encrusted with sewer mud and smelling like a camel. I needed minor medical attention, a shower, and a meal.

After finding the nearest McDonalds drive-thru, we made it home with a few cuts and bruises. My purple and green ankle revealed itself after I showered off the mud, and I iced it for a few days. A wicked, blistering sunburn made me itch and peel for weeks. Kathy had an infected cut on her foot that festered, and a bad sunburn as well. *Oh, how we suffer for our music!* We joked to each other. We were willing to endure hell to see our favorite bands and even if it took weeks to recuperate.

Mötley Crüe was worth it.

A week or so after the show, Mötley Crüe made the cover of Rolling Stone—the first time a "metal" band had done so. The feature article disclosed Nikki's real name: Frank Carlton Serafino Ferrana, and that his real father was Sicilian. I was totally blown away. I took it as a sign—we had something in common! When I'd told my mom that he was Sicilian, she mentioned that *that* was why he was so handsome and talented. Of course it was.

Kathy and I started to wonder if we could move to LA together, someday. Graduation was only two years away. What were we going to do with ourselves? Neither of us had plans for college, at all. How could we make LA happen?

I started my junior year with a new goal: figure out how to move to Los Angeles and meet Mötley Crüe.

Three years later, I'd be sitting in Tommy Lee's house.

6.1

Guns N' Roses also released their debut album, *Appetite for Destruction*, that summer of 1987. Once I saw the *Welcome to the Jungle* video on MTV at 2am, I was completely and totally hooked. They were like nothing I'd ever seen or heard.

Kathy and I went down to the Ohio State campus, the center of all things edgy and cool in central Ohio, and bought *Appetite for Destruction* on vinyl at Singin' Dog records, right on High Street. I only knew one song, but I loved the artwork, the lyrics, the whole package. I studied the album with the same intensity that I had all the Mötley Crüe albums. It was dirty and disturbing. After the slick polish and tepid production of the *Girls Girls Girls* album, GnR sounded so fresh, authentic, raw and angry. You could tell these guys were young and hungry. I loved every single song on the album.

As soon as I got into GnR, something in me shifted a bit, and I began to view Mötley Crüe a little differently—they were rich rock stars, with rock star problems, and they had these themed albums that now seemed so contrived. Guns N' Roses went back to the basics. They had great songs. The production was raw, capturing the dynamic of the musicians without taming them too much. Song arrangements were instinctive and emotional.

As I listened to and memorized the album tracks on *Appetite for Destruction* in the order they appeared, I began to understand that it was story. It was a story about Los Angeles. The struggle to survive, the reality of living rough and hungry in Los Angeles. The desperation to make it, the humanity and the inhumanity, the exploitation, the sex, the addictions, and the rock n' roll.

Guns N' Roses. There were no mansions or fancy cars for these guys, at least not yet. They were slumming it compared to the guys in Mötley Crüe. Their authenticity exploded what was becoming a very slick "metal" scene with overproduced, poppy albums from bands like Mötley Crüe, Bon Jovi, Def Leppard, Whitesnake, Poison, and Ratt.

Guns N' Roses shifted everything toward "more authentic." They were angry, they were honest, and the music rocked my soul. The album spoke some kind of universal truth about humanity. Many people thought it was "thrash" at first, but no—it was straight melodic rock n' roll.

Even though the poppy "hair metal" scene continued on for a while longer, everything seemed to change after GnR. Things went darker, a little harder. Authenticity did start to matter, and more bands with no makeup, costumes, or themes started to become more popular. Metal incorporated more of a punk ethic. Thrash metal had been thriving for years with their own underground scene and would soon know mainstream success, and for me, it seemed that GnR bridged a gap to the harder, heavier, angrier stuff.

Guns N' Roses were the right band at the right time, and along with a few other bands, they completely changed how I thought about my life and my future. They were preaching the gospel, telling their story of Los Angeles, and I loved it so much.

6.2

Music was the thing that Kathy and I bonded over, so we took an elective music theory class together our Junior year. We thought it might be fun to try to start a band. There really weren't any women doing what we wanted to do—no one our age, at least. We didn't want to be Vixen or The Bangles or Lita Ford. We wanted our music to be heavier, and we didn't want to have to wear spandex and hairspray and corsets. We just wanted to rock. Maybe like an early Heart, meets Tesla.

Up to that point, I was still into Mötley Crüe, along with GnR, RATT, Faster Pussycat, Cinderella, The Cult, Van Halen, Dokken, Tesla, and Metallica. I also listened to Heart, The Doors, Led Zeppelin, Ozzy, and Dio. I'd heard heavier stuff, like Motorhead, through my friend Kevin Amici. I also explored some punk, and darker bands, like Venom and Possessed, but they weren't quite my thing. Mostly, I liked music I could sing to.

Neither of us could read music, though, and we thought we probably should if we really wanted to start a band. She'd bought a Fender Telecaster and was teaching herself to play. I had an acoustic guitar, and was saving up to buy a bass and amp. We practiced singing and harmonizing to various rock songs while Kathy plucked out rangy chords. Our voices naturally complimented each other, and we thought we sounded pretty good.

Plus, we'd heard that music theory was a fun class to take, which is always a bonus during the drudgery of high school.

Mr. Kenreich, our music theory teacher, was very cool. He had a large head and narrow shoulders, a long, angular nose, framed by a neat, steely haircut. He always wore a pert bow-tie, a dress shirt, and a tweed suit jacket with elbow patches. He had mischievous eyes and the hint of a smile at the corners of his thin lips. He was very patient and pleasant, always calm and steady. He seemed to float by in a bubble of tranquility as if he were composing a concerto in his head. If we were goofing or whispering in class, he'd pause and give a raised eyebrow smile and continue, but he never got nasty or held a grudge. He repeated lessons to us on the piano with a great flair and humor. I began to understand the fundamentals of music, chords, and beat. I'd never had any formal musical instruction other than what I received in public school music classes, singing in Girls Glee in middle school, and through listening to the radio and my records.

Music is an emotional, dynamic experience for me, not an analytical one, so it was strange to me to see music written on paper, in a two-dimensional form, being studied and analyzed like a math problem. This was a language I could not speak and never fully understood. I had never been really great at formulas, or following instructions, so I struggled in that part of the class, when we'd have to write out music and harmonies and scales. Just like in my algebra classes, when I'd have to write out math problems, I struggled to wrap my mind around the symbols. It was always just out of my grasp.

So, I had to fake it to some degree. I could "feel" the music and sing the music, I just couldn't "read" or write the music.

But as promised, the class was fun. We had a lot of metalheads and misfits—Mike M., Ray, Jeff, Vince. Some had years of formal musical training already, and some were already playing instruments. One of those guys was a senior, named Aaron.

Aaron was tall, with a dark, glossy mullet, and striking blue eyes. He was funny and dorky and really cute, and we hit it off immediately. He was a huge metalhead, and soon a bunch of us in class—Ray, and Mike, and Jeff, and Ian, and Kathy and Devon—were all hanging out together after school. Within a few weeks, Aaron and I were good friends, finding excuses to go do stuff together. It didn't take us long to fall for each other. He was my first love, and my first real boyfriend.

Aaron was also a very good guitar player, and a music enthusiast with an open mind. He had a versatile, deep voice and could imitate James Hetfield spot on, which made me love him even more. He also liked some

Country music, some Rap, and of course—Metal. In addition to liking Metallica and Anthrax and Queensrÿche, he introduced me to Soundgarden, and Slayer, and to all kinds of new music—mostly heavier stuff. He was a big fan of DRI, COC, Trouble, SOD, Mercyful Fate, Sacred Reich, Flotsam and Jetsam, and Armored Saint.

As I sat on his basement floor flipping through all his vinyl, I noticed that many of the bands had one thing in common: they were on a label called Metal Blade Records, in Tarzana, California, and produced by a guy named Brian Slagel.

His name also flashed on the screen when Aaron and I watched the movie *River's Edge*, starring Keanu Reeves. Much of the soundtrack to the movie were Slayer songs, and Brian Slagel was the guy who put the soundtrack together. I noticed his name right away in the credits.

Aaron was a fan of all things Metal Blade, and soon, I was, too. There was so much "corporate rock" happening—Bon Jovi, Whitesnake, Dokken, etc.—that Metal Blade was refreshing. No power ballads, no spandex, just metal. Liking Metal Blade bands was like being a part of a small club.

Aaron's band, Prophecy were starting to get gigs in smaller venues, and I'd go to every show that I could. Aaron was silly and dorky and sweet and affectionate, but when he looked over and snarled Metallica lyrics to me while playing his hot pink BC Rich Warlock, he looked dangerous and sexy, and I absolutely swooned.

6.3

In order to get a proper demo tape made, many local bands in the Columbus area used the studios at The Recording Workshop. The Recording Workshop was a vocational school for sound engineers, a five-week, on-site program, located in the deep back hillbilly woods of Chillicothe, Ohio.

I drove down there with Aaron and his bandmates Andy, Jim, and Jeremy to get a tour of the facility. As a student there, you got a small wood cabin next to the studio, very rustic, and pretty high on the spooky factor. I could just imagine Jason from the Friday the 13th movies lurking in the dense southern Ohio forest, ready to gut us all with a scythe.

Still, despite the creepy factor, if you had a band and were willing to drive the 60 miles south, you could get a demo tape done for free at the mercy of the students learning to become audio engineers, and that's exactly what Prophecy did.

I was fascinated by the production aspect of music, and imagined that it would be such a cool thing to do—to work with bands in the studio, laying down tracks, building a song. Seeing the process and watching Aaron work was inspiring to me. I'd been to a recording studio with Kevin Amici when I was a few years younger, but his band had fucked around too much with partying for me to actually see much of the process. With Aaron's band, I sat with the students at the mixing board and I could hear how the tracks were laid down and I could fiddle with the knobs.

Even though I always thought about being a writer, I didn't actually know how to be one. I was still a shitty typist. Meanwhile, I was always tinkering with amps and speakers and electronic things. Being an audio engineer sounded like fun, and I thought maybe I had an ear for it.

And here was a school, not too far away, where I could learn a real skill. If I could figure out how to pay for it, I could go to The Recording Workshop after high school, and if I survived the five weeks of living in the spooky forest, maybe I could find a job as an audio engineer, working in a studio somewhere. Somewhere like Los Angeles.

6.4

I lost my virginity to Aaron in his basement bedroom while listening to Armored Saint's new album, *Raising Fear*. Aaron was a huge Armored Saint fan, and I was becoming one, so I didn't mind at all. We used a condom and a tube of KY Jelly, bought by me at the Kroger Sav-on on Schrock Rd, where my mom had worked in the seafood department.

The sex itself was painful, sweet, and mercifully quick, but we kept trying. The second time we did it, we listened to *Appetite for Destruction*—my request. The third time, we listened to *Shout at the Devil*—also my request. The fourth time, it was Slayer's *Reign in Blood*.

I lost track after that. The more we did it, the better we got at doing it. When we were together, the music was always on, we were planning on what to eat, and we were figuring out ways to find some privacy.

Aaron was a great first boyfriend.

We would hang out all weekend long if we could, and it was over at Jeremy's house during a Saturday practice that I sat watching TV when Megadeth's *Peace Sells* video came on. I sat bolt upright, turned it up, and was completely enthralled by this song.

I'd not heard anything like this, this Megadeth. So raw and powerful. Dave Mustaine, snarling. This wasn't sex, drugs, and rock n' roll party music. This was serious, personal, and defiant. Punk, even. There were no abstractions in this song—it was a one-sided conversation between Dave Mustaine and "The Establishment" or "The Man". It was political, and sounded threatening and menacing. It perfectly captured the anger and ambivalence of my generation, years before we were labeled as Generation X slackers. It seemed like a big "fuck you" to the Reagan mentality and the frivolousness of the music scene and to authority in general. I loved Megadeth immediately. Turned out, Aaron already had the *Peace Sells…But Who's Buying?* album and we listened to it on the way home that night.

A few days later, I went to the Record & Tape Outlet and bought my own copy of *Peace Sells…?* I found out that Megadeth had just released a new album: *So Far, So Good… So What!* and I purchased that album, too. I bought them both on cassette, just for my Walkman.

I spent the next few weeks listening to them over and over again.

And then, my little world fell apart.

6.5

Of course, it wasn't Megadeth's fault that I was a shitty student making bad choices, but within eight weeks of buying those Megadeth albums, my report card showed the usual C's and D's and my mom found out I was smoking pot occasionally. Then, she found out I was having sex with Aaron. After making Aaron come over to our apartment and reading him the riot act and scaring the shit out of him, she drove me to the Planned Parenthood in downtown Columbus, where I endured a pelvic exam more painful than any sex I'd had, and she made me go on the pill. I felt totally violated by the whole situation, and by the stupid doctor at Planned Parenthood who stuck her finger all the way up my butthole without warning.

During all this, my folks had plans to move into a new rented condo, across town. Instead of letting me stay at Westerville South and arranging a ride, my mom and step-dad insisted I try to straighten myself up with a fresh start at the new school, Westerville North, where I could take the bus from our new condo. To them, it wasn't punishment, it was just convenient, and for my own good. Tough Love.

And then, for whatever reason, Aaron and I broke up.

I was beyond sad, and pissed at all of it. I didn't want to go to a new high school.

So, I pushed back against my mom and step-dad. Fuck them. Fuck them with a capital F.

I promptly started dating a new long-haired boyfriend, Johnny, at the other high school, and sleeping with him as well. I was already on the pill, so Fuck them.

Then, there was family group therapy with my mom and Dick because they thought it would be helpful to the family if I shared my feelings about all these issues in a "safe" environment. I was snarky and bitter with the therapist. Fuck them.

I retreated from my mom and step-dad on every level. I ate cereal in my room instead of having dinner with them. I stayed out too late with my new boyfriend and we smoked a lot of pot and stole beer. I had been a mediocre student at Westerville South; at North, I didn't even try. I refused to do homework altogether. I skipped class. Fuck all of them.

I wanted to see how far I could take it. I was committed to the cause of being a bratty pain in the ass. I felt harassed by—and fearful of—the ex-wife, held to standards I had no clue how to achieve, and made to participate in a drama that I wanted no part of.

And now, I was the one being punished with a new high school.

Seriously. Fuck them.

I listened to a lot of Megadeth and Metallica and Mötley Crüe up in my room. I turned it up as loudly as I could until my mom would thump the ceiling with a broom from downstairs to tell me to turn it down. I'd ignore her until she had to walk up the stairs and knock on my locked door. Then, I'd just laugh at her frustration with me.

My new school was a joke. I made some new friends quickly, though. My new boyfriend was a guy that I had known in middle school, before he had moved into a new apartment across town with his mom. Johnny and I were inseparable, he'd pick me up and take me home from school in his tiny Honda Civic, we'd listen to all of our favorite bands together. He was a child of divorce, like me, and for some reason, we clung to each other, wrote beautiful love notes, and shared our dreams of moving to LA together. He was the only bright spot in my world. Otherwise, I was failing out of my junior year of high school with a vengeance.

The harder my folks pushed me, the harder I pushed back. After years of freedom, I was sick of them trying to parent me. Making me attend a new school just to be assholes. I'd known some of my high school classmates since the third grade when I'd first moved to Westerville. Even though I hated school, I was immensely sad that I wouldn't graduate with my friends.

I was sick of Dick's shit with his ex-wife and ridiculous custody battle for his kids. His ex was running us into the ground, and it always seemed to escalate into something more unbelievable. More court dates, more lawyers, more money we didn't have. Fuck them.

The icing on the cake was that I found out that the small amount of money Papa had left to my mom when he passed had been spent on lawyer's fees for my stepdad. It had been about six thousand dollars, not much, but my mom had tucked it away, always telling me that she would use it to help me with college.

Truthfully, I didn't really know the purpose of college. It was just something I heard people talking about. I knew it meant more school. I wasn't thrilled with the idea, and I didn't know if you could go to college to be a writer. I didn't actually know *what* a person could be by going to college—my mom had a college degree, but she worked retail and sold insurance.

Maybe I could've used the bit of money for cosmetology school, or maybe the Recording Workshop. Something that I could go earn a living with. It had been just enough to cover the expenses for either of those options.

But now that seed money was gone, spent on useless lawyers. Whatever hope I had for my future was gone. It upset me more than anything else, because somehow, I felt completely abandoned. My future felt abandoned. What if I actually did want to go to college? Or cosmetology school? They took the choice away, before I could even make it. Putting up with all the shit they threw at me, these adults and their divorce drama, the resentment grew in my heart.

My step-dad's kids were on soccer teams and had dance lessons and went to summer camps. His kids each had a robust college fund. His ex-wife lived in a four-bedroom house and drove a nice car.

I had never even lived in a house, and I wouldn't until I was 35 years old, when I bought one for myself. My mom drove a car for years that had a cardboard box as a floorboard. I never even had a bike as a kid. The irony and unfairness of it all was not lost on me.

I stewed in my anger for a while, but then, I started to think differently. I'd have to survive life on my own, and they couldn't tell me what to do. I came to think of my own independence. I didn't want to owe anyone anything, anyway. Fuck them.

Not having that money meant I was completely free to make my own choices once I turned 18. I wasn't obligated to listen to anyone's opinion. Their influence in my life would stop once I became an adult. No one could guilt me into doing anything I didn't want to do.

Not having any financial ties to them meant I could just walk away.

And I wasn't afraid of working. I'd worked since I was a kid at the Giftique, and for Earlene at the fair, and I'd just gotten a job at Sister's Chicken & Biscuits. I was a shitty student, but I knew I could take care of myself. I wouldn't hesitate to earn my way in the world. I came to accept that whatever I wanted to do with my life was completely up to me, and it was my responsibility, no one else's. It meant true emancipation from this whole situation. I started feeling happier, knowing that I was in control. I was in charge of my own life. I didn't need their money. It felt like blood money, anyways, after all the drama.

There is dignity in not asking for help, or accepting a handout.

7.0

[Public Enemy #1]

January, 1988. Westerville.

My mom was kicking me out of her house.

After months of my open and bitter rebellion, failing school, and smoking pot, my mom threatened to call my dad to come straighten me out. I exploded when she made the threat.

"My Dad? You're going to call my DAD??? To straighten ME out? You guys are the ones who are fucked! Who the hell is HE? Fuck you! FUCK YOU!!!!"

I screamed at her in frustration which tore at my vocal cords in a way I'd never felt before. I almost choked on my own venom, it burned so bad. "I fucking dare you! My dad doesn't give a shit about me. He fucking couldn't care less about me and never has! Fuck you! Fuck all of you!!!!"

My mom stood there and took it all, and smiled.

She looked me right in the eye and said, very low and calm:

"Oh no, honey. YOU'RE the one who is fucked."

***

When he arrived and rang our doorbell and was standing in the living room of our condo, I realized that I had never seen my mom and my dad in the same room together, ever. I'd never even seen a picture of them together.

I also realized that I was in some pretty deep shit. My dad wasn't there for a visit. He was there to pick me up to take me to Michigan to live with him. He was living there now, closer to his parents, the grandparents I'd never heard from again.

I'd visited my dad only once, in Michigan, a few years before. He'd called out of the blue, as a part of his Alcoholics Anonymous recovery, 10 years after the last time I saw or heard from him. I also met my half-brother, Zac, who came in from California. The alien baby who'd also been abandoned by our mutual dad. He was a nice kid, but the whole visit was hard. My dad was a stranger to both of us. I didn't feel connected to him at all. I wasn't raised with Zac, so it was hard to think of him as my brother. These people didn't feel like family.

The thought of going to Michigan again was almost unbearable. I cried and begged my mom not to go through with it. I said everything I could think of: That I'd do better, that I'd run away, that I'd set the house on fire, that I'd kill myself. She wasn't budging. I had to go. She was done with me. My mom called him on Wednesday, and he drove the six hours down from central Michigan to central Ohio in a Mercury Lynx station wagon on Thursday.

I was, indeed, fucked.

I was being put out like the trash. I felt stabbed in the heart. My chest was tight and it was hard to breathe through my tears.

I really thought my heart was going to break in two.

She threatened to call the police and have me taken to juvie, which, not knowing if this was possible or not, and knowing how stubborn and fierce she is, I fully believed to be a real threat.

So, my choices at that moment were to go with my dad, who was pretty much a complete stranger, and drive to Michigan with him, or deal with police and possibly go to juvie. A small part of me wanted to be a motherfucker and go down in a blaze of glory and get sent to juvie.

But the slightly more rational and curious part of me knew I had to go with my dad. It had taken my mom only two phone calls to find him, and he was here. My dad, the ghost, the phantom. He had materialized out of the ether, it seemed. But he was a real, live, human being. And he was here because some small part of him really did care about me.

They gave me an hour to pack. Weeping, I packed a big duffle bag, unplugged my stereo and wound up the cords to my speakers. I took a few posters off my wall and folded them carefully, tucking them in among my crate of vinyl albums. I packed all of my cassettes, tucking some of them into my purse for the car, along with my Walkman. I packed up my makeup and blow dryer. My boyfriend Johnny dropped by, in shock as to what was happening, to say goodbye. They left us alone for 15 minutes up in my room. I shut the door and locked it, and we had quick goodbye sex on the floor of my bedroom while my parents sat downstairs, finishing their coffee.

I hugged and kissed Johnny and told him I'd write and call as soon as I could. Then, I got into the car silently as my mom and step-dad stood on the sidewalk. My step-dad was smiling, so smug, it seemed. Fuck him. My mom was crying, and I refused to look at her as we pulled away. I had a wad of tissues, and sat quietly weeping for the first two hours of the drive. Finally, after flipping through the radio stations, Dad asked if I wanted to listen to anything in particular.

I rummaged through my purse for a tape. I pulled out Megadeth's newest album, *So Far, So Good…So What?* I reached over and popped it into the cassette player, and found track six: *In My Darkest Hour*. I turned it up and the low, fierce rhythm filled the car. Mustaine spoke the words, and my dad didn't flinch. Instead, he stared straight ahead and clutched the wheel, listening as the song got more intense. It was like the song was written just for me, to my dad, and all the wondering I'd done as a child about him.

After the song ended, my dad stopped the tape and glanced at me with his sad blue eyes.

"Wow, that was heavy. It reminds me of Vietnam." He lit a cigarette and looked back at the road.

"Yeah? Well, it reminds me of you," I said. He looked at me again, his bright blue eyes meeting my steady brown ones, swollen from tears.

Fuck you and every other adult in my life, I thought to myself. *Fuck you all.*

We sat in silence a little while longer as we drove north up Route 23 across the cold, barren flatlands of Ohio.

***

We stopped outside of Toledo to eat an early dinner at a Bob's Big Boy. I was starving, so I ordered a double hamburger, with French fries and coleslaw and a big coke. I finished the whole meal, and my dad nodded at me, impressed.

"I've always been a good eater," I told him. "Probably because I was always a little hungry as a child." I wanted him to feel guilty. How would he know this about me? We were still strangers to each other. Still, I felt better after eating. I was going to survive this shit, no matter what. I would give no one the satisfaction of taming me or breaking my spirit. I would do my time and make a plan and get out. Fuck them.

As the server brought the check, dad asked for a chocolate milkshake to go. He looked at me and asked if I wanted one.

Upping the ante, I said, "Sure—but make mine a chocolate malt."

His eyes opened wide and he said to the server, "A chocolate malt! Yes! Make that two chocolate malts to go!" He was pleased, and smiling at me, like it was the most brilliant idea, ever.

Like, *you really are my daughter.*

He reached across the table and gave my hand a squeeze. I squeezed back.

We carried our malts to the car and drove north into the Michigan dusk.

7.1

We arrived at his house after dark and unloaded the car, trudging everything up to my new room in the attic. He had already made up the bed for me. I met his wife, Mary, and she welcomed me and made sure I was all set for the night. I cried myself to sleep, and then slept like the dead.

I woke Sunday morning and had breakfast with them with swollen eyes and a scratchy throat. They showed me around their little, plain homestead, under chilly gray skies. It became clear to me that I was truly in the middle of nowhere, on a long country road surrounded by cornfields and pine forests. Coleman, Michigan was cold and muddy, and my dad and Mary lived at the end of a dead-end road on a couple of acres, 3 miles out from the one stoplight in the middle of downtown Coleman, and 20 miles from the small city of Midland. His neighbors were a half-mile away in either direction.

Monday morning, he drove me to the local high school, enrolled me, arranged for me to ride the bus home, and left me there to start classes. With my heavy eyeliner, teased up hair, black GnR t-shirt, and ripped jeans, I felt like an exotic, colorful bird that landed amongst these plain country folks, some of the kids straight off the farm in their overalls, and a few Amish. Many openly stared at me.

The entire high school had 150 students, and the whole town was in the middle of nowhere. It felt like I was in *Children of the Corn*.

The land was so low and flat, the school bus had a flasher on top that I could see out the living room window, across the cornfield, and all the way across the highway as it headed onto the over pass, making a turn, and barreling the two miles down the road toward my dad's house. It gave me a few minutes warning so that I could finish breakfast, rinse my dish, grab my lunch bag and backpack, and walk down the 800-foot mud and gravel driveway to meet the bus. Dad's old hunting dog, a golden retriever named Blue, would walk with me down the driveway and sit at my side until I got on the bus.

There was a run of thick pine forest across the road from the house, and on cold, misty mornings, sometimes

Blue and I would see a few deer crossing into the woods as we waited. I always thought it was a magical thing, like a visitation from another world. They'd pause and peer at me with their gentle brown eyes.

It's going to be OK, they seemed to say.

I wish I could follow you into the forest and disappear, I thought.

***

Mary was my dad's third wife, born and raised in Midland, the daughter of a prominent doctor. She was low key and kind to me, very much an earth mother and hippie. She loved to garden and cook, she was a great softball player and tomboy, and she loved animals and camping and hunting.

As I lived there, I found out that, along with my dad, she was also an alcoholic. She had a thermos filled with Jim Beam and flavored Kool-Aid that she carried around with her everywhere.

She was a kind drunk, though, and would get sillier and more affectionate as the day wore on. She picked me up at school one day, and she stopped the car in the middle of the road to save a turtle from being crushed, and only when she lurched back to the car did I realize that she was hammered.

She also loved Skoal Bandits—a little plug of chewing tobacco wrapped in what looked like a teabag filter that she would tuck between her cheek and gum. Although they were a little neater and dare I say, more ladylike, than wads of chewing tobacco, there were still spit cans all over the house full of these things.

As I got to know her and her family a bit, it turned out that her mother was related to Frank Zappa. I took it as a holy sign from above, like Mama sending me a sign. Despite her quirkiness and problems with whiskey, Mary and her entire family were exceptionally kind to me—and I was now, by way of a shaky, dysfunctional, alcoholic marriage, some kind of third cousin by marriage to Frank Zappa. I knew it was a slim connection, but it still felt a bit cosmic. It felt like a confirmation of sorts, a signal on the road. Even in the backwoods of Michigan, there was a bit of magic to be had.

Dad's house was a still work in progress. He had bought it in shambles after a fire, and he was rebuilding it, cobbling together building supplies and salvage. He was an expert carpenter and had worked construction for years, so he did most of the labor himself. The kitchen was in rough shape, with plywood sheets on the floor, unfinished drywall, a fridge from 1952, a two-burner propane hotplate set on pieces of slate dug right out of the Michigan earth, a microwave, a coffeemaker, and a sink. We also used the gas grill quite a bit, located just outside the kitchen door on a small concrete pad.

He built the cabinets and counters himself, and had used wood salvaged from an ancient, abandoned barn a few miles away to craft beautiful patterns on the countertop, all varnished to a high gloss. He used clipped brass bullet casings as decorative detail to cover nails. The cabinets had no doors, just simple open shelving, and we did most of our prep work at the kitchen dinette with the Formica top.

The house was on well water and heating oil, both of which were strange to me. My dad refused to treat the well water, so it turned everything rust orange with its high iron content: the washing machine, the toilets, the bathtub, and everyone's hair. I went to school with many blonde girls who had auburn spots on the backs of their heads where their hair met the shower stream. The water had a rotten egg smell to it. We drank a lot of Nestea, Country Time, and Kool-Aid to cover it up. After a week, I started buying gallons of purified water to drink, but my dad wouldn't touch it. Too fancy, he thought.

Dad had two acres of land, and a huge garden. He and Mary both had a green thumb and preserved whatever harvests they had. Delicious garlic pickles and relish, canned green beans, jams and preserves.

A lush blueberry thicket, planted in a circle like a donut, is where he grew his marijuana plants, hidden right in the middle of the thicket and completely concealed from the road. A couple of large trees helped to hide it from above, in case they were buzzing him, he said. He had all the space and necessary equipment to grow and preserve his harvests, both legal and illegal.

In his crude basement, he had dug out a small room, about a 10x10 space, which had a few shelves, a small table, and lots of clothesline strung up. He had a few grow lights and dozens of coffee cans full of dirt. It was where he started his pot seedlings, and where he hung his pot plants to dry. It was like a little pot dungeon, completely hidden.

Not only did he smoke pot, but he had a lot of buddies who did, too. All of them Vietnam veterans. Anyone who needed some, he pretty much gave it away. He took donations of whatever could be afforded, but only accepted if he knew they could spare it. He might be an alcoholic, but he wasn't a drug dealer, he told me. He told me he got many of his plants from a buddy of his at the University of Michigan, where they had some secret research going on, he said. He knew how much pot helped him with his pain and anxiety, and he thought it only right to share what he grew easily on his land.

Of course, though, he was paranoid, so he rigged his electric meter not to show the spikes in electricity while growing lights were on the seedlings, and he always had an ear for low aircraft. He wasn't for sure, but suspected that he was under some kind of surveillance. In general, his paranoia was a symptom of PTSD, but I didn't know this at the time.

I didn't know what to think of any of it.

So, I'd pinch off some of his pot and toke on it, too. I smoked my dad's homegrown pot on a backwoods homestead in rural Michigan, and dreamed about my future, knowing for sure it wouldn't be there.

7.2

My dad had refinished the attic of his small house with new drywall and a new, large carpet remnant, and I had the two small, sloped rooms to myself, just like when I was a small child living in the walk-up apartment with my mom in Ashland. Once again, I felt like the orphan in the garret, like Sara Crewe in *A Little Princess*. I could even hear field mice scratching around in the insulation above me at night.

I had the back room, away from the stairs and a bit more private, with a door that closed. The front room was mostly storage and boxes for my dad, some of his guns and winter clothes and stuff from Vietnam. It would have made a cozy den or office. The back room was brighter, with a small closet and two windows that looked out over the cornfields, a lonesome highway, dark, flat pine forests and low gray skies. I promptly plastered the bare drywall with my colorful posters of Mötley Crüe and Guns N' Roses. I set up my stereo and organized my music collection. I wrote letters to Kathy and to Johnny. And I cried, and I cried, and I cried.

Those first few weeks in Michigan were some tough times. Coming to terms with what had happened, why I was there, the indignity of being sent away and being taught a lesson. I felt completely heartbroken, lost, and angry. Roaming a new high school in a daze, feeling like a freak, and lonely.

I truly didn't belong there. I didn't really belong anywhere, it felt like.

Having to live with a father who abandoned me as a child, and sent away from a mother who had abandoned me now, I felt cast away, literally, to the wilderness in this shithole of a town.

For the only time in my life, I contemplated what the world would be like if I wasn't in it. How the best revenge on my parents would be to die a bloody death by wrist slitting, bleeding all over my dad's shitty little house, and him having to tell my mom that I was dead. For a few minutes, the cruel thought of my parents' sorrow and guilt comforted me.

But of course, I couldn't do it. If I had really wanted to kill myself, I just would've found a gun to use. They were plentiful around my Dad's house.

I dreamed vivid dreams of my grandmother, Mama, and of the ocean she crossed to get to this country, of the family she left behind in Sicily, and of the life she created in a new land. What had she felt as she approached the coast of the United States in September of 1931, holding her nine-month old son, and not speaking a word of English? How had Mama survived living in a completely new place, a new culture?

There was a small glimmer of hope in my heart, wanting to find out what was next for me, for my life. I didn't want to give up on myself. I wasn't quitting my life over this shit. This is all temporary, I kept telling myself.

I wanted a real, adventurous, wholesome, happy life. I wanted to find a way to disappear from this world and live a life of my creation in a new world, a new place, and on my terms. I did not want to be broken by this.

I cried in that attic room for weeks, listening to Mötley, GnR, Queensrÿche, Heart, Megadeth and Metallica, writing letters to my friends and my boyfriend, dreaming of escape. The whole time, my dad didn't bother me. He called me honey and patted my hand. My step-mom, Mary, was sweet and empathetic, too. Eventually, my mom and I started to patch things up by talking twice a week. She wrote often, too, with encouragement and articles clipped from the newspaper, or a sweet card with a $20 tucked inside.

I started to think of Michigan as a vision-quest of some kind. What was I here to learn? Endurance? Humility? Resilience? Transformation? I didn't know for sure, but there had to be something better ahead, and I was determined to find out. My heart finally settled down, and I found some peace: My dad loved me the best he could, I loved him the best I could, and I knew I wouldn't be in Michigan long.

I hung on to that with stubborn hope and moved forward.

I finally reached a place of acceptance and resolve: I had to survive this.

My dad was exceedingly fair and kind with me. Eventually, I let him hug me as I cried the last of my heartbreak out. He had the kindest blue eyes, so sad at my suffering. He understood. He had suffered, too. As he began to tell me his stories about Vietnam, I realized how little I really knew about this man.

Vietnam changed him forever. It fucked up a whole generation of young men, beyond anything I could really understand at the time. I just didn't comprehend it. But as I grew older and my dad and I continued our relationship, the horrors that he went through as a soldier were revealed to me. It explained everything about why he couldn't be a real father to me, how he had been dealing with this trauma since before I was born.

I didn't know at the time that he had been brutally sexually assaulted, gang-raped, by a group of four older officers during his first week in Vietnam. He was, quite literally, "fresh meat"—18 years old, straight off the farm, overly friendly and naïve, with a penchant for booze and bullshitting. He was an easy target. He knew who his assaulters were, and then had to live in camp and serve his time in Vietnam with them, which compounded his torment, guilt, pain, trust issues, and his inability to deal with reality up until the day he died, many years later. One of these men had even contacted him after the war.

But as a sixteen-year old kid, I didn't know any of these things yet. We didn't know what war and sexual violence does to a person. My dad was a poster child for PTSD—not only from the war itself, but from the assault, and all the issues that come with it—survivor's guilt, addiction, paranoia, sexual dysfunction, violence. My dad tried hard over the years to live a straight life, to get sober, to deal with his issues—he tried and tried again, and ultimately, he failed.

My dad's troubles, to a great degree, were not his choice. He lived his entire adult life through the lens of trauma, violence, and assault. And so, it would remain the greatest paradox in my life until the day he died: I finally understood the horrors of Vietnam and how the trauma had impacted him for decades—but I still couldn't ever quite forgive him for leaving me.

7.3

For the first month I was at my dad's, anytime we had red meat, I just assumed it was beef—and I wondered why the beef had a different taste up in Michigan. One day, I mentioned this curiosity to my mom on the phone, who burst out laughing. *Oh sweetie, you're not eating beef, you're eating venison*, she'd said.

I was horrified at first, and kind of pissed, and then I felt silly. How had I not clued in? My dad didn't have the heart, I suppose. But then I got over it when I realized that venison was pretty tasty, and we had a freezer full of it, harvested by my dad and prepared well.

He was an avid fisherman and often competed in tournaments around the state. We had trout and other fish on occasion. One time, he went up north, and netted five big coolers full of smelts, which are smallish fish that are quite abundant up in those cold waters. I spent the better part of four hours, hunched over buckets and newspaper with a pair of sharp scissors—snip, snip, slice, scoop—which is how you clean a smelt. We beer-battered them and fried them up and ate them like French fries that night, and my dad made tartar sauce with his homemade garlic relish and real mayonnaise, which was the first time I ever tasted real mayo and not Miracle Whip—I was instantly hooked. It was a delicious treat and worth the effort of scooping fish guts. The rest of the smelts he froze in Ziplock bags full of water for our later enjoyment. Hunting, fishing, preserving and farming, being frugal and making do. My dad was a homesteader. This is what everyone around us did, too, and I was learning.

My dad was a Marine-trained expert marksman, and he had been hunting since he was a boy on a farm, roaming the forests of north central Ohio. He had been raised in the country and had been around animals, hunting, and farming his whole life. When he went to Vietnam, they made him a medic—a "crackerbox" ambulance driver. He said it was because he had the stomach for the blood and guts of the battlefield. He knew death. He knew anatomy. He knew how to butcher animals.

Somehow, this qualified him, at 18 years old, to pick up bodies and the body parts of his friends and fellow soldiers in the jungles and battlefields of South Vietnam. By the time I lived with him, he was 37 years old and 85% disabled according to the VA. He had taken some shrapnel to his knee, and it was never the same. He had been one of the early activists regarding Agent Orange injury, and his medical history was fraught with numerous skin conditions and surgeries. His feet were still infested with the Jungle Rot.

For a while, he was the president of the Vietnam Veterans Association chapter in Midland, and he marched in parades and volunteered where he could to help other soldiers. He flew an American Flag from an enormous flagpole in the front yard, with its own spotlight. He collected his disability benefits and took some college classes in Saginaw and worked his homestead and tried to make it work with his third wife. He was a functional alcoholic suffering from severe PTSD but—he did make an effort to teach me, to be a good father to me, at least for the time I was there.

7.4

In late April, he came home with a deer in the back of his Ford pickup.

The deer had jumped out in front of a car and gotten hit and died instantly. Dad saw it happen, and pulled over to help the driver. He talked to the state troopers, and they helped him load the deer carcass into his truck even though he didn't have a tag for it. They told him they considered it a public service, and they hated to let the meat go to waste. Within the hour, he hauled it home and strung it up in the middle of our roughed-out kitchen with a spread of old newspapers underneath. As I walked in the door from school, my eyes got big as I saw the carcass hanging there, dripping, from the ceiling. Then my eyes went to the floor. The last bit of guts from his crude road-side field dressing.

I put my stuff down on the kitchen table.

"Hi Sweetie, how was school?" Dad was cheerful and ready for me. Before I could answer, he handed me a knife and nodded at the deer and said, "Go wash up. I'll show you where to start cutting."

As grossed out as I was at the reality of what I was about to do, I took the knife.

Dad and I rendered the deer that afternoon and evening. I helped him slice it all into cubes, steaks, and loins. He packaged and froze the bones, labeled everything, and started a batch of marinade, to make jerky. We listened to the local rock station, which mostly played John Cougar Mellencamp, ZZ Top, and Foreigner. Dad made coffee for us, and we kept going. He told me he'd take me in to Kmart to buy me a new pair of jeans, since my good school jeans were all bloodied up.

"You're a country girl, now," he chuckled. "You've got a pair of proper work jeans."

I denied it and said "No way, no how—I'm not a country girl." I was secretly pleased. There were things you just couldn't learn by reading a book, and if anything, I knew I was learning things, living there with my dad. Learning things for survival. I learned firsthand that homesteading was damn hard work, and that you don't wear your nice jeans to do it in.

That spring, I planted a garden in those stained work jeans. I helped my dad haul wood, shovel manure, and plant new trees along the road in them. I caulked windows and painted house trim and planted flowers in them. We went target practicing in the woods with his rifles in them, I learned how to drive his old Ford pickup truck with a stick shift, and how to get it out of the thick Michigan mud in them. Those jeans saw a lot of action.

I didn't mind all this physical, outdoor activity. I secretly loved learning how to run a homestead, tend a garden, and take care of things. Shoot things. Chop wood. Take care of myself. It all felt very Laura Ingalls Wilder to me, and I jumped in with both feet. I learned that homesteading, ultimately, was about creativity. How to plan the garden, how to lay the fence, figuring out how to build things and improve your land and use the resources that were around you. How to barter with neighbors and swap favors and services.

Dad was always working, tinkering, building, and improving the place. Every day, a new project.

He sat down a few times a day in his favorite old chair in the garage to smoke a joint and drink a beer. Even though he wasn't sober most of the time, he was pretty mellow and steady. He kept his addictions to himself, and was discreet and polite about it, but I saw the empty bottles and cans overflowing in trash bags, waiting for my dad to haul them back in for the glass deposit. I knew how much he was drinking, and Mary, too.

I never saw any angry outbursts, although he did get jumpy if he heard any type of helicopter or gunfire from the woods. He'd get a wild look in his eye, his radar up and on alert. He always kept a loaded gun up near the door, just like Pa Ingalls had.

"You just never know," he said to me. "We are out here in the middle of a cornfield, miles from town with an interstate just across the field. Plus, shooting dinner from my front porch is fun," he'd grin.

The entire time I was there, he was kind and patient and fair with me, even if sometimes a little slurry. He was proud of me, but I didn't let him get too proud. I told him that I just enjoyed my chores. It gave me time to think, to dream, to plan, to let my mind wander with possibilities. It reminded me of my old babysitter, Sarah, who had trained me to do housework. Doing chores at her place had been peaceful, too.

As I tilled the sandy soil and planted two long rows of seed potatoes in thick manure on my hands and knees, I thought about Nikki Sixx, formerly Frank Ferrana. I'd read somewhere that he'd spent time on a farm in Idaho. I wondered if he'd ever planted potatoes? As my mind wandered and imagined, Los Angeles flickered, and came into focus.

I sat back on my heels for a minute and breathed in the clean Michigan air and warm dirt smells. The breeze picked up for a moment, and the trees in the forest across the road made a big whooshing rustle. If I closed my eyes, it sounded almost like ocean waves. The pine trees and dampness almost smelled like the ocean. *Almost*. I breathed deep.

California.

Most of the kids I went to school with in Michigan were straight off the farms or out of the trailers that dotted the countryside, and that is where many of them would stay for life. The longer I was there, the more I knew for sure that I'd not stay in the Midwest. I wanted to be in a big city. Bigger than Columbus.

Was it possible? I whispered to the stars in my attic room, *please help me find a way*. Meditating on posters of Axl Rose and Nikki Sixx, like they were saints. My tribesmen, orphans and refugees, dreamers. Their stories—escaping their shitty childhoods, heading to LA on a Greyhound Bus and then making it big—were like fairytales to me.

I believed in the magic and mythology of their stories. Dreams could come true, and I was willing to pay whatever price was asked of me. I had nothing to lose. Anything was better than being stuck in the middle of Nowhere, Michigan.

7.5

My dad had a big road atlas, and I studied the routes to Los Angeles. Would I go the north, middle, or southern route? What kind of car would I have? How much money would I need? I wrote in my journal of all the possibilities. I knew that ultimately, and eventually, I had to get away from my parents.

Los Angeles. It felt far enough away. And it was somewhere. Somewhere important.

I was at rock bottom. I was on my way to being a high-school dropout, living with two alcoholics on the outskirts of a one-stoplight town called Coleman, 20 miles northeast of Midland, three hours north of Detroit, three hundred miles from Westerville. I was isolated, trapped by distance from everything I cared about.

I didn't know what I wanted to *do* in Los Angeles. I just knew I had to *get* there. On the map bump-out of Southern California, I memorized the freeways, suburbs, and orientations of the city. I imagined myself there, living out my life, meeting Nikki Sixx or some other handsome rock star to marry and settle down with. I wanted a new life, a new family, a different destiny than what faced me here, or in Ohio. My future felt far more certain in LA.

I knew I needed to get back to Ohio for a while, to get a job, to graduate high school, to save money. I'd be 18 in less than two years. It seemed like forever, but I knew it wouldn't be long at all.

Day by day, I'd be closer to home. Closer to something better.

I only made one real friend while in Michigan—Lisa. She was tall, with sharp blue eyes, the youngest of many siblings to a local dairy farmer. We met in Algebra. She tried in vain to help me pass the class, but I was born to struggle at math, it seemed. Her efforts were appreciated, but I was always hopelessly lost.

She was friendly and ironic and funny, and she loved hard rock and a bit of metal, too. We started hanging out more, and she'd just started driving, which was great. We were now able to go a few places—into Midland, to the mall, or over to Mt. Pleasant to the hippie shops and book stores near CMU. I didn't feel quite as trapped, and my dad let me roam a bit.

When she found out that Guns N' Roses were coming to Saginaw, Lisa drove straight over to our house to ask my dad directly if I could go with her. Shockingly, he agreed on the spot.

But we needed to hustle and drive into Midland to get our tickets at the record store before it closed. I asked my dad if I could skip dinner at home that night. My dad peeled off twenty-five dollars from his money clip, handed it to me, and told me to have fun and be careful, and to be home by nine.

The cash covered the ticket price to the show, a brand-new issue of *RIP Magazine* with GnR on the cover, and a trip to McDonalds. Lisa and I clutched the tickets and giggled in disbelief on our way home.

Guns N' Roses were coming to Saginaw in six weeks on their first real tour for *Appetite for Destruction* as headliners, and we were going. I couldn't believe my luck.

Guns N' Fuckin' Roses!!

8.0

[Starry Eyes]

Friday, May 6, 1988.

Wendler Arena in Saginaw held about five thousand people, and as Lisa and I pulled up to park, we could see the excitement on everyone's faces as they walked in.

This Guns N' Roses concert was a general admission show. Growing up in Ohio, I knew of the horror that unfolded at a Who concert in 1980 at the Cincinnati Coliseum when a bunch of people were crushed to death in a stampede; as a result, GA shows over a certain capacity were outlawed in Ohio.

But this was Michigan. They had no such law, and it was quite normal to go to a GA show of this size in an arena.

Despite my fears of being crushed in a mob, we found a spot right up at the security barrier at the front of the stage, and we stood our ground pretty well trying not to get jostled out by bigger guys.

I felt like I was having déjà vu of the David Lee Roth show when a swarthy looking roadie—this one with longer, greasy hair—approached me and said hello.

"Hi ladies, how are you tonight? Do you want to meet the band?" he asked.

I looked at Lisa and stuttered, "Uh, yeah! We'd love to meet the band!"

He held up two after-show sticky passes in one hand, and two fingers on the other.

"They cost two blow jobs."

I laughed out loud and said, "Are you serious? For real?"

He raised an eyebrow, smirked and nodded. He kept holding up the two fingers. He was dead serious.

I shook my head in disappointment and disbelief.

"No, sorry man. I can't do that." He shrugged and kept moving. Lisa and I looked at each other with raised eyebrows. *Oh well.*

What a fucking scam.

I wasn't about to blow a roadie—or a rock star, for that matter—in order to meet Duff McKagan. There was just NO WAY I was missing this show.

A few minutes later, I saw the same roadie approach two other girls down the line from us. Maybe they'd be agreeable to his terms.

Fuck him. Fuck them. I was there to watch the band.

I was certainly not there for sex or for someone's amusement.

I was there to rock out. And boy, we did.

A band called Zodiac Mindwarp opened the show, and they were fun and energetic. The lead singer was wearing a pair of flappy black gym shorts, with no underpants underneath. His hairy dick was flopping around in front of us when he'd put a foot up on the monitor, which choked us with laughter. He wagged around with no shame and it was funny as hell.

After Mindwarp was done, we felt the energy of the crowd shift in anticipation. The lights dimmed and the buzz grew louder. When Guns N' Roses finally hit the stage, everyone surged forward and got caught in a giant, moshing frenzy. It was automatic, like a murmur of birds, moving in unison.

We tried to find shelter along the edges but—in a moment that I had already known would happen—I ended up getting trapped and crunched against the metal security barrier and having to be pulled over by a huge security guard. Lisa and I were separated for a minute but then we spotted each other. We made our way to a safer spot, a little farther back. My sternum was bruised and I was shaking, but I was OK.

The view was better from a little further back, anyway.

The show was magnificent. The sound was perfect and they were amazing.

I couldn't believe I was seeing Guns N' Roses. I knew that I was witnessing history—the first tour of one of the greatest rock bands, ever.

And this is a show I would have missed if I hadn't come to Michigan.

This show was added at the last minute. If I were still in Columbus, there was no way my mom would've let me travel on a school night, even if I had been behaving. They hadn't played Columbus on this tour. They had played Cleveland the night before and were on their way to play a string of shows in Canada.

No—this was meant to be. After months of being trapped in Michigan, this was my reward. They were like travelling preachers, praising the gritty, truthful glory of Los Angeles—and I was in.

I was ALL in.

I knew it, standing in the arena that night as they closed with *Paradise City*. I was moving to Los Angeles. The feeling hit me in the gut, a knowing, deep in the belly, that I was going to be OK. I was going to LA and nothing could stop me. I was 16 years old and I knew it as sure as I've known anything in my life since then.

Tears streamed down my face for no good reason as the band closed the show. I staggered out of the arena in a daze, bruised and scratched and totally inspired.

There was no denying it. I was moving to California, somehow, some way, some day.

It turns out, someday was just 23 months later.

8.1

June, 1988.

After the GnR show and as school got out for the summer in Michigan, I had to convince my mom that I was ready to move home and be a good kid. We talked about it on the phone and in our letters to each other. I had to keep a B average, get a job, get my license, and save for a car. I had to be respectful and be a part of the family. I negotiated for a midnight curfew on the weekends, and she agreed to it. I felt ready to do all that, or at least to fake it. If I could fake it and play nice, then maybe I could get through it. I was still angry and disappointed. But I also didn't want to stay in Michigan, so I made the deal.

My mom and I patched things up as well as we could, and on June 9, just a few weeks after Megadeth played Columbus, she drove to Michigan to pick me up. My dad had offered to let me stay if I wanted to, but I didn't. There was nothing for me in Michigan.

I know it disappointed him that I was leaving. He wanted to make up, in some way, for being such a shitty dad to me. But it didn't matter, really—that time, my childhood, was lost, gone.

Part of the deal for me coming home to Ohio was to be allowed to go back to Westerville South for my senior year so I could graduate with my friends. In return for that, I promised to buckle down and keep my end of the bargain, be respectful, and not do stupid stuff.

I got my job back at Sister's Chicken & Biscuits, and started saving up my paychecks. In six weeks, I had about $200, and I started looking for a car. I wanted a car that I could get to California in, but most everything that was even remotely suitable was $800 to $1000. I kept looking.

Dick, my step-dad took me out for driving practice that summer, in an old parking lot by the local dam—Hoover Reservoir. In addition to my dad's old Ford pickup, I learned most of my driving skills in my mom's white four-speed manual Ford Escort. As Dick and I spent a few hours together, we began to talk and understand each other better. He really was a nice person, and he adored my mom. They were two people really just meant for each other. As much as I still hated the situation with him and the ex-wife and kids, I accepted it. I was getting the fuck out, so it didn't matter. I might as well go peacefully and let them live out their drama.

I got my driver's license in July, and I bought my first car a week later. I'd spotted a 1973 VW Super Beetle in the classified ads for $300. Dick got really excited at the idea—he told me about growing up in Hawaii in the 50s and 60s, and driving his old Beetle around Oahu, surfing and camping. We went to look at the car, skeptical that it would be worth our time.

It wasn't much, but it ran and had a solid engine. It was mostly a dark blue car, but the back, right bumper was a rich, eggplant purple. The driver's door was a festive bright orange, and it had two tinted windows, also mismatched in color. Across the back window were the dancing Rainbow Bears. A Grateful Dead blessing. That must mean good vibes, right? It had no radio, but it did come with two speakers, with wires conveniently sticking out near the gear shift. I was pretty sure I could splice up my old Walkman to the wires, to rig it as a makeshift radio/tape deck. The windshield wipers were dubious and smeary, and there was no AC, only a rigged-up vent in the back that blew hot air, no matter the time of year.

It was a patchwork of issues, but it roared to life like a little beast as Dick and I took it for a test drive. It snorted and backfired a few times, but then drove just fine. It was actually quite peppy. Dick inspected everything closely and thought it was just a little moisture in the gas line. He taught me how to drive this particular stick shift, with the reverse in a different place than I was used to.

Once I gave it a spin around the block, I was having fun, laughing at how ridiculous this little car was. It was so ugly that it was cute. You could hear me coming from a mile away, and I loved it. I think Dick loved it more. He seemed almost giddy.

Then, Dick made me an offer I couldn't refuse—he'd pay for half the car for me. He was going to chip in $150. That way, I'd have a little gas money, and I'd need to start paying for insurance, anyway. I said yes, immediately, and the deal was done. I drove the Escort home while he drove new little Beast, to make sure there were no major defects. I took my mom for a spin when we got home, and she was bemused, at best. Dick drove with me to the Ohio BMV to get the title and registration stuff done.

Although I loved my new little car, my step-dad loved it a bit more than I did and always wanted to drive it. Eventually, I gave it to him and I drove my mom's old Ford Escort for a few months—with its own list of issues—until someone hit me at an intersection. I was fine, but mercifully, the Escort wasn't.

Then, a for sale sign appeared on a little blue 1980 Toyota Corolla, right in our neighborhood. It was a cute, two-door coupe with a 5-speed stick, and zippy. It was in good shape with 80k miles on it. They were asking $1200, but I offered $800, and they took it. Two weeks later, I about choked when I had to replace the clutch, brakes, and tires, but other than that, it seemed fairly reliable, with a radio, good wipers and signals, and no mismatched parts or rust. I'd spent most of my savings on it, so I started over again—this time with my eye on the prize: getting to Los Angeles.

Before school started, I worked for Earlene again that August, and I drove myself to the fairgrounds every day. I loved my freedom, and getting the chance to make some "real" money—a bit more than the $3.50 an hour I made at Sister's.

I turned 17 in September, and in November 1988, I started working at a Victoria's Secret distribution warehouse which was only a few miles from our apartment. I had to pick orders for the stores, and I'd get tasked with counting out hundreds—thousands—of pairs of underwear to fill boxes to go to the stores. Just after graduation, I moved over to the Catalog division and started taking phone orders on the night shift, from 6:30pm to 3am. It was a fun job, talking to people from all over the country about clothes, upselling. We didn't get commissions, but we did get perks and bonuses based on our sales volume, our "dollars per minute" call ratios, and I did pretty well at that. The access to super-cheap clothes was a great benefit, too.

8.2

Johnny and I broke up while I was in Michigan, but Kathy and I picked up our friendship when I got home like there had been no separation, and we started our senior year at Westerville South, determined to get through it with as little drama as possible. While in Michigan, I had practiced my singing, and she had been playing her guitar.

We started harmonizing and playing music together, thinking maybe we could start a band of some kind. I dyed black streaks in my hair, and mastered the art of bleaching Kathy's dark hair to a bright, white blonde. Heart was having a comeback, and we thought we'd package ourselves as a younger, more metal Ann and Nancy Wilson. There weren't a lot of chicks playing hard rock. We also started going to a few live shows to see our high school friends play in their own bands.

With a few of our guy friends from our old music theory class, we formed a band where I was the singer. Kathy wasn't quite ready to play in front of others, and to be honest, neither was I. Somehow, my little band, Gun Shy, performed one song at the Westerville South talent show that year. After that live performance, at which I had been absolutely terrified, I decided that maybe I wasn't meant to be a performer. The thought of doing it again gave me nightmares, and honestly, our band wasn't good enough to really stick it out and get better. We had fun rehearsing, though.

So, Kathy and I practiced in the safety of our bedrooms, with our guitars, bass, and vocal harmonies, recording ourselves on a boombox. Maybe I'd be braver as a singer if she and I were on stage together. We both paid for guitar lessons, and I started taking vocal lessons from an old jazz singer named Michelle Horsefield. Michelle told me I had a solid three octave vocal range, and that I was lucky because most rock singers didn't. I was just happy to be able to sing along to Ann Wilson and Don Dokken.

8.3

Columbus, Ohio is sort of a plain-Jane city. It doesn't sit on the shore of a beautiful lake, like Cleveland, and isn't nestled into the hills above the mighty Ohio River, like Cincinnati. It has none of that flair. Columbus sits on the beginnings of open prairie, just outside the last of Appalachia, along a medium-sized river, the Scioto, (pronounced "Sigh-o-ta").

Columbus is the bellybutton of Ohio, and the city is divided into four quadrants by its interstates, with I-70 running east and west, and I-71, running north and south. Surrounded by the I-270 outer-belt. Columbus is shaped like a giant pizza—although if you've ever eaten local pizza in Columbus, you'd know it's cut into squares, not slices.

Columbus seems to straddle the line between the North and the South, and is a musical crossroads between rock music and country music. A little bit Nashville, a little bit Cleveland. Back then, it seemed that if you lived north of I-70, you listened to rock. South of I-70, you listened to country, or at least that is what it felt like. Musical culture runs deep, all throughout Ohio. It's one of the best-kept secrets about the Buckeye State, I think—how many people are musically literate.

Columbus is a small big city, white collar and business oriented and wholesome, home of Ohio State University and Buckeye Nation. For having no professional football team, it's a town that is obsessed with football. It's never had a national music scene, either, but it has a thriving musical culture that supports local and regional bands: The Godz, Rosie, McGuffy Lane, Scarlet, Lollipop Factory, Shock Tu, Bad Reputation, Nasty Action, Madd Moxie, and Ronald Koal. And there were Cleveland bands that played Columbus often: Michael Stanley Band, Spoyld, Kidd Wikked, Priscilla, Easy Street, and dozens more—way too many to name.

All of them played the Alrosa Villa and/or the historic Newport Music Hall on a regular basis. All of them easily packed venues on the circuit of 300-1200 people.

Ohio in general has been a breeding ground for music stars, for sure; Maynard James Keenan, from Ravenna; Marilyn Manson, from Wooster; Trent Reznor, Janey Lane, Boz Skaggs, Dwight Yoakum, Joe Walsh, Chrissie Hynde, Devo. There have been many big-time national acts to come out of Ohio. Ohio is a place where great musicians and song writers can gain a following and get paid to play original material to good crowds.

A small part of it is probably the general climate and weather in Ohio—it felt gloomy to me, like I was living in a fishbowl. It felt like I could go for weeks without seeing the blue sky. Columbus is a as rainy and gray as Seattle. The summers are nice and humid and thunder-stormy, the winters cold, humid, and dark. So, people go out to see music, they go out to restaurants and bars and to football games, and they support the local music scene.

A bigger reason, at least from my experience, that musicians thrived in Ohio, is that music education and appreciation was strong in Ohio public schools. It's mandated in the Ohio Revised Code. From the time I was in kindergarten, music was a part of my curriculum. There were instrument donations and low-cost music instruction through the elementary school. Glee club or orchestra were required in middle school, which fed into the high school marching band and drama club.

Marching bands are a breeding ground for great musicians and performers, and are promoted heavily in high schools—all of which feed into The Ohio State University and The Best Damn Band in the Land. These kids go on to keep playing music, for fun or otherwise. We are the grandchildren of immigrants, a melting pot of European cultures that valued a strong work ethic, as well as music and the arts. Our ancestors listened to opera, polka, and Irish and German drinking songs while settling and building the great state of Ohio on their farms and in the factories. Of course, I didn't really know any of this while I was growing up, it was just always there. My mom always played music and enjoyed live music, as had my grandparents.

Finally getting to go out to see bands—local bands, my friends' bands, and some national acts— was always a lot of fun. Despite these late nights, I still got up to go to school and work. It was part of the deal. I always told my mom where I was, who I was with, and when I would be home. She'd even let me go up to Cleveland to see shows with my friend Anne, who lived up there, and who I'd met at the Alrosa.

I managed to keep my shit together, and I didn't once violate my word. Michigan was behind me, and the future was bright.

8.4

In addition to Pamela Des Barres, the other woman to spark my imagination and confirm my resolve to go to Los Angeles was the director Penelope Spheeris.

On a chilly and rainy Friday night, I picked up Kathy and we drove over to High Street to a small art-deco film theater called the Drexel North. I'd heard a movie mentioned on MTV that was about metal and Los Angeles: *The Decline of Western Civilization part 2: The Metal Years*. We weren't sure what to expect—it was a low-budget, independent film by this chick filmmaker—but it looked interesting.

The movie blew me away. It was like a clarion call to me. It was a documentary about the Sunset Strip and the metal music scene in Los Angeles. I hadn't seen anything like it before. It was gritty, seedy, sad, and absolutely captivating. Watching Chris Holmes drink himself into a stupor as his mom looked on. We didn't know at the time that it was staged—we thought it was for real. Or, that determined, hungry mindset of Dave Ellefson of Megadeth—and they played my song—*In My Darkest Hour*.

The movie featured the band London—Nikki's earlier group—Faster Pussycat, Odin, Ratt, bits of KISS, Ozzy, Aerosmith—all bands we liked. Women were not depicted favorably, mostly as brainless ornamentation.

The whole movie reeked of desperation, of exploitation, with underlying misogyny thrown in. It was a snapshot of Los Angeles and what was going on there. In many ways, it was a visual parallel to Guns N' Roses' *Appetite for Destruction*. I finally understood the habitat in which some of my favorite music was made.

Instead of being repelled or disgusted by what I saw, I was motivated. *Things are happening. I've got to get there.* I wanted to see it all for myself, in person.

I spoke the words to myself almost every day: *I'm moving to California. I'm moving to Los Angeles. I'm moving to Hollywood.*

I was going to talk my future into a reality.

***

Mom and Dick asked me what my goals were after graduation, and I never deviated from my plan: I'm moving to Los Angeles. I knew they didn't take me seriously, but I didn't care. I wasn't under any obligation to take their advice. They both thought that I should consider going to cosmetology school—something practical, a skill that I could use to make money with. I could be up and running in a year or so, doing hair, and it was a skill I could take anywhere.

Sure, it was a great idea. I could dig doing hair. My folks weren't quite as keen on the Recording Workshop idea because they didn't think it was as practical.

Working in a recording studio or a hair salon, it didn't matter—I was pretty sure that either would be a practical skill set to have in Los Angeles. I finally told them to stop bugging me—that I just wanted to get to Los Angeles first, and I'd figure it out from there. They weren't offering to help, and I wasn't going to ask.

Once I turned 18, I really didn't owe them an explanation. I was going to live my life on my terms.

Until then, though, I was going to have fun and go to as many shows as possible.

8.5

Ohio. February, 1989, senior year.

One late Sunday morning, Kathy and I went to Coyle, a guitar and instrument store, to buy strings for her guitar, and to look at a real Stratocaster. I had my red Fender bass with me and had pulled it out to see if the guy could adjust the bridge. Kathy had the new guitar in her hands and was sitting down.

We were there for a few minutes noodling around, and then, like out of a movie, Kip Winger and Reb Beach walked around the corner and up to the counter.

They looked over at us with instruments in our hands, and they said hello. We recognized them immediately. They came over and introduced themselves and asked about our gear. I guess they weren't used to seeing many girls with guitars.

We knew they were in town for a show at the Newport that night, but we had purposely decided NOT to go because, you know, it was Winger. I was into Megadeth and Metallica by this point. We weren't huge fans of Winger. They were all over the radio with their hit, *Seventeen*, but now, here they were in person, and suddenly, we were fans. Kathy and I exchanged glances—HOLY SHIT—and remained calm.

The two men were beautiful, I mean REALLY good-looking guys. Kip was movie-star gorgeous and

Reb was taller and super cute as well. The other guitarist/keyboard player for Winger, Paul, was also lurking around, and seemed to home in on me. He thought it was really cool that I played bass and sang. He was pretty cute, too, but not like the other two. I got a bit of an off-vibe.

Kip was friendly and gracious, and asked if we were going to the show.

"No, not yet!" I said, smartly.

Kip smiled and said, "well then, how many should I put you down for?"

I told him three tickets would be great, knowing that one of our friends, Laura, was a big fan and would appreciate the invite. Paul asked for my phone number, and I gave it to him, not thinking much of it, but curious.

I got home and called Laura who was totally stoked to go to the show with us. We made our plans to meet up.

An hour later, Paul actually called me. It was near sound check time, and he was making sure I was still coming down to the show. I was surprised and flattered, and a little bit creeped. My mom had answered the phone.

Laura, Kathy, and I parked down on campus and made our way to a bar right next to the Newport, called the Street Scene. We planned on getting a bite to eat before the show, and they had decent hamburgers. Laura was old enough to buy a bucket of beer, too, which is part of the reason we brought her along. We sat down and started to look at the menu.

Suddenly, as we were being seated in a booth, my name was called from across the dim dining area, and there was Paul, and the guys and crew from Winger, at a big table. Kip waved and stood up, Paul scootched chairs, and pretty soon the three of us girls were wedged in among the band and crew, who were all friendly, funny, and very sweet. Paul was intent on having me talk to him, so we chatted and I ate an enormous bacon swiss cheese burger. I felt like he was studying me intently as I wolfed down my food, like I was the most fascinating creature, ever, although I secretly hoped he'd lose interest in me. I just kept eating, trying not to feel too creeped, and hoping that my whole-hearted dedication to my messy burger would turn him off.

Laura, on the other hand, was stammering, sweating, and giggling shamelessly, sitting next to Kip. I couldn't believe my eyes—my smart-ass, know-it-all friend was losing it in front of these rock stars. I was a little embarrassed for her. The Winger dudes graciously picked up our food bill, and we told them to have a good show, and thanked them again for dinner and the tickets.

Paul kissed me on the cheek and asked, very seriously, if I'd meet him at the bus after the show, and I said sure. I was in no way attracted to him. He just wasn't my type. He was a lot older than me. But I was curious, and thought it was kind of cool, too. I'd never considered myself a "groupie," but it felt like that kind of scenario.

Only, I wasn't committed to the path—I was just seeing how it would play out.

The show was fine, really, but not my kind of music. They were free tickets and the guys were obviously good musicians and performed well. There were a lot of women at the show, a parade of sturdy cornfed Ohio girls hanging around in skimpy outfits. One of these women was a notorious local groupie who had sex with animals, according to a legendary Polaroid picture that had circulated around the Alrosa.

Paul found me in the crowd outside the back of the Newport. As he was being pawed by other women, he grasped my hand and pulled me toward the bus. I stopped and shook my head at him.

"Man, I'm sorry, but I'm not going on the bus. It's just not my thing."

"Come and have a drink! It's no big deal," he tried to convince me. More women spotted him and started circling.

"It's OK. I have to get up and go to school tomorrow." I'm not sure he understood that I was still in high school.

He seemed disappointed. I felt bad, and appreciated how nice they were, and I was grateful, but...no. I thanked him again for the tickets and we drove home.

Paul called me two more times that next week, and then I never heard from him again, which is a good thing—because I really was only seventeen.

9.0

[Dancing On Glass]

Los Angeles, Summer 1990.

My first weekend in Los Angeles was a success. Stacy was great, and she invited me to move in to the tiny studio apartment and split the rent. I'd have a futon to sleep on, a spot on the street for my car, and an address, all for $200 a month. Mario gave his blessing, and I made a quick trip back to San Jose to grab a few more things from my Aunt's house. She was understanding, and was willing to store the rest of my stuff until further notice.

The city of Los Angeles welcomed me with sunshine and possibilities. I was in love with Laurel Canyon, and Stacy was an enthusiastic tour guide, showing me all over the cool parts of the city. We were going to the beach a lot, and out to various clubs, and we were at The Rainbow with Mario, Jr. a few nights a week to eat and drink for free.

Mario, Jr. and I got to know each other better over these first few weeks. He was quirky, but he had gentle brown eyes and a tender heart. He always had a bit of cocaine around. I'd tried cocaine only once before, in the bathroom of the Alrosa Villa in Columbus just a few months prior. I didn't feel much of anything from it except a tingly nose. I tried it a few more times with Mario, but I still wasn't impressed. It made me feel tacky and fake. I wasn't a coke head, and I didn't want to be. I got a better buzz from a strong cup of coffee. I'd figured out by now that a bit of weed and a few drinks was my limit in terms of intoxication.

Mario was literally the first person I met, and the first person I slept with in Los Angeles. I was 18, and he was 42, older than my own father, but it didn't bother me. My heart even skipped a beat when Mario peeled off my bathing suit bottoms on the edge of his bubble-filled hot tub under a canopy of tall trees.

Mario and I hung out and talked and drank and, occasionally, we had sex. Some nights, he had dinner delivered for us, other nights I drove us down to the Strip and we sat at the table in The Rainbow kitchen and ate and laughed and visited with his friends and family.

One night, he told me he had been invited up to Sam Kinison's place, so he navigated as I drove us up a spooky and dark Nichol's Canyon. We kept climbing up until we reached a dead end on Solar Drive. We saw some cop cars parked around the white, modern house that Mario said was Kinison's place, so we turned around and found a place to park at the end of another canyon road. We watched the city lights for a bit and talked and talked. Some nights, I'd stay over and sleep in his bed, and some mornings, I'd get up and fix us an egg and toast breakfast.

For the first time in my life, I felt truly free and happy. Los Angeles was everything I had hoped for, and it all seemed to sparkle like a new jewel on my finger, showing itself off while I admired it. I was learning my way around the City, and I was trying to forget Ohio. I was finally free to be myself, in charge of my own destiny. I had no backup plan, no idea of what I really wanted to with myself. Whatever I figured out about my future life, I was sure I'd be doing it in LA.

The summer of 1990 stretched out before me without a plan or pressure. I tracked down and called my old friend, Kevin Amici, from high school, and it turned out he was staying less than a mile from me in the Canyon, in a tiny little bungalow up on Weepah Way. We met up a few times and had meals together and caught up; he was working at an asbestos removal company during the day, playing in his band, and doing the sound at Gazzarri's, at night.

Stacy introduced me to a few of her friends. Robin, a waitress at the Body Shop, was one of them. We clicked immediately. We roamed the City together, me and my new friends who felt like sisters, who welcomed me and showed me the ropes and shared their knowledge and laughed at some of the absurdities of living in the big city. It was all so spectacular: the eternal sunshine, the ocean and beach, the stoners, junkies, orphans, and freaks that roamed the boulevards and hills and canyons in the city of my dreams.

9.1

One night at The Rainbow, Mario introduced me to Sean Lewis, the guitar player in legendary Sunset Strip band, London. Sean stopped by our booth to say hello and was so friendly and sweet. In a blink, he asked me out and made plans for us before I could even politely refuse. Mario didn't seem to mind.

Sean and I went out on a few dates over the next couple of weeks, and he was a true gentleman, a lot of fun, and a really smart guy. I almost couldn't believe how nice he was, plus, here I was, seeing a guy in London— Nikki Sixx's old band.

Unfortunately, I wasn't really physically attracted to Sean, and the band seemed to be more famous for its past members than its current overwhelming talent. They were out there still scraping it on the Strip while their peers in other bands went on to platinum glory. I wanted to love the band, and I wanted to be attracted to Sean because he was such a nice guy, but I just didn't and wasn't. I've never been a good faker, and he was too nice of a guy to jerk around.

I began to realize that I always liked the bad boys, the dangerous guys, the older men.

I was already sleeping with Mario, and I didn't want to hurt his feelings or have it get weird. I told Mario all about Sean, and he seemed touched. He thought maybe I should be dating someone my own age, rather than an old man like him. So, I asked him, *Mario, are we dating? Or just having some fun?* He winked at me and kissed my forehead and didn't answer. I knew what he meant.

Mario asked me to accompany him to Las Vegas for his daughter's wedding later that month. She was three years older than me. I was honest with him when I told him I felt a bit strange about it, and that I didn't want to be a distraction at a family event.

I knew how Italians were. He knew I was right, and he went to the wedding without me.

9.2

I'd been looking for work for a couple of weeks but wasn't having much luck, so I asked Mario if he could help. He couldn't put me at the restaurant because I had no experience other than fast food, although I was willing to bus tables. I didn't take it too personally because I knew how it can be with a family business. Especially an Italian family business—politics can be tricky. So, he made some phone calls and told me to contact his friend out in the Valley, an Armenian guy named Serj, who owned a car dealership up on Victory Boulevard.

I called Serj and arranged an interview, which wasn't really an interview. I showed up, we talked, and I started the next day. Three weeks after arriving in Los Angeles, I was answering phones in the Valley for the Armenian mafia for $7.50 an hour.

I didn't know if it was true or not, but it did feel quite shady. The dealership was located north on Laurel Canyon then, east on Victory. There was an old brick building and a small car lot with used cars for sale, although I didn't see any customers, ever. I did file paperwork with the DMV that had customer names, and I filed signed sales contracts, but I never saw customers make these purchases.

I just did the filing that appeared on my desk, took phone calls, made bank deposits, and ran personal errands for Serj and his guys. Otherwise, there was a lot of sitting around with an assortment of Armenian and Russian men. I knew a few Russian phrases from my old friend, Julia, and they were happy when I greeted them in it. They were all very charming and polite, chauvinistic, but respectful. It almost seemed to be a competition among them, who could be nicer and more generous toward me. I went in at 10am and was usually done by 4pm, but they paid me for 40 hours a week.

My first day on the new job, I packed a PB&J sandwich for my lunch and a banana, not sure of the food or break situation, and hoping for a soda machine. When it was near lunchtime, they decided on Chinese delivery and Serj asked if I wanted anything. I said no, pulling out my meager sandwich, somewhat smooshed from the banana in my purse.

Serj started laughing. "What you eat?" he asked.

And I showed him. "Peanut Butter and grape jelly," I said.

He shook his head. Not acceptable. A scowl.

Handing me the menu, he insisted I order something. I ordered sweet n' sour pork, the very cheapest thing, not sure if I was paying for my lunch or not. I never wanted to assume anything, but Serj waved my money away with his thick, hairy fingers.

"You no pay," he said.

The next day, I packed another sandwich, just in case, and Serj told me to put it away. He looked me in the eye and said very seriously, "We buy your lunch now."

I nodded, understanding. Sometimes, I'd have to go get lunch for everyone, but from then on, they always paid for it. And honestly, it was a real treat to be taken care of that way.

They fed me well and paid me cash every week to hang out with them for a few hours a day.

Serj asked if I liked dogs, and I said yes, so he took me to a breeder in Sun Valley and I helped him pick out two Rottweiler puppies to act as guard dogs for the dealership. I went out with his credit card and bought all the doggie equipment they'd need to be comfortable while at the dealership, which was wonderful, since I loved animals and didn't mind hanging out with and training new puppies.

When I came down with a terrible sore throat, I told Serj I needed amoxicillin, and his friend showed up with it the next day. Another of his friends was starting a skin care business, and they gave me a year's supply of wonderful products. The guys made sure my little Toyota had new tires and an adjusted clutch. When Serj saw that I was using an old spiral notebook as my phone book and day planner, he sent me to Staples to buy a proper Day-Runner with all the accessories, his treat. They would let me leave early on Fridays, and they often slipped me an extra $50 to go have fun with over the weekend.

I never felt in danger, and I was never sexually harassed or bothered, but I was aware that something was a little off. I didn't question it, though. I just played dumb and showed up every day, smiling and happy and ready to help. Maybe they just liked having a pretty girl around the office. I was always polite and deferential. I spoke up when asked, but otherwise let them be the gentle chauvinists that they were. I made myself as useful as I could be, running errands, arranging reservations, doing paperwork, helping them shop for their girlfriends, taking care of the dogs. I knew it was a cherry gig, but was I careful with how much they knew about me. A cash arrangement was good for everyone.

9.3

My new friend, Robin, was a gorgeous, glossy brunette with a tight body, big blue eyes, and a sweet, flirty nature. Despite some family money and a small trust fund that covered some of her basic monthly expenses, she was a child of addiction, having survived many turbulent years with an unstable home life. She had escaped to Los Angeles, too, trying to get away from her family. You'd never know any of this about her at first, though. She was open and fun, a big-hearted Leo, an animal lover and a sweet drama queen that loved the rocker boys. She and I had great chemistry and a lot in common.

Robin was two years older than me and had been in LA for a year. She seemed to know all the cool places, and all the cool people. We had a similar sense of humor, and we could talk for hours about our deepest secrets and stories, and laugh our asses off at our own antics. And there was always juicy speculation about all the rockers we'd run into and party with. She took me to get my first manicure, and we roamed through vintage stores down on Melrose. She waitressed at night at the Body Shop to make extra money, and went on auditions during the day, hoping for a break into acting.

I was still living with Mario, and despite his initial paranoia with who came to the house, it seemed that an awful lot of strange people dropped by to visit him. One Sunday morning, while I was sleeping in my underwear on the futon in the studio, I woke to a large, long-haired, bearded man, with leather arm straps like a Viking, standing at the unlocked patio door.

I didn't know how long he'd been standing there, but he apologized for startling me. He handed me a brick-like package wrapped in brown paper, and told me to make sure Mario received the delivery. Then, he handed me a small envelope with five joints inside of it— my reward for making sure the package arrived safely. Mario got the package, and I appreciated the smoke, but I was creeped out by the visitor.

After a couple of weeks of hanging out and partying with Robin, I mentioned that I didn't feel quite safe at Mario's place after the Viking handed me a brick of who-knows-what-probably-coke. On the spot, Robin invited me to live with her for a few months. She'd moved into a bigger apartment for the dogs and was alone in the city, too. She felt a little safer having a roommate and someone to help out with her pets and just to hang out and have fun. She was a kindred spirit, a soul-sister for sure, and I said yes immediately.

Robin lived in a nice apartment building on the corner of Fuller and Hawthorne with Hollywood Blvd. to the north of us, Sunset to the south. Rock n' Roll Ralphs, the grocery store, was just down the street, and a hiking path into the hills just up the street. It was a great location.

The timing of the move was good, too. Although Stacy and I had been fine living in cramped quarters up at Mario's, she had gotten some news from home about a family member, and she was moving back to Jersey as quickly as she could. I had to make a fast decision, and I knew I couldn't afford to live in Mario's studio by myself, nor did I want to. I didn't want to owe him any favors or be at anyone's mercy. I was sleeping with him and paying rent and working a job that he'd arranged. Probably not an ideal situation.

Moving in with Robin solved all of this immediately. For the same $200 that I was paying in the Canyon, I could get a safe, secured building in the heart of Hollywood, with a parking spot in the garage, and my own clicker. She even put me on the lease, so it was official. I was a resident of California. I was so grateful. This arrangement felt much more civilized than sleeping and parking rough in Laurel Canyon, with strangers coming and going at Mario's small compound.

Robin's two dogs were a big Red Doberman named Judas, and a beige Cocker Spaniel named Haji. Judas the Dobie was a big baby and a sweetheart, always looking for a snuggle and a snack, and Haji was a brat—

territorial and snappish, a little son of a bitch who was only occasionally very nice. Robin and I both took turns walking the dogs, and I was happy to help her out with it. We'd walk them up to the end of Fuller, and hike up into the hills, where we could explore the remains of Errol Flynn's old house in Runyan Canyon.

Other times during our dog walks, we'd see rockers, like Taime Down of Faster Pussycat. He looked rough during the day—a gothic, pale mess wearing last night's eyeliner, and pushing a shopping cart like a bag lady in the parking lot of Rock n'Roll Ralphs. Robin would say hello, and he'd stop to chat with us, pet the dogs, and talk about his upcoming shows.

We ran into Stephen Pearcy of RATT, along with some of the guys from Warrant, one night at Denny's on Sunset (also known as Rock n'Roll Denny's.) Stephen slid out of his booth and came over to give Robin a big hug. Stephen looked great—tan and sexy.

Wow. There he is, in person. After years of having his posters on my wall, here he was in his full glory, handsome and intense. Robin had dated his friend, Joel, so they knew each other socially and had partied a few times. Apparently, one drunken night on the way home from the Cathouse, Stephen accidentally broke the windshield in her little black sports car, and then paid to have it fixed. I shook his hand as Robin introduced us. She was always gracious and polite like that.

I was still boggled at meeting him, when, the next day, Stephen called and left a deep and sexy message on Robin's answering machine:

"Robin, Anna-Marie, this is Stephen. It was great to see you last night. I'm having some people over at my place tonight. Why don't you girls come up and join us? Sometime after nine." Click.

I looked at Robin in astonishment. She rewound it and played it again.

"Can you believe that shit!?! Stephen Pearcy actually remembered my name! Oh My God!" I blurted out. People always got my name wrong—calling me Anna, Anne Marie, Anna Mary, Annabelle, Rose Mary, Rose Marie, but no—Stephen Pearcy nailed it. "Anna-Marie."

"I know, right?" She knew him better than I did, and even she was still a little impressed at the invite.

She rewound the tape and we listened to Stephen's sexy voice one more time. Even though she knew people and had been in LA longer, she wasn't too jaded—there was still a special aspect to all of this, being on the scene and mingling with these rocker boys when our friends back home still had posters of them on their walls.

Robin and I didn't even discuss it. We were definitely stopping by later to hang out with Stephen Pearcy.

9.4

Stephen lived close, Robin told me, straight up Fuller, a little north of Franklin. Taime Down lived in the same building, too, she informed me. Hollywood in 1990 was still crawling with long-haired rockers who'd gone gold and platinum, living in regular apartments like everyone else.

Instead of worrying about parking the car, Robin and I just walked the half mile slightly uphill to Stephen's place, a little after dusk. Walking around old Hollywood at night felt quite safe, I thought. Los Angeles was starting to feel comfortable to me.

The apartment building that Stephen rented in was at the end of Fuller, right where it dead-ended into Runyan Canyon. The apartment itself was spare. There were a few cushions set up on the floor near the stereo and a huge music collection. We all plopped down on the floor. Stephen brought us a beer, and then we passed around a joint and relaxed a bit. My thighs were still burning from the walk uphill, although I wouldn't admit it.

My radar was up as I observed my surroundings. I didn't understand how the lead singer of RATT—one of the biggest bands of the 1980s—could be living in this state of affairs. I didn't want to be impolite and ask the question, but almost as soon as I had the thought, he explained that this was just his city crash pad. He had a beach house down in the South Bay. He used this place at his convenience, when necessary.

"See?" He took my hand and led me to his room. "I stay here pretty regularly, but I don't really need furniture because everything I need is in the bedroom," he said.

Oh wow. He is a pro, I thought to myself. *Very slick.*

I played along out of curiosity. *I am standing with Stephen Pearcy in his bedroom. Holy shit,* I thought to myself. *He's hitting on me.* His room was small and cozy, with a comfy looking bed, more music, a closet full of clothes, and an attached bathroom. We chatted and I lounged on the bed. I eyeballed all of the albums and asked if he minded if I looked at his music collection.

"Sure," he said. He rolled a joint on the bathroom counter. I started flipping through all of the vinyl he had.

A moment later, from behind me, he says, "You've got a great ass. Has anyone ever told you that?"

"No, not quite like that! But thanks." My back was turned toward him as I leaned over and inspected his albums, and when I looked back at him, he had squared his hands and was actually "framing" my backside in his visual sightline, sizing me up.

"I'd like to see more," he said, smiling.

Ugh. I *was* slightly flattered, I had to admit. I mean, really, if I'd come to Los Angeles to bag rock stars, he would have been a big trophy.

But that wasn't why I was here. I wasn't sure *why* I was here, but I knew it wasn't for this. I did not want to fuck Stephen Pearcy. I thought of Steve Jones and his weirdness. I wondered how many girls actually took them up on their out-of-left-field propositions.

Probably a lot. Probably a shit-ton.

I had spent years as a music fan, and to some girls, this may have been a dream come true, having a rich and handsome rock star proposition them. It was exciting, for sure. In that moment, though, it felt gross and seedy, almost scripted to a RATT song. It was too easy.

Couldn't we have a meal first like two normal people? Does it have to go straight to this? I thought to myself. Most men I'd ever been attracted to had made me laugh. I'd never gone for the pretty boys so much as the ones who were funny and goofy and sweet and would talk to me like a person. I wanted connection. Mental before physical.

Sex wasn't a big deal to me, and in fact, I'd been fairly promiscuous since my first boyfriend. I loved the attention from men, I enjoyed flirting with men, I liked men, period. I didn't have to be "in love" to have sex with someone, but I did have to like them. I'd slept with older men and guys my age, cute ones and some homely.

I'd done a few guys out of mercy, as a gift to them for whatever sweetness they'd displayed. Sex was a curiosity to me, and I was detached from much of it, moving from lover to lover without shame or remorse. In this regard, I'd always felt more like a man than a woman. I wanted a real connection, and love would be great—I always hoped for it—but the friendship and sex was good enough, almost an intellectual endeavor, something to study and achieve.

Except, right now, all my curiosity was turned off, and the last thing I wanted to do was have sex with Stephen Pearcy.

I'd had pictures of him on my wall and I knew all his music. He sang in one of the biggest bands of the 1980s—I knew most of their albums by heart. *Out of the Cellar* and *Invasion of your Privacy* were in a constant rotation in my life for a few years there. He was 15 years older than me, and very obviously, an experienced player. He'd had thousands of girls—I could only imagine, and I'd heard the groupie stories even in Columbus.

Ultimately, though, I knew I wasn't one of those girls, and I didn't want to be.

The rocker boys were fun and all, but I was a music fan for the music. Even though the music made me feel sexy and rebellious, I didn't want to get vulnerable with a guy who had so many other options. I'd always dated musician types—they didn't have to be famous. Being played by a player wasn't fun for me.

Still, Stephen was very nice to me after I said no, and I almost regretted it.

"I have to get up and go to work," I said. "But I'm honored that you think I have a nice ass. I know you've seen multitudes." I was teasing, and he laughed. I figured that if he was really interested, he had Robin's number. Who knows? He might've had me after a meal and a real human connection.

But that didn't happen.

We joined the others back in the living room, I drank one more beer, and Robin and I walked home around midnight.

Thank God it was downhill.

9.5

I was still answering phones in the Valley for the Armenians when Robin told me that she'd heard that the famous strip club, The 7th Veil, needed a couple of new servers. She was thinking about leaving the Body Shop after some kind of drama had gone down. I thought it would be no big deal to serve cocktails in a strip club, but I had never actually been in a strip club. How hard could it be?

I was curious about the places that Mötley Crüe had mentioned in *Girls Girls Girls*. I wanted to see all the places where Nikki Sixx had been.

I dressed in a button-down shirt tucked into a tight black mini skirt with high heeled boots and sheer black tights. I opened the buttons on my shirt to reveal a peek of my black bra underneath. Robin wore a similar outfit, but she'd had her boobs done and actually had some professional cleavage to show. Although, by Hollywood standards her rack was quite modest—a nicely placed C cup on a size 4 body.

We showed up at the 7th Veil at dusk, and a Middle Eastern looking man sat at the door. We told him we were there to apply for the waitressing jobs. There were no applications to fill out, though. It was more like a try-out. He looked at Robin and nodded in approval, then looked at me, and then down to my chest. He unbuttoned another button of my shirt and placed his hands under my breasts, giving them a lift. My B-cups were barely sufficient. Then he looked me in the eye and shrugged and said, "Eh, you can try. You've got nice face. You need better bra. Go see the bartender." He nodded toward the door.

With that reassuring endorsement, we made our way inside and talked to the bartender, who gave us small black aprons and cork-bottom trays. Then he told us how to work the room. Robin was an old pro, having waitressed before. I turned around, completely petrified, wondering what the fuck I was doing as I approached the first table.

There was a dancer in the middle of a circular stage, elevated, spotlighted in pink, surrounded by men. She was completely nude, with her legs spread open, thrusting her hips into the air and masturbating for the audience with a cellophane-wrapped cigar. The vision hit me like a punch in the head. *Wow, there it is*. When Robin had said it was a nude bar, I didn't really comprehend that it meant nude-nude, spread open pink nude.

Now, I understood.

'Something to drink?" I offered to a guy with an empty glass, almost choking on the words. They didn't serve booze or alcohol of any kind—just soda and juice. State law. I suppose it kept things from getting too crazy. The men couldn't touch the dancers, but they were still within poking distance, right up close. It all felt very dangerous to me. Like they could pounce at any minute.

The men sat around calmly, though, docile and smiling, nodding at the spreads before them. I felt like I was approaching a lion's den, but they barely paid me notice and usually didn't even look at me when ordering. I was distracting them really, having to get them $8 cups of watered-down orange juice to meet their drink minimum.

I had never considered myself a prude, but I was deeply embarrassed by all of it. I felt self-conscious, a bit ashamed, and very vulnerable. I wanted to be cool and comfortable with the display of nudity and sexuality. But I wasn't. It felt personally degrading to me, and I was fully clothed with tights and bad bra.

That, and I had to learn to balance drinks on a tray while wearing heels. It was harder than it looked.

Still, the tips started coming in as I worked the floor that night. The other waitresses gave me and Robin the stink-eye and ignored us. There were no assigned tables, so it was every server for themselves. Some of the servers loved up the guys a bit, trying to get bigger tips. That felt degrading, too. I don't mind flirting a bit, but it didn't feel normal with a woman thrusting herself upon a cigar three feet away.

The bartender was helpful, but not overly friendly. Servers like us came and went, I'm sure. After some time working the floor and sharing the bathroom/dressing room with them, I realized that many of the dancers were wasted and high. They ignored us, too, looking glazed and snorting cocaine between sets and stages.

I wondered about the dancers, where they lived, where they were from, why they did this, how they coped. The mood in their dressing room was sad and low. They were of varying ages, ethnicities, and body types, but the one thing they all had in common was a bare-bald pussy. I wondered how that was possible without razor burn. Later, I asked, and Robin told me they waxed, which was something I'd read about in Cosmo, but had never seen. It was the early stages of hairless-pussy culture, for sure, with Brazilian waxes becoming popular shortly after. I always kept my bush trimmed tight, neat and groomed, but yanking all the hair out by its roots to complete baldness seemed really, extremely painful to me.

Then I saw the clit and labia piercings on the dancers, and my mind boggled. I didn't even know people would do that. I had no idea that people would pierce their genitals and wear jewelry in it. I had never heard of such a thing.

The first night, I made $150 in about two hours. The Middle Eastern man said I could come back the next night, but to wear a better bra and get a manicure. So, I did. I was still hopeful that I could make it work.

The second night wasn't any easier to bear. As I watched a girl spread her ass cheeks and flex her big brown butt-hole for her audience, the thought hit me— I don't need to do this. I don't need to bear witness to another human being's loss of dignity. I couldn't think of any circumstance under which I would find myself in the position of having to pretend-fuck a cigar for a live audience, or show anyone my butthole for money. *Ahh, Los Angeles. Am I built for this?*

I thought that I'd just go get a job at an In-N-Out Burger, instead. That was an indignity I could bear if I had to. I'd worked fast food before. But hustling drinks in a nudie bar? I knew I couldn't do it. I didn't want to do it. Even just as a waitress, with clothes on, I didn't want to do it.

I didn't go back to the 7th Veil after that night, even though I'd made good money. The place had bad energy. The dancers made me sad. I was just as lost as they were. Who was I to judge people? They were making great money at a premier strip club, and this was their choice, I assumed. I'm sure many women there felt free and empowered by it, and I understood that dynamic as well.

But the women I met at the 7th Veil didn't seem free or empowered. There was a cloak of sadness, of damage and hopelessness in that club that I could feel, but couldn't explain. Exploitation, maybe.

All I knew was that I didn't want it on me. Shit like that clings to your soul. I didn't want to bear it. I didn't have to participate. I wasn't that desperate.

It all sounded so glamorous, the strip club life, glorified like it was something special in the Mötley Crüe song. But it wasn't. It wasn't glamorous at all.

9.6

Los Angeles. July, 1990.

Life at Robin's was fun and easy for the next month or so. The apartment building had a pool on the roof, so we went up there during the afternoons to work on our tans. We drove up to Zuma beach in Robin's black sports car with the dogs, and went out almost every night if we could, even if it was just to go have dinner at The Rainbow, or El Compadre, or out for sushi.

I tried sushi for the first time at the place just across from The Rainbow. It was a little rough to start, and Robin had me do three shots of sake when I gagged on my first bites of raw fish. But once I was a little drunk, I made it past the texture of avocado and ditched the boring California Roll—and then I was hooked. That summer, I maxed out my Discover card on sushi and Mexican food and drinks. I was still driving out to the Armenians in the Valley and making easy cash, but I had no clear plan other than living each day as it came. Luck had carried me far, and strangers had been kind to me.

There was freedom in that uncertainty, and the sushi was delicious.

***

Robin's mom lived in Phoenix, and Robin invited me to fly home with her for a quick weekend visit for her birthday. Also, Faster Pussycat and Mötley Crüe were both playing in Phoenix that weekend, and Robin got us on the list for both shows. It was my first time in Arizona, my first time feeling the heat of the desert in full, early August summer, and I loved it. We stepped off the plane onto the hot tarmac at Sky Harbor, and it was a welcome, shocking, blast of the devil. It felt good on my bones. Exotic and luscious. Her sister picked us up in her BMW, my first time in one, and I soaked in my new surroundings. I loved Phoenix.

We stayed with her mom in Chandler, and we partied hard that weekend. We saw Faster Pussycat play at a club in Tempe, and then we ended up at a resort on South Mountain, in a pool at 2am drinking margaritas with some rocker types—guys from Faster, Dokken, and band called IKON. Robin seemed to know everyone, both on the local scene in Phoenix, and in Hollywood. The Mötley show was the next day, but we were both too hung over to drag ourselves out of bed.

We barely made the flight back to LA.

Still, we hadn't celebrated her birthday in LA, so with the help of her friend, Debbie from The Rainbow, and with Robin's blessing, I planned a small birthday party later that week. I wanted to show her my appreciation for her friendship. I planned for 10-20 people, bought beer and chips and vegetable trays, and about 50 people showed up—rockers of all kinds, guys from Faster Pussycat, Badlands, various other players and promoters from bands on the strip, a couple of actors who were on TV shows.

It was quite surreal to me. I was in the kitchen for a few minutes refilling the ice, and I started chatting with Brent Muscat of Faster Pussycat. I mentioned that he might know my friend Kathy, from Ohio, who'd hung out with Greg for a while on their last tour. He did remember her, and told me what a sweetheart she was. I really missed my best friend.

After mixing and mingling and meeting all these strangers with familiar faces in our apartment, I took a minute to catch my breath and sat down on Robin's black leather sofa, right next to a dark haired, slightly chubby older man with a friendly face.

I smiled at him and noticed his beautiful blue eyes, and his smell. He smelled really, really good. He leaned in, and we started chit-chatting and shook hands. He patted my hand as we talked. He told me I was a pretty girl, thanks for having him, and that his name was Ron. I liked Ron immediately. He was funny, kind, and an engaging conversationalist for the few minutes I sat with him. He kissed me on the cheek when he left a little while later, bidding me farewell, as gracious as could be. I wondered if he was gay? It didn't matter. He had good energy and had made me laugh.

Later that night, as Robin and I were cleaning up and chatting about the evening, I told her that I really liked the Ron guy, seemed very nice, and quite a character.

"Oh, yeah, that's Ron Jeremy. He does porn," she said, matter-of-factly.

I hadn't really watched a lot of porn. I wasn't against it, or offended by it. I'd seen snippets here and there, and although the curiosity factor was high, there was a cheesiness factor to 1980s porn. The women seemed to have hot pink blush and stiletto heels, the men all had moustaches and a lot of body hair.

Oh, my gosh. Ron had a moustache, and a lot of body hair. Then, it hit me.

I said to Robin, "You mean, like, he stars in porn movies?" The thought astounded me for a minute. "He's not the producer or director?"

"Well," she said, "he might produce or direct, I dunno, but—he's in the actual movies. He stars in them."

Then I understood why it was so easy to talk to him—he was a stud, a sexy beast. He knew how to fuck women, and he made money doing it on camera.

"They call him *The Hedgehog*," Robin informed me with a straight face, doing air-quotes with her fingers.

I hooted in laughter, snorting, howling at the image in my mind. Robin joined in the giggle fit.

I'd made a real, momentary mental connection with a nice older man, and it turns out, he was a famous porn star.

Los Angeles did not disappoint.

9.7

In mid-August, Robin and I went out one night to a club called New York City. It was attended by a lot of rocker types, and I spotted Glenn Danzig of the Misfits, and Kirk Hammit of Metallica almost immediately, talking in a corner near the bar. Just as I saw them and elbowed

Robin, I spotted another familiar face across the bar, someone I knew. In a flash, we connected eyes and made our way around the bar to each other, arms open for a big girlie hug.

It was Starlet! Beautiful blonde party girl, earth mother hippie chick, and a pal from the Alrosa Villa in Columbus. We'd said our goodbyes at a Shock Tu show the previous spring because she was moving to LA, and now here she was, in the flesh, in front of me at a club on Hollywood Blvd. She was always very sweet to me, but she seemed to have difficult, jealous, mean girl-type friends, so although I liked her a lot, we'd hung out only a few times in Ohio.

She was funny and quirky and a flirt. Bumping into her in LA was a great treat—we made plans to get together the next day. She lived right in Hollywood, not far away. She asked me if I remembered Deron, from the band Nasty Action in Columbus—how could I forget Deron?! Deron was a funny bird, and a talented guitar player. She told me that Deron was taking classes at the Guitar Institute in Hollywood, and that they were now roommates. Their other roommate was a guy named Dale who was also a musician, and from Heath, Ohio.

Over time, I ran into a lot of people from Ohio and eventually realized we were a part of some kind of Great Western Rock n' Roll Migration.

I hung out with Star and the boys a few times, and then she asked me if I wanted to move in with them. I was hesitant, at first, but I talked to Robin about it. Her sister was coming for an extended stay in a couple of weeks, so the timing was good for me to move on, and we remained good friends.

Star and the boys lived in an apartment that was in a rougher part of Hollywood, off Las Palmas and

Fountain, just north of Santa Monica Blvd. Living on Fuller Avenue with Robin had been in a luxury building with a pool and a gym, but this building was definitely not luxury and had neither. There was a Mexican convenience store on the corner that Star told me was pretty scary, and it wasn't the kind of neighborhood for moonlit Hollywood walks. But at least we lived with two men, and I still got a clicker and a secure spot in the garage. Most of the time the garage door worked. It was safe enough.

Star and I shared one bedroom and a bathroom, the boys shared the other bed and bath. My rent was $200 per month to sleep on the floor in Star's room. A friend of Star's gave me an old futon, and I spent $60 to get a new pad for it. I had a small, cardboard dresser, two feet of closet space, a used futon, a Walkman with a small cache of cassettes, and an old blue Toyota Corolla with a tricky clutch.

I had no plan and a few hundred in the bank. A few hundred dollars between me and homelessness.

Still, I felt really lucky.

9.8

Deron and Dale were my first boy roommates, and they were great. Deron had played guitar on the scene for years in Columbus, so I knew him socially and from going to see his band, Nasty Action, usually at the Alrosa Villa. He was 6'4", with a beak of a nose and corkscrew curls down to the middle of his back. Deron was one of those naturally funny people, with a Muppet vibe—almost like Big Bird meets Jeff Spicoli.

Dale, my other roommate, was smaller, quieter, cuter, and we hit it off like long lost siblings. As I settled into life on Las Palmas, Dale and I did everything together—grocery shopping, dodging the drunk bums at the coin laundry, splurging on El Compadre every so often. We went to shows and clubs, for hikes around touristy spots, and down to the Santa Monica Pier and the beach. We often did 2am Del Taco runs in old Hollywood, and one time, he even helped me color my hair. He was a big sweetie, and a good friend to me.

***

One Saturday morning, we all packed up Dale's beige minivan and set out from Hollywood at 8am. We were headed to a tiny secluded beach down near Laguna that they had all been to before. We were planning on staying for the day, and we brought sandwiches, Doritos, and apples for a beach lunch.

It was sunny and close to 90 even on the coast that day, and it felt wonderful. The sky was bright, no haze at all, and the ocean sparkled. I had on a black bikini, with my hair in a long French braid down my back. I wore an old pair of cutoff jean shorts and a loose white t-shirt over my suit. We hiked in our flip flops down a steep, rocky path, and the boys offered their hands to help us keep our balance.

We arrived to a small beautiful cove, covered with abundant sand. We took a few minutes to set up our blankets and stake out a space. The beach had a few people, but it wasn't crowded at all. I watched, smiling, as Deron and Dale ran toward the water. Whooping and hollering like little kids, they threw themselves onto the boogie boards and caught the first waves. After a minute in the intense heat, Star and I waded in, but stayed nearer to the shore. The water was chilly on my hot skin, but it felt good to wash the road dust off.

Being on the beach reminded me of visiting Lake Erie as a child, with its relaxing warm water, gentle waves and endless sandbars. But only for a minute. The Pacific was dangerous in a way that Lake Erie had never felt to me, and it was cold. Colder than I expected. I waded in further and the cold took my breath away. After a few minutes, I got used to it as Star and I bobbed around waist deep, where I felt fairly safe and not too freaked out by the kelp that occasionally bumped into my leg.

The boys met us in the water and we floated around and chatted for a minute. Deron offered, and I refused, and then he talked me into trying the boogie board. I was an OK swimmer, but I'd never swam in the ocean before. Lake Erie didn't have waves and swells like this. At all.

"I'll be out there with you to help you get going. You won't get hurt, girlie," he said, his long curls dripping down past his broad shoulders and off his big beak of a nose. He was completely unselfconscious, funny and serious at the same time, and his tone made me want to try.

"All right," I said. I was a little scared, but it looked like so much fun.

And oh boy, it WAS so much fun. We waded out to the deeper water, where it was almost over my head, but only chest high on Deron. I clung loosely to his arms and shoulders as we got ourselves ready—he explained that I needed to heave myself up onto the board, and we'd wait for a wave. At the exact right moment, he would push me toward the shore. The swell came and I braced myself as he launched me onto those beautiful waves, shouting *ride, girlie, ride!*

I loved it. It all worked perfectly. He gave me four awesome pushes onto smooth waves, and I laughed and hooted the whole way in, feeling a wildness in my belly that reminded me of sledding down a steep hill after a good snowstorm.

Eventually, I started getting tired, so he asked, "One more ride, girl?" Deron was a good sport.

"Sure, one more and I'm pooped!" As I made my way back toward him in the deep water, he reached out for me and we grasped fingers as he pulled me toward him.

Just then, I saw an unusually huge wave coming up right behind him, and I said, "WAVE!"

Deron ducked safely under the water. For some reason, though, I let go of his hand and jumped high, trying to clear the wave.

Instantly, I realized my mistake.

The wave met me square in the body just as it broke, and it slammed me under, under, under. It felt like forever. The wave rolled me out of control through the water. My arms and legs flailed until I was dizzy and out of breath. I felt myself being scraped by the sand on the ocean floor as I tumbled like a rag in a clothes dryer. I didn't know which way was up until the wave spat me out near the shore, on my hands and knees, dripping, coughing, bleeding, with my bikini top askew and my breasts hanging out of it. As I peered up, I could see that I was only a few feet from some nasty looking rocks sticking out of the sand. Even through the daze, I was grateful I didn't land on them.

Deron rushed out of the water to help me, shielding me from the people on the shore with his body in a big, hovering hug, close up to me, as I repositioned my top and tried to keep my balance. He grinned widely when he saw my boobs, and then reached around and tied the back up for me. He held my hand as I wobbled up to the blankets.

"Girlie, why'd you go high? You gotta duck the waves and go under!" Deron said.

I didn't know why. I guess I hadn't known, and nobody had warned me. Lake Erie didn't have waves like that.

I was dizzy, and I had water in my ears. I collapsed face down on a towel on the hard sand and fell asleep for an hour, which is the only thing I felt capable of doing. That ocean tumble exhausted me past a point I'd ever felt before. I had to lay down and sleep. I slept a deep sleep while the sun baked me stiff and my arms went numb.

When I woke up an hour later, Star told me that I was seriously scraped up. I could hardly move. I had abrasions on my shoulder and on my lower back hip and butt cheek—and a deep 10" scrape down the bones of my spine, like a zipper, along with a raw knee and elbow. It's like road rash, but from the ocean. An ocean bite.

I felt it all start to sting when I sat up and the salt water trapped in my thick braid dripped into the wounds on my spine. To top it off, I'd gotten sunburned badly. Star helped me rub lotion onto my exposed parts, but it was too late. I was scraped up and bloody and salty, and fried up like a chicken-plate dinner from Sister's Chicken & Biscuits.

We were all sunburned, though, by the end of the day. As we drove the 90 minutes back to Hollywood through the Southern California sunset dusk and traffic, Dale's van started belching black smoke. Star and I looked at each other—we were about to be stranded somewhere, we thought. Dale shrugged it off and laughed. The van was a piece of shit, he said, but it always kept running.

And, somehow, it did.

We had eaten our picnic lunch earlier, but of course, by later in the day, we were all ravenously starved. We went through a Del Taco drive-thru and made our way back to the sketchy apartment in our rough, rude mini-van, with bags of cheap Mexican food. We ate our feast on the floor, picnic style again, still in our sandy suits with soggy towels and t-shirts. My white t-shirt was streaked with watery bloodstains.

I dabbed Vaseline onto my scrapes, and for many weeks after, I walked around sore and scabbed up. If I moved my body the wrong way, the scabs would break open and ooze a little blood onto my clothes.

My sunburn turned into a deep, beautiful tan, except for where the scabs were. The scabs healed up and would eventually flake off, but I was left with a pink scar midway down my spine that would take almost twenty years to fade away.

Within a week of taking that wave, Star told me there was a receptionist position opening up where she worked, so she asked me to come in and talk to her boss. It was incredibly generous of her to offer me the chance, and I jumped on it.

I interviewed at Errol Gerson and Company in late August 1990, my scabs from the ocean still fresh and raw.

It was the beginning of another wild ride.

10.0

[City Boy Blues]

September 12, 1990.

He popped his head around the corner, and I looked up from the desk of my small cubicle. My heart skipped a beat. "Hi, Dave!" I squeaked.

I had only been on the job a couple of weeks and it was my first time seeing him in person, but I knew exactly who he was. His lanky frame approached and I introduced myself when he asked my name. Then he said, "Hey, may I use your phone to make a call?"

"Sure, go right ahead," I said. I came out from behind my little cubby and moved to the side. Dave Mustaine brushed past me and sat down in my warm chair, picked up the phone, and smiled.

"Thanks," he said, "I'll just be a minute."

He was taller and more handsome than I had expected. I'd only ever seen him in videos, and in the movie documentary, *The Decline of Western Civilization, part II – The Metal Years*, that had come out two years prior. That movie was one of the reasons I was in Los Angeles. It had showed the gritty, seedy side of the music industry in LA, the excitement of the scene, the reality of trying to make it in the music business.

It was a documentary about my people. Megadeth had been featured in the movie, and actually getting to listen to these guys talk had been amazing. I had watched

Dave Ellefson speak with such certainty and focus, yet he seemed so vulnerable. I was already a Megadeth fan, and the movie had cemented it, as it showed them in the recording studio playing "In My Darkest Hour." It was a masterpiece of a song that had carried me through some tough times.

I already knew from the interviews I'd read over the years that Dave Mustaine was a smart guy. He seemed like a no-bullshit dude, not one to suffer fools. My boss, Errol, told me that he was "high maintenance," but it was no surprise. He had that reputation. Seeing him in person made me terribly nervous, but I knew I had to keep it cool and professional. He wasn't the first rocker I'd ever met, but I kind of wanted to freak out. *Dave Mustaine*!!

I pretended to go to the mailroom with a purpose, but I really just had nowhere else to go. I could sit in the front lobby with the new receptionist from the temp agency, or I could go putter around the mailroom, which was a long, narrow galley full of cabinets and office supplies, along with a small sink, coffee pot, microwave, and mini-fridge. I started a fresh pot of coffee, my hands shaking a bit as I poured the water. We had a phone extension back there near the postage meter, and I could see that Mustaine was still on the call, so I called Errol.

"Mustaine is here and is making a call on my phone," I half-whispered to him. Errol told me not to worry. He sounded relaxed, reassuring with his clipped accent. With no quick rescue from my boss, I knew I had to keep my cool and do my best to keep Dave there for the meeting.

Errol ran a financial management company, and I'd only been working for him a couple of weeks. He was South African, Jewish, educated at USC, and was just a bit older than my mom. He was tall and broad shouldered, handsome, with gentle brown eyes and a cropped, salted beard. Our office was located at the west end of the Sunset Strip, on the fourth floor of the 9229 building, two blocks west of The Rainbow.

When I found out that Mötley Crüe's management, Doug Thaler and Top Rock, was located in the same building, I just about fell over. Of all the places to start working my first real job in LA, I end up in this building, with Mötley Crüe potentially roaming around. Maybe I'd get to meet Nikki Sixx in person! Holy cow.

I was introduced to Julie Foley, who worked for Doug Thaler, and who's name I recognized immediately from old Mötley Crüe album credits. Turns out, she was dating David Ellefson, of Megadeth. I'd only meet David a few times in passing. He was polite and focused, and they seemed like a great couple, very down to earth.

We had many other clients other than Megadeth, of course. Peter Frampton, a few guys associated with the KISS organization, record company presidents, actors, writers and producers, photographers. But Megadeth was Errol's biggest client, to date. He handled all the money and taxes and touring support of the corporate entity known as Megadeth, as well as the personal finances of some of the band members, but it was his first time doing that for a band about to break so big.

During our first meeting and job interview, I had used my best manners and acted as charming as possible. Errol had asked me if I knew who Megadeth was. I laughed, and said, *Yes! Of course I know who they are.* I named each of their albums. I knew their history. I mentioned the movie. I knew they were fresh out of rehab, and I thought that Marty Friedman was an awesome addition to the band.

I knew all the current bands on the metal scene. I had prowled the Sunset Strip for the last few months, going out to local clubs to get a general feel for who was who, at least as a fan. Errol loved it.

We clicked right away. He was an ideas guy, and I guess I answered his questions smartly enough. My education and work history up to this point were nothing remarkable: I'd been a mediocre student in public schools, and almost failed out of high school. I had only worked a fast food job, a warehouse job, telephone sales, and retail, with a few temporary office jobs sprinkled in. I was a slow typist at best. I told him I could type 40wpm, but it was probably half that. For whatever reason, he gave me a shot as the new receptionist.

Within a week or so, I became Errol's assistant. We met for 20 minutes every morning over coffee to discuss his appointments and schedule, and what he needed done for the day. He was patient and gracious as he taught me his routines. He mentioned that he wanted to expand with new account managers, and perhaps he could train me and eventually feed me clients to manage. Considering my love of music, and Megadeth, and the fact that I was now in possession of a maxed-out Discover card with a bank balance of under $200—I was thrilled to find an opportunity like this in Los Angeles.

So, I'd moved to the cube with a window looking out onto Beverly Hills, right beside Errol's door. This was where Dave Mustaine now sat. In my chair. On my phone.

Holy shit.

A few minutes later, I took a deep breath and wandered past my cube to check on him. He was still talking, relaxed, with his feet up on my desk. He looked up at me and waved me over, took his feet down, and motioned for me to sit in the extra chair I had up against the wall.

And so, I took a seat in the guest chair of my own cube as he finished up the phone call. I squirmed and tried to sit up straight. My cuticles were a mess. My cheap, old Payless boots were scuffed. I wished desperately that I had worn more eyeliner.

Trying to wrap up the call, he motioned with his hands and rolled his eyes a bit, then smiled at me as he said goodbyes into the phone. He hung up and apologized for his feet on the desk.

"No problem," I said. "I do it all the time."

"Really?" he said, squinting.

"No." I shook my head, and we both chuckled. I mentioned that Errol was running a few minutes behind. I offered him some coffee or a snack. He declined.

And then, we started to chit-chat, settling into an easy 15 minutes of conversation.

It felt like a dream.

"Are you going to the show tomorrow night up in Ventura?" He asked. "It's my birthday, should be a good show."

September 13, 1990. This would be the second show of the giant tour that was about to unfold for Megadeth's new album, *Rust in Peace*. He would be turning 29 years old.

We are both Virgos, I thought. *No wonder he's so easy to talk to.*

"Yes! I'm going to the show. Errol had invited me to drive up with him." I told him.

Trying to keep the conversation going, I mentioned that the day after, Friday the 14th, was my birthday. He asked how old I was, and I told him I'd be turning 19. We did the math real quick, and we figured out we were born a decade and a day apart.

"Wow," he said, "you're young."

I could tell that he was sizing me up. He was very direct, and he looked at me with a squinty-eyed interest. "What are you doing for your birthday?" he asked.

I told him I had tickets to go see KISS down in Long Beach. That I'd been a fan since I was a kid and this was my first time seeing them.

He was very intense, perceptive, and intimidating, and yet, I was comfortable talking to him, person to person. He asked me what other kinds of music I liked, and I told him—hard rock and metal. I mentioned that I had moved to LA from Ohio. He said his girlfriend's family was from Ohio, the Cincinnati area. We talked about the old Newport Music Hall in Columbus, and that I'd missed their last show there because of some trouble at home.

He told me he thought the Newport was a cool venue to play. He asked how long I'd been in Los Angeles, and I told him for 3 months, since early June.

We were having a real conversation and he was listening to me, engaged, so I gave him the basics. Single mom. Absent dad. Latchkey kid. I told him I was in high school, getting kicked out of my house when Megadeth's last album came out, and his music had helped me during that time, one of the hardest times of my life. He said he appreciated hearing that, and that music always made him feel better, too.

I held back from going any further. He was there for a meeting regarding his money and tour, not a sob story from his business manager's assistant. The new album was a monster, and I told him so. He said that he was proud of it, and he hoped it would sell well.

He told me he understood about going through hard times. We kept talking, and he told me more about himself.

So many metalheads seemed to have a similar story. An unstable home, moving around a lot, an alcoholic or absent dad and a working mom, or some other version of parental instability or heartbreak. He had a fierce survival instinct and street smarts. I recognized it. He told me a bit about how he grew up, and that he'd had some rough times after he got kicked out of his last band, Metallica.

I think he said this to test me, but I already knew the history of him being fired from Metallica, and the ongoing animosity. I simply said, *yeah, I heard about that*. During our conversation, I'd made it a point NOT to say the word Metallica—and it was hard not to.

Kathy and I had seen Metallica on their last tour, for the *And Justice For All* album. They were an amazing band, and had blown me away with their fire and fury and sheer power. His humiliating dismissal from Metallica was the stuff of metal legend.

He was a man on a mission now, for sure, strong and confident, out to prove himself, but maybe still a little raw and fragile at the corners. There was a lot at stake with this album, and a lot of responsibility on his shoulders. Both he and his partner, David Ellefson, had just gotten out of rehab for a heroin addiction, had found two new bandmates, and had written the album of a lifetime to try and salvage what was left of Megadeth.

After hearing the record they'd just recorded, there was no doubt that this was a monumental, genre-defining album. Truly an instant classic. With this album,

Mustaine had proved his point—he was a talented guy in an amazing band. *Rust in Peace* would drop in stores in a few weeks. Thrash metal was going mainstream, and Megadeth were at the top of their game, setting the bar high, riding the crest of the wave, tight and fierce and ready.

And there I was, chit-chatting with Dave Mustaine, a few moments of easy grace with him, just before *Rust in Peace* exploded. It was an amazing album, Megadeth in their finest, most precise form. An album I became obsessed with, by a band I already loved.

At this point, though, no one knew how big *Rust in Peace* would be, there were only high hopes. It would go on to earn a Grammy nomination and garner some real mainstream crossover. They performed on the *Arsenio Hall* show in February of 1991. My mom called me the next day and told me they were "really good!"

Errol's business was growing and he was hopeful for networking opportunities and more business from musicians. Mustaine was in a good place, hopeful for a good tour and sales after yet another lineup change in the band. He mentioned again that he was in a relationship, with a nice girl named Pamela, whom he'd go on to marry six months later.

I was hopeful for my future, too. I was in Los Angeles, I had this new job that held promises for a better life, and my boss, Errol, was very good to me—kind, concerned, and fatherly, even. Life was good, so good.

I realized that things were on the upswing for the both of us, and I said, "It's been a lucky year so far, and I can't believe all that's happened."

He nodded and squinted and paused before saying, "Yes, but we also make our own luck, you know? You have to take action."

I smiled and held his gaze for a moment. Oh, this man was wise. He was so right. It was true. I'd had no big advantages in life, and neither had he. Kids of poverty and divorce. Nothing had been given to us, and we expected nothing. I was making my own luck, just as he was making his. Our paths were different but the concept was the same. Creating something out of nothing. I was trying to build a life—one that I didn't have clear vision of quite yet—but I was sure that life, my dream life, was here in Los Angeles.

Anything was possible.

"You're right, but sometimes, it feels like there are other forces at work, too," I said to him.

He nodded his head; he understood.

"I mean, I'm sitting here with you! This is proof that magic exists!" I joked to him.

Errol came rushing out of his office just as Dave and I paused.

Dave got up out of my chair and said flattering things about me to Errol; Errol shot me a look of gratitude and thumbs up. He winked and nodded, and I brought him a cup of fresh coffee with four lumps, just as he liked it, and bottle of water for Dave. They went into Errol's office and emerged 45 minutes later, all smiles.

Dave waved and said *Goodbye, see you tomorrow night*, and we wished each other happy birthdays.

I sat back down in my chair, buzzing from the magic of meeting Dave Mustaine. Then I stood up, and stepped into the sunshine blazing through the south-facing window, warm on my skin.

It was a crisp and clear September day, with no haze or smog. I could see the ocean, dark but sparkling like a disco ball between buildings, just a few miles away. Toward the east and looking down the Sunset Strip, I could see the big mountains beyond, shimmering somewhere along a distant highway. It was magnificent.

Somehow, I was here. I was in the middle of it and Los Angeles was at my feet, smiling at me.

11.0

[Louder Than Hell]

September 13, 1990. Los Angeles.

The Megadeth show was in Ventura, so Errol picked me up at my Hollywood apartment in his giant black Mercedes for the long drive up the 101.

It wasn't a date, although for a minute I let myself imagine it as I settled into the plush leather of Errol's car. But it was strictly business, all night, which was great. Errol was fun, a good guy to me, and a decent boss.

We talked all the way up the 101, and then we stopped to have a steak dinner before heading to the Ventura Theater. It was Errol's first-time seeing Megadeth, too. They'd been on a break from touring while going through rehab and recording. They'd just signed on with Errol while they were producing *Rust in Peace*.

We had great seats in the balcony, and I was on my feet as soon as they opened the show. I think Errol was stunned at what he was seeing, the raw power of it, their precision. His eyes were wide as he looked at me from time to time and just said "Wow!" I nodded in agreement.

I was blown away, too. I'd seen Metallica on their last tour for *And Justice For All*, at the Ohio Center with Kathy, so I had an idea of what a "thrash" show was like—but Megadeth surpassed all my expectations. I soaked it up, feeling the drums on my body making my chest thump. Megadeth circa 1990 was really powerful stuff.

We watched Dave Mustaine, David Ellefson, Nick Menza and Marty Friedman just completely shred it. There seemed to be a technical snafu during the encore, which soured the mood a bit, but otherwise it was an awesome show.

Errol and I wandered backstage afterward and said our hellos. We had a piece of Dave's birthday cake, met Nick Menza's mom, and said hello to Julie Foley, Dave Ellefson's girlfriend. We gave hugs and kisses to Ron Laffitte, Megadeth's manager, and his awesome assistant, Sondra.

I had come a long way in three short months. I had left Ohio just 12 weeks prior, landed in the middle of Hollywood not knowing a soul, met and lived with Mario, Jr., worked for the Armenian mafia, and now I found myself backstage at a Megadeth show with a VIP pass.

It all happened so fast, it seemed. I didn't even think about what was next, what I wanted to do. I didn't care about going to cosmetology school, or studying audio engineering. Who needed a plan when fate was providing all this?

We drove back to Los Angeles, and Errol was buzzing. He couldn't stop talking about Megadeth. This album was going to be huge, he predicted. It was great for his business.

I was buzzing, too. The past few days with meeting Dave and seeing Megadeth for the first time—I couldn't believe how it had all aligned.

11.1

Amazingly enough, a couple of weeks prior, when I'd first started with Errol, Dan the roadie from the Poughkeepsie trip—the nice guy who helped me out when JJ got drunk—called in.

Of course, I didn't know it was Dan at first. A man called in asking for Gary, one of our account reps. Gary wasn't available, so I asked if he'd like me to leave a message.

He said, sure, it's Dan so and so. He told me he was calling from a hotel, and left the hotel and room number. I knew Gary had been working with a contractor on the KISS tour.

I recognized Dan's name and voice and put it together immediately. Just as we were about to hang up, I said to him, "Hey, I know this is weird, but this is Anna-Marie. We met in February in Fishkill, at Ace's studio. I'm from Columbus? I borrowed your hotel room. Do you remember me?"

"Holy shit, girl! What are you doing in Los Angeles?!" He hooted at me over the phone. He was in total shock.

"I moved here in June! I'm working for Errol. Where are you?"

"I'm in Montana," he said. "I'm out here with KISS. I'm so glad you said something! What a coincidence. How are you? Hey, we'll be there in a couple of weeks, down in Long Beach, do you want to come to the show?"

"Awesome," I said, "that would be great!"

It was a huge bonus that it happened to be on my 19th birthday. Slaughter and Winger were opening, which I thought was interesting. It might be kind of fun to run into those guys.

There couldn't have been a better way to spend my birthday. I invited Star, and of course, she was on board to go with me.

11.2

September 14, 1990. Long Beach.

I still had to go to work that day, even after being out late with Errol at the Megadeth show, and even with it being my birthday, but Errol did let us leave a bit early so we could make traffic for the KISS show. After running home to change, Star and I stopped for an early dinner at El Compadre, and then we drove down to Long Beach. I don't remember much about the setlist or the show itself, other than that there was a giant sphinx involved, and some pyro, of course. It was a KISS concert, exactly what I expected when I had imagined seeing them as a kid.

After the show, we were hanging out in the VIP section backstage, drinking free drinks and looking for my friend Dan. A small, sweet guy with a giant bush for hair came over to us and talked to us for a minute. He asked us if we were having a good time. Star and I giggled when we realized it was Eric Carr, the drummer for KISS, as he walked away. He'd been so nice and sincere, and just slightly too awkward for a rock star.

Gene Simmons had come out, and was stalking around saying hello to a few people. He was big and tall and handsome and ferocious looking, his hair longer than I ever remembered it. He worked quickly, shaking my hand, saying hello, and moving on. There was no chit-chat, it was all business. He was gracious, but didn't loiter.

STILL! *If only my mom could see this*, I thought. I touched Gene Simmons!

What a birthday gift.

Gene Simmons, in my mind, had always been my surrogate father. He was the reason I loved music, the reason I loved heavy metal. The God of Thunder. And here I was, meeting HIM in the flesh, on my 19th birthday.

I wanted to tell him all of it, how I'd loved him as a child, how I thought he was my father, how much I loved his music. But I didn't. I was just grateful for the show and the tickets and passes.

A few minutes after shaking his hand, I turned around, and in my face, with wide blue eyes and a friendly smile, was Pete Reveen, the guitar player for Salty Dog, whom I'd last seen on a hotel bed in Cleveland after seeing their show with my friend Anne. We recognized each other at the same time.

He pointed at me, I opened my arms for a hug, and he exclaimed: *CLEVELAND! WHAT ARE YOU DOING HERE???* We fell into a big warm hug and laughed at the chance meeting. He was so cute. It was great to see him there. Mike Hannon, the bass player in Salty Dog, was from Ohio, a local boy who made it big—getting a record contract with Geffen.

The last time Pete and I saw each other, we'd passed a joint and hung out for a bit while his singer was nodding off and throwing up from drugs in a hotel room after their show. We talked about the whole big mess of life. Two complete strangers, yet he felt like an old friend.

Sometimes people just click, and Pete was a really nice guy.

We exchanged numbers and promised to keep in touch. I told him I was working for a business manager, the guy who handled Megadeth, and to let me know if he knew anyone who might need an accountant.

I couldn't wait to tell Errol that I was hustling for business. Pete was a cutie, and still signed to Geffen Records, so who knew. If any label was going to break a hard-rock blues band with a singer similar to Axl Rose, it would be Geffen Records. Salty Dog had put out one good record and were a great live band. Maybe he'd need financial services at some point in the future.

No one really realized at this point that Seattle Grunge was in the pipeline and barreling toward us.

Moments later, I found Dan the roadie and we hugged and he wished me a happy birthday. I thanked him from the bottom of my heart. This sweet man I'd met by chance in Fishkill, New York, who'd been so chivalrous, offering me his hotel room and genuine concern when I'd been almost stranded on that road trip from hell with JJ.

And now these birthday tickets and backstage passes and meeting Gene Simmons and seeing Pete. I didn't know how to thank him.

He had to get back to work, so he hustled through quickly and promised to keep in touch.

Just as Star and I decided to head out for home after the show and our backstage social hour, I spotted Paul Taylor, from Winger, but I decided not to bother. Even seeing him from afar, I thought…nah.

My 19th birthday was perfect as it was, already.

12.0

[TNT (Terror In Tinseltown)]

October, 1990, Los Angeles.

I felt so lucky going to my first "real" job in Los Angeles, where I paid taxes and got real paychecks. I commuted west through the city, usually down Fountain, then up to Sunset onto the Strip, and it seemed very glamorous to pull into the 9229 building every day, even if I was in my crappy old Toyota. Errol graciously paid for my spot in the parking garage.

Star introduced me to Frank, a new assistant working for Top Rock. Frank was cute, with long curly hair just past his jaw, only a couple of years older than me. He could be a bit bitchy in a hilarious way, yet he was open and friendly, and we got along great. His dad, David Chackler, was an old music-biz pro, having worked with artists such as Fleetwood Mac, and 2LiveCrew, one of the bands that had been targeted by the PMRC back in the day. His dad also happened to rent a small office in Errol's suite, so Frank would pop in to say hi and hang out.

Frank and I started going to lunch, then going to shows, and just having fun in general. He was a good guy with a lot of connections, and he seemed to know everyone, including some of the Guns N' Roses guys, and many others on the scene.

Frank had worked at Columbia records just prior to working for Top Rock. One afternoon, he played me a demo tape of his favorite new band that had an album coming out soon: Alice in Chains, from Seattle.

Oh my God. I was instantly, totally obsessed.

I loved Seattle music. Hendrix, Heart, Queensrÿche, I'd started listening to Soundgarden in Ohio, and now there was Alice in Chains? Awesome. Soon after, Frank passed me a shiny promo copy of their first album, *Facelift*. I was so in love with that album—listening to it almost every night to fall asleep to. I'd lay there on my futon with my Walkman, in a shared bedroom in the middle of Hollywood, after driving to my glamourous job on the Sunset Strip, not sure what was next, but feeling positive that it would be good, as everything up to this point had been.

***

One night, in early October, Frank picked me up in his Celica and told me that we needed to pop in on his friend's birthday party for a few minutes. We drove to El Compadre. As we walked in the front entrance, I spied Tommy Lee at a table, spotlighted like a unicorn in the dim, golden pink interior lighting. My heart flip-flopped at seeing him.

That's Tommy fucking Lee!

Suddenly, Tommy got up from the table and was hugging Frank, and shaking my hand, welcoming me to the table. Stunned and nervous, I realized—it was *Tommy's* birthday, and this was *his* birthday dinner with friends that we were popping in on.

Holy Shit.

Frank and I ordered some food, but I wasn't sure who was buying, so I ordered small. I watched Tommy Lee and laughed along and tried not to make a fool of myself in front of strangers, especially him. When my plate arrived holding a single chicken enchilada, for the first time in my life, I could hardly eat. Tommy was in a sober phase at this point, and had to explain to the pushy waitress that he only wanted brewed iced tea, not Long Island iced tea, because he had a drinking problem and was in treatment and *please don't ask me again if I want alcohol* in the nicest sort of way.

I was eating dinner with Tommy Lee. My mind struggled to wrap around the thought, even as the evening went on. To top it off, we were invited to attend his real birthday party—the big, official one, happening at a pool hall down on Santa Monica Boulevard few nights later, where I'd meet Heather Locklear. I felt so incredibly lucky, like it was a dream.

Part of me couldn't believe that Kathy wasn't here with me for these moments. Although we had fantasized for years and I'd written short stories about adventures like this, it was better than anything I could've ever dreamed up.

12.1

Not long after Tommy's birthday, Frank's car had to go in the shop, so on a Friday morning, I picked him up at his apartment on Santa Monica Blvd. and drove him to and from work that day as a favor. As I dropped him off at home, we made plans to go out to dinner and a movie later on, since he was stuck at home otherwise. I went home for a few hours, to shower and change. We had fun together, so I didn't mind a night on the town with him at all, or chauffeuring us around. When I picked him up a bit later, he told me that we had to drive out to the Valley first, to drop something off to Tommy.

"Holy Shit, man. *Holy shit.*" Frank just smiled at me.

"What? Do you mind? It's just a master tape of some of their new songs…"

I knew he was teasing me.

And so, we drove out to Woodland Hills, up into a fancy, gated community, and rang the buzzer. Tommy's voice crackled on the speaker.

"Duuude," said Tommy Lee.

"Duuuuddde! It's Frank." He was leaning over me to talk into the speaker. It made me giggle, hearing them be silly.

The gate opened. Frank navigated through the neighborhood to a big, traditional looking house with four garage bays. I parked on the street in front of the house, not wanting to leak oil on the nice driveway. Tommy came bounding down to greet us, shaking my hand again and leading us in. I walked into the house, which had a giant foyer and a grand, curved-banister staircase on the left.

The wall up the stairs was lined with framed gold and platinum Mötley Crüe albums.

I'm going to need to take a look at those, I thought to myself. Otherwise, Tommy's house was like something my mother would decorate. Window treatments, marble columns, fluffy pillows, tassels, flower arrangements. Kind of Dynasty-ish, which I found ironic. There wasn't much of a "heavy metal" feel to his house, at all.

There were a few small dogs that followed us around, which was amusing as Tommy hustled them along. Tommy asked if he could get us anything. I was thirsty, and I had to pee. Tommy poured me a glass of water in the kitchen, and showed me the half-bathroom, nearby. The dogs waited for me outside the door, and I gave them all scratches and belly rubs when I was done. Tommy apologized for them being annoying, but I told him it didn't bother me at all.

Frank was carrying the master tape in a case, so Tommy led us up to the small recording studio tucked into his bedroom, which was located by walking through his bathroom and closet. *I'm in Tommy Lee and Heather Locklear's closet*, I thought. *Wow*. It was all pretty normal. Fancy, but normal. The studio felt like a little treehouse above the garage.

We watched Tommy struggle with the reel-to-reel machine, trying to load the tape correctly. He couldn't get it to work. He laughed at himself and threw a few *fucks*, and finally got it right. He was naturally funny and a sincere person. I liked his energy. And oh my goodness, he was more handsome in person than I ever thought he'd be.

He played us a segment of drum and bass tracks for a new Mötley song.

Three years ago, I was in the crowd at Buckeye Lake, in the middle of a muddy cornfield, watching Mötley Crüe. *Kathy is not going to believe this*, I thought.

I myself could hardly believe it.

We hung out with Tommy and listened and chatted for 45 minutes or so. As we wrapped up in the studio, I asked if he minded if I looked at the collection of gold and platinum albums on the way down the stairs. He said it was no problem, and he and Frank paused in the lofted hallway so I could take a few minutes. I told him I'd seen him at Buckeye Lake, in Ohio, on the *Girls Girls Girls* tour. He remembered the gig.

"It rained and there was a lot of mud," he said. I laughed and nodded.

"Yep, that was the show!" I was happy he remembered it.

He took us out by way of the garage, and lit a cigarette. Frank wanted to check out the new Ferrari. Tommy glanced out at my old, homely Toyota, lurking yonder on the street near his mailbox

"I parked on the street so it wouldn't leak oil on your driveway." I said to him.

He took the lit cigarette out of his mouth, looked me straight in the eye, and flicked it onto the carpeted floor of his fancy garage.

"Pfftt, no big deal." he said with a smirk. He smashed the cigarette with his foot and grinned. There were other burns and butts on the carpet, too. He didn't say it verbally, but I knew what he meant: *Your shitty little car doesn't bother me. Nothing too fancy, here.*

Heather was filming a new TV series and was driving the big Mercedes sedan that night, he told us. In addition to the black Ferrari, there was a Porsche parked there, along with a motorcycle and a couple of 4x4 ATV's. "I bought one of these for Mick, too, but he won't ever get on it," he said. I about died at the thought of Mick Mars on an ATV.

We waved and said our goodbyes to Tommy as we got into the Toyota. I was grateful and a little stunned. He had been so gracious and funny, even knowing I was a fan who'd braved mud, injury, and disease to see his band.

We left Tommy's house and went to Frank's favorite pizza place, where we talked and talked. Then, we caught a late movie at Universal Center on our way back to Hollywood. I was buzzing from the good energy of the evening, of meeting Tommy and hanging with Frank and enjoying the city.

For a few hours, it was pure magic. About a year later, I'd hear the song Tommy played to us, in full. I recognized it immediately when Frank played it for me—*Primal Scream*.

Honestly, probably my favorite Mötley Crüe song of all time.

12.2

The buzz around Alice in Chains was growing. When they did a show at the Hollywood Palace, opening for Extreme, Frank got us on the list. Our amazing balcony seats were right next to Tommy Lee and Heather Locklear. Oh my gosh. Champagne was delivered to the table, and glasses poured all around. Heather was enjoying a glass of it. She was a lovely, radiant woman. And she was as nice as could be to me.

Meanwhile, Tommy was "forbidden by Heather" to drink, according to my source (Tommy), who used air quotes and whispered it to me across the table in a gossipy way when Heather got up to use the restroom. It gave me a little hint that all might not be well in the marriage.

I nodded at Tommy and made a face—"that's not fair!"

I set my glass down on the table, and felt bit guilty for drinking the champagne in front of him. He leaned back and said, waving his hands "No worries, lady! Drink up!"

This was my third time meeting him in the last four weeks, and he was easy and friendly with me. Maybe he thought I was Frank's girlfriend, which was fine. I liked Frank a lot.

Still, I couldn't believe it was all real—sitting in a balcony seat in an amazing old Hollywood theater, drinking champagne with Tommy Lee and Heather Locklear, watching Alice in Chains play one of their first shows for the *Facelift* album and touring cycle. It was the very beginning of the wave of music from Seattle that would change hard rock and heavy metal as we had known it up to this point. But no one knew any of that, yet. Still, it felt like a convergence.

There was a raw, dark authenticity about Alice in Chains that I hadn't really seen since Guns N' Roses. There were a lot of fakers and copycats and hype on the scene—even the biggest bands were figuring out their next "theme" or concept. Copycat bands were copying copycat bands. Mötley, once so cutting-edge, seemed like a slave to the trends, posing for fashion shoots with expensive Harley Davidsons and Playboy Playmates and other displays of wealth and excess. I had just been to Tommy Lee's house and saw it all firsthand.

Alice in Chains—they were the real deal. Sweaty, flannel, working class, dreadlocks, monster riffs and tuned-down guitars. No posing. Amazing howls from Layne Staley. Blistering solos from Cantrell.

LA crowds can be tough, sometimes. As I watched the audience, I could tell were unfamiliar with AIC, and people were just a bit indifferent, and didn't quite know what to make of them. Regardless, they were tight and precise. I grooved and sang to the music, already knowing the songs by heart. They were powerful to watch live. They reminded me of a heavy metal riffing

Crosby, Stills & Nash. I felt that music in my heart and belly.

It was the first wave of grunge to really hit Hollywood, and for a few precious months, it felt like something really, really special.

12.3

The day to day of working for Errol was always interesting. I started to understand how business was done in Los Angeles, and how deals were made. I learned who the VIP's were, and started to understand how accounting and taxes were done, the concept of royalty checks, the way we'd pay our client's bills every month. We would send them a packet, summarizing expenses and spending and bank statements and ledgers, as well as other legal documents.

We had a courier service—a new concept to me—where you could dispatch a person to pick up and deliver documents to people. These courier drivers were usually young, desperate, and driving uninsured clunkers—but grateful for the work. Todd was no different.

He was bleached blonde with black roots, kinda cute, short, and Polish. He was a drummer, from Cleveland, and we became friends over the few weeks when he picked up and dropped off courier packages. He was living in a shitty studio apartment off Cahuenga with a girl named Doreen who was from Oklahoma.

Todd and Doreen were not romantically involved, but best friends, brought together by the whims and fortunes of a typical Hollywood scratch existence. Soon, Todd and I were meeting at Denny's for coffee and hanging out, going to shows, and it wasn't long before we started sleeping together.

His friend Doreen was a dancer, a stripper with a good heart and a southern accent. She was whip-smart and funny as hell. Four years older than me, she was a former paralegal, and was dancing because she actually enjoyed it. She liked the money and the bit of freedom from the stressful 9-5. She worked a few nights a week at a topless club out in the Valley. She glammed it up for her shifts, made decent money, and by day she could have been mistaken for a schoolteacher.

Doreen was not at all like the dancers at the Seventh Veil, or the Body Shop, or any other idea about strippers I'd had up until that point. She had tiny boobs and refused to get a boob job, and her hair was wild, dark, and curly—unbleached and uncoiffed, and her bush, trimmed but natural. She danced in a G-string, and her butt was perfect and her legs a mile long. I loved Doreen immediately, her happy, sensible, good energy. She and I became friends easily, and by the end of November, the three of us decided to be roommates.

We found a beautiful 3rd floor apartment on Lanewood Avenue, a pretty little street right next to Hollywood High School, between Hollywood and Sunset. Smack dab in the heart of everything, Lanewood was lined with large, old pine trees that seemed to shelter the street, and it was as quiet as you could find in the literal middle of Hollywood.

I moved out of Star's apartment and said goodbye to my boy roommates, and Dale helped me move over to the new place. At the new place, Todd and I were planning to share the larger room and the attached bathroom. Doreen had her own, smaller room and bathroom for a larger cut of the rent. We signed a six-month lease. We celebrated Thanksgiving together, and between Doreen and I and an old gas stove, we managed to scrape together a pretty good and proper Turkey dinner for a small gathering of people, all of us away from our families for the holidays.

Right after our Thanksgiving feast, I went down to my car and found it sitting immobilized, booted with a giant yellow tire claw. The Los Angeles Parking Mafia was out terrorizing people on Thanksgiving Day, because of stupid unpaid parking tickets.

I wanted to cry. What the fuck?

Doreen drove me to the parking violations office the next day to pay the tickets to get my car unbooted. She was a good sport, and had dealt with the same shit from the Parking Mafia.

The roommate situation worked out well, for a couple of weeks at least, But then Todd started drinking a lot, and we had a falling out about something very minor, something I don't even remember. All of a sudden, he was beyond angry at me for reasons that I didn't fully understand.

I came home one day and he was pissed at me, and it was over. I was really hurt by his anger, but I was stuck in a lease with him for five more months. The large bedroom we shared got divided by three bookcases that he bought and put together himself in a frenzy, trying to separate himself from me. He slept on the floor on one side of the bookcases, and I slept on my little futon on the other side.

Even Doreen thought he'd gone off the deep end, and was worried about him.

Meanwhile, she'd started dating a guy named Chad, a drummer from Canada. He moved in. Then the three other guys in his band, who were all living at their rehearsal space in West LA and using charity of friends to shower, were getting evicted and needed a place to crash. Of course, they started sleeping on the floor in the living room. With all of their music gear, and sometimes, their girlfriends. All of them shared Doreen's bathroom.

Meanwhile, Todd brought home a new girl, barely legal, an exchange student from France who spoke very little English. She slept on the other side of the bookshelf with him for the entire week, and I had to share a bathroom with another woman. They made love loudly and grossly, and I couldn't believe the rudeness.

Then, the next weekend, Todd and Frenchie went to Vegas and got married. Doreen and I were completely shocked. She was barely eighteen, and here on a student visa, completely vulnerable in a strange city—it was just weird.

It was only then that I realized that Todd was emotionally unstable, moody, alcoholic, and prone to irrationality. A Gemini to the extreme. When Frenchie wasn't around, he graciously left me huge turds in the toilet, unflushed, just to be rude.

Then, with all of these people crammed into the apartment on Lanewood Avenue, my dearest former roommate, Dale, called me in a bit of trouble. He'd had a falling out with Deron, and he needed a place to stay. I didn't have much to offer him, but I was happy to do whatever I could.

I know he wouldn't have called if he hadn't really needed the help. He came with a pillow, a towel, a rucksack with a few clothes, two guitars, and a swollen black eye. Also, he still had the beige minivan that blew black smoke. He set up camp in my small space, and we shared my small double futon at night, snoring next to each other like babies in a cot.

He really was the first guy I felt totally at ease with, someone I could be myself around. I'd always felt judged by my sexual worth, I think, and Dale didn't do that. He was a friend, a true friend. He was cute and gentle and funny—everything I would want in a boyfriend, but still. I didn't feel romantic about him at all. Or maybe I wasn't ready to.

When we weren't working, Dale and I were hanging out. He also loved Queensrÿche and the Doors and Mötley Crüe, and he was a huge fan of RATT. He was a reader, too, so he'd pick up cheap paperbacks for us to share.

Dale needed a job, so I called my old friend Kevin Amici, who was working for an asbestos remediation company. It was dirty and dangerous work, but it paid pretty well, so we'd splurge on payday and go to El Compadre for a real meal and fancy drinks, or go out to see a band. When money was tight, we'd scrape together our loose change and go to Del Taco at 2am for bean burritos. Dale was the most peaceful and generous person I knew, but he wasn't afraid to get into a scuffle either. He was protective, a Leo, and I felt safe with him. We looked out for each other and pooled our resources.

In many ways, by going to Los Angeles, I cobbled together the family that I needed—people who were dreamers, seekers, orphans in the world—who loved me without judgment, or an agenda. Kevin, Dale, Doreen, and Frank all felt like family to me, at least for a time.

12.4

Christmas was approaching, and I decided to take a quick trip up to San Jose to spend Christmas Eve with my aunt

Linda, and to grab the last two boxes of my things from her house. I didn't stick around long on Christmas day though. I felt weird being away from Los Angeles, almost anxious.

So, I spent Christmas morning with my aunt and her two kids, had a good breakfast, and hit the road around noon, hoping to be back to LA at dusk.

Halfway through my trip and with the music loud, the Toyota made a noise and I felt a clunk under my foot, and suddenly, I was losing speed and power. An exit was coming up and I steered the car down the long ramp, and straight to a gas station, somewhere near San Luis Obispo. I filled the car with gas and asked an annoyed clerk to come out and look at it.

The clerk confirmed my worst fear—my transmission was busted.

The clerk, offering no suggestions or help, went back into the station.

Fuck me. Who the hell was I going to call on Christmas day? My aunt was three hours north with her two kids. My mom was in Ohio. My roommates were three hours south, all with shitty cars. A tow truck would cost me hundreds of dollars. I had no money in my bank account, and no room on my Discover card. I had less than $40 in cash. I ran through every scenario in my head, not feeling brave enough to hitchhike, seeing no great options. I was stuck. There was no one I could call to come rescue me on Christmas day. Flat broke. Busted tranny. 200 miles from Hollywood. 2000 miles away from Ohio.

Merry Fucking Christmas.

Los Angeles—I felt like she was taunting me.

What the fuck am I going to do?

But.

But, but, but...what if?

I stood there for a moment, with my arms crossed on the open door. I closed my eyes. The wind touched my face. It was a gray, chilly day and I could smell the ocean, not very far away.

California, you are breaking my heart.

Tears pinched my eyes. I got back in the car and started it, gently revving the engine as I eased up the clutch. I pushed it through the gears, trying to see if there was anything there.

I hit fourth gear, and the car moved forward, slowly. I kept coaxing it along, pumping my tricky clutch. Revving, pumping, revving, pumping, gently up the exit ramp. *C'mon motherfucker, come on!*

I couldn't believe it. I literally prayed to God and Jesus out loud as I built up speed. My pumping and revving technique worked enough to get me back on the road and up the exit. Within seconds, I was back on the 101, not believing I was really doing it. I was actually driving the car without a full transmission. I took a deep breath.

I merged into traffic. I could break down any minute along the side of the road, but I didn't.

Somehow, by some goddamned miracle, my fourth gear held the line for the next two-hundred miles. I drove 55mph all the way back to Hollywood, not hitting any clogs or stoplights. I clenched up through the Valley at dusk, during the only real traffic slowdown, trying to maintain speed, but otherwise it was like the path was paved open just for me. I drove straight off the 101 at the Highland exit, coasting through old Hollywood, revving and pumping the clutch, and making every light until I arrived to my parking garage on Lanewood Avenue. I had to open the door and push the car over the small hump down into the building and into my parking spot.

Fuckity fuck fuck fuck. I made it. Almost out of gas and with a busted transmission, the fucking Toyota made it.

I was back in Los Angeles. Fates be damned.

12.5

The New Year approached, and I weighed my options on how to get the Toyota repaired. I arranged rides to work with all of the various people in our apartment who did have cars. Dale chauffeured me around, too, and life continued on as normal, except without my own car. I hated it. But, even though all of us roommates were driving clunkers in various states of disrepair, there was always a car to borrow if I needed one, and I never did have to catch a city bus.

Dale still took guitar lessons and music theory classes at GIT, and he had been invited by one of his classmates to drop by and hang out on New Year's Eve. The classmate lived with his mom and dad out in the Valley, and his dad was an actor of some sort. Dale and I made plans to drive out to Encino for a bit, and then we could figure out what to do with the night from there.

We found the house and knocked on the door of the beautiful white Spanish hacienda. It had a courtyard and a fountain and lots of greenery and Saltillo tile. The door opened, and there he was—The Actor himself—Edward James Olmos. Suddenly, I was being embraced and kissed on the cheek in a gracious welcome to his home. His friend's dad was Edward James Olmos?

Holy shit. What a total surprise.

Dale and I stayed for two hours. We ate from a beautiful buffet and drank champagne with the Olmos family. I was dazzled and amazed. Mr. Olmos was funny, warm, and gracious. So handsome and distinguished. His wife was beautiful, with dark eyes and pale blonde hair. I couldn't believe I was sitting here with them. We clinked glasses and swapped kisses all around to greet 1991.

I couldn't wait to tell my mom. I thought back to just a few years ago, of watching all the Miami Vice episodes in our basement in Ohio, thinking about how cool he was.

Dale and I made it back to Hollywood, buzzed and tired. We passed out on the futon for a few hours, and later, for the first day of the New Year, we drove to Santa Monica and ate breakfast at Denny's, then to the ocean and where sat on the cold beach and relaxed for a while. We laid low and hung out all day.

First day of 1991. *What would the year hold for me?* I wondered.

It had all been fucking amazing up to this point. My car was busted, but I was OK. I just had to figure out how to get it fixed, and I didn't want to ask for help.

12.6

One Saturday, Dale asked if I wanted to go to a party with him, out in Reseda. It was being hosted by some of his friends from Ohio, whom I hadn't met, but I was glad not to be stuck at home. We made the drive out to the Valley and found the little bungalow. Dale's friend greeted us at the door, and they soon disappeared into the backyard. I hung back, feeling a little anti-social, as usual. I spotted a table full of snacks, soda, and beer, and I helped myself to a fistful of Doritos and a Corona.

The house was a typical 1950s Valley bungalow, with nice wood floors and purple walls. Of course, being in Reseda, I thought of Miss Pamela. There was a black velvet sofa with crumbs all over it, but no one was sitting there. I brushed away the debris and sat down, content to just rest for a few minutes and get my bearings. The kitty of the house lurked, and soon I was petting her as she nosed my neck from the back of the sofa. I've never met a kitty I didn't like. She nestled into my lap for a good rub.

A few minutes later, as the kitty purred and I was lost in my own thoughts, I looked up and realized a guy was staring at me with laser blue eyes.

As soon as he caught my eye, he jumped up and introduced himself.

"Hi, I'm Matt. Who are you? Has anyone told you that you look like Linda Ronstadt? Who are you here with? Where are you from?" He came over and sat next to me, right in my space, with the whole sofa empty next to us, and peppered me with questions.

The kitty got annoyed and jumped down.

Matt zeroed in on me and I kept up my defenses. But he was pretty cute. He reminded me of a cross of David Hasselhoff, with a little Kurt Russell and Patrick Swayze thrown in. He had long, blonde, wavy hair. He was very funny, and very much a flirt.

I was cool to him at first, answering him directly. I knew he was laying it on thick, trying to charm me. *Good grief.* But after we kept talking and he kept flirting and I kept drinking, I felt like the most important person in the world. He wanted to know all about me.

The Corona flowed, and by the end of the evening we were giggling and nuzzling and glomming on each other like crazy. He smelled good. He was sexy and confident, with a sharp wit. It turned out that he was from Ohio, too, and had been in one of the big legendary bands on the Columbus circuit in the 1980s, Scarlet.

Of course, I had heard of them—they were on the scene before I was, though. He was nine years older than me, also a Virgo, and a generation ahead. He had lived in LA for a few years now, and was a professional musician in two working bands, plus he had done studio and touring work for a variety of artists over the years.

He had played on Star Search and Johnny Carson, and toured with a popular top-40 artist. He did all this and it sounded glamorous, but the reality is that he still had to work as a drywall finisher during the day to pay his bills.

He had just broken up with a long-term girlfriend, and had a string of women and sordid tales behind him from years of minor semi-rock stardom. I didn't care, though. He was sweet, he cared, he called. We spent the next day together, and we were together from that point forward. We fell into a sweet romance, and I had myself a new, cute boyfriend.

He had some problems though. At first, I thought it was just new-relationship awkwardness. He was generous sexually, although he refused to climax with me. Otherwise, though, he was affectionate, loving, and sweet. I figured he might have some left-over baggage from his last relationship, and I tried not to let it bother me.

We called each other 'Pookie' and enjoyed being together. He made me laugh, and we were always doing something—going out to eat, going places, going to movies.

After I picked up a used copy of *Helter Skelter* to read again, we went on a field trip to find the Sharon Tate house on Cielo Drive. We pulled up and walked up to the driveway, hoping we weren't too conspicuous. After looking at the pictures in the book closely, we realized we were standing in front of the same gate and gate buzzer with the bloody fingerprints from that horrific night 21 years ago. We couldn't see the house, but the gate was still the same and hadn't been altered, which spooked both of us. We scooted back to our car and got out of there.

If anything, I had a new partner in adventure, a good friend and someone I could talk to, someone who encouraged me and told me he loved me.

12.7

As a treat, Matt splurged and bought us two tickets to the premier of the new *Doors* movie down at the Cinerama Dome on Sunset. This was the Oliver Stone movie, starring Val Kilmer, and the buzz was great since it had been filmed around Los Angeles. Plus, I LOVED The Doors. One of my all-time favorite bands.

An older, grizzled guy stood behind us in line, dressed with scarves and chains. He was wearing a vintage denim and leather vest with patches on it. As we stood on the sidewalk leading into the theater, he and Matt started chatting. He told us that Jim Morrison himself had given him this particular vest, that they had been friends back in the day, and that he had helped them with equipment at their early gigs.

Matt and I stood there, not quite sure what to believe. Matt bullshitted him a little, but the guy didn't seem like he was bullshitting us. He was one hundred percent sincere, and seemed to be of sound mind.

The two possibilities were either that he was stark raving mad, or telling us the truth, at least his version of it. There was no way to tell. You just never know who is who in Hollywood. He took off the vest so we could look at it closer. He showed us the label—and some clue that I can't remember. There was some feature of this vest that was "solid proof" that it had been Morrison's—and it all sounded completely plausible. Why not? Maybe I actually did get to touch Jim Morrison's vest. He had roamed the streets of Los Angeles only 20 years prior.

The Cinerama Dome movie theater was a real treat. It had a very modern, *Jetsons* feel to it, with velvet seats and plush carpet and huge curtains and a stellar sound system for an amazing soundtrack. The movie completely engulfed us. Stylistically, the movie was great, using the music, the vibe, and the portrayals of Los Angeles and the music scene to show how Morrison evolved as an artist. The Doors had to be one of my top three bands ever, and there was no way for me to separate my feelings about the Doors from my feelings about Los Angeles. They loved the city, I loved the city, and the movie had been filmed in the city not long prior.

But the movie bothered me, too. Kilmer portrayed Morrison much more sinister than I ever felt him to be. His Morrison felt on the verge of serial killer, psychopathic, sociopathic, almost. Charles Manson-ish. There was a certain heartlessness in the character, a cruelty.

Then, I realized that in some ways, Kilmer wasn't just portraying Morrison, but was also acting as a reflection of Los Angeles. Beautiful, glittering, dreamy, like an Angelyne billboard, but with a dark empty mystery underneath. He played to the void. We all have two sides to us—the light and the shadow. Los Angeles had a shadow. I was beginning to really feel it.

I walked out of that movie feeling empty and melancholy, the story reminding me of how I'd felt alone my whole life. Jim Morrison died two months before I was born, in the summer of 1971, not quite 20 years prior. Despite having money, status, talent, and fame, he died alone in a bathtub in Paris.

And here I was in Los Angeles and I felt…*so alone.*

What I really wanted down at the very heart of it were the things that I couldn't yet verbalize. I dreamed about feeling normal. I wanted a family. I wanted a partner that loved me, and wouldn't hold back. And I began to think about someday, maybe, being a mom.

I didn't want to be alone. I realized that I probably didn't have a future with Matt. I would always be second fiddle to his career. I wasn't sure Los Angeles could give me what I needed, either. She was fickle, and sometimes, a real mean bitch.

***

Not long after seeing *The Doors*, we went to see the new *Silence of the Lambs*. It was being shown at the historic Warner Pacific Theater, on Hollywood Blvd., a few streets north and not too far from the Cinerama Dome.

Where the Cinerama Dome had felt modern-retro and a bit space-agey, the Pacific was in an older style—not art deco as I expected, but more like an Italian opera house—with ornate carvings and coffered ceilings and huge chandeliers. Walking into this theater was like stepping back in time. I immediately felt the ghosts in this building—it was a strong, dark presence to me.

I had just read Anne Rice's *Interview with a Vampire*, and I half expected to see the Vampire Lestat drifting down the staircase in a dusty tuxedo, or corseted ladies emerging from the shadows. The seats were a dark red velvet on cast iron, ancient and heavy, bolted to an old wooden floor underneath ornate, but threadbare, carpeting. The floors echoed as you walked into the theater. There were grand columns and staircases and faded brocade wallpaper and old gas lamps. It was a magnificent and beautiful antique, elegant, out of time and place.

Of course, *Silence of the Lambs* was the perfect movie to see in such a setting, being so dark and gothic. The movie scared the shit out of me.

It had started raining while we were in the movie and when we emerged, it was a cold Pacific deluge. We were soaked and chilled by the time we trotted the few blocks back to Matt's truck. As we made our way through the streets of old Hollywood in the cold rain, I thought of the Black Dahlia, and what kind of sick and deranged bastard would kidnap, torture, and mutilate people. Predators. I had just met two of them in this movie, and Clarice Starling was my new hero.

12.8

Within a few weeks of meeting Matt, Doreen and I were at The Rainbow one night and we met a guy named Cookie. He was an older guy, well-groomed and tan, who asked us if we would be interested in making some money attending parties. I was skeptical, but we took his number anyway, and tucked it away. It seemed shady.

But with my car still busted and no ideas on how to fix it, I thought about it for a week or so, and called the number for Cookie. Again, he told me I could make a few hundred bucks by attending parties. He told me to call his friend Heidi, who was looking for some new girls to work her network.

Heidi wanted to meet me, so I borrowed a car to drive to her place down off of Robertson, right on the edge of Beverly Hills and West Hollywood. Her house was a beautiful little Spanish bungalow. She was small, tan, dark haired, older than me, and bit "hard" around the edges. She reminded me a little of Mackenzie Phillips. Still, she was friendly enough, businesslike. She invited me in, and I was totally charmed by her house—the white plaster walls and wooden floors and built-ins. It was a proper Hollywood bungalow, for sure, and it felt very chic and cozy.

She told me she had an assignment for me, but it was in San Francisco. I was to accompany an Asian businessman to a company dinner and cocktail party. She told me I would clear $1900, after her $600 fee, and that my plane ticket would be paid for. I was to be picked up at the SF airport, and dropped back there 24 hours later. She wasn't sure if I'd be staying in a hotel, she explained.

Of course, it sounded too good to be true, so I asked her bluntly, "Am I expected to sleep with this guy?"

She looked at me and paused before speaking. "If you want to, you can," she said, carefully. "That's up to you."

At least I know what I'm really getting into, I thought. *Who knows, maybe it really is just a business dinner.* I agreed to

Heidi's terms. She told me to wear business slacks, heels, and a nice blouse. Her friend drove me to LAX in a gold Honda hatchback.

I arrived in San Francisco, and just as promised, a blue Mercedes with a driver picked me up and took me to a beautiful, remodeled modern Victorian row house with stunning views. This is where I met Yoshi, my date for the evening. He was pleasant, polite, and didn't speak great English, but I was patient and we were able to communicate well. He was super polite, and very sweet, and even funny.

Once again, a feeling came over me and I realized in a moment of mild panic that no one in the world really knew where I was at that moment. Matt knew I was going, and Doreen knew, but I could disappear and no one would start looking for a few days. I fought the urge to call my mom. She wouldn't understand why I was in San Francisco, and I was afraid that I might break down and tell her about the mess I'd gotten myself into.

But no. I was going to get through this without calling my mom or freaking out.

It turns out, there was no business dinner. Instead, it was just an old-fashioned American date. We went to Alioto's at the Wharf—the only restaurant I could think of to suggest when he asked what I wanted to eat for dinner. We walked around and ate chocolate, watched sea lions, and then went to a bar to have a drink. When we made it back to his place, I asked about the guest room and he just smiled, and invited me in to his bedroom with a small bow.

I'd actually had a good time with him that evening. He wasn't completely unpleasant looking, either. Although I've never been attracted to Asian men, I thought hey, he's not horrible. I'd had a few one-night stands with guys who were less fun, and who turned out to be real jerks. Yoshi was nice, and generous, and kind of cute.

I understood in that moment exactly what choice I was making.

I needed to get my car fixed.

The sex wasn't terrible or remarkable in any way. I've had much worse sex in my life, and for worse reasons, and with worse lovers. It was awkward, but he was small and gentle, he wore a condom, and he came rather quickly.

I thought of Matt. I'd told him about this trip in an effort to get my car fixed.

He didn't even try to stop me from coming here.

It was all fine. No big deal, I told myself. I slept in Yoshi's bed beside him, and he didn't snore.

The next day we woke up and I showered. We went to breakfast down at a cute, hip diner. Then he drove me himself down to the airport, handed me $3500 in cash, and kissed me on the cheek. *Easy-peasy.* I felt weird, though.

Once I got to my seat on the plane back to LA, I finally relaxed. I was both happy and sad. I'd crossed a line but I wasn't sure what it meant, if anything. I wasn't ashamed, just sad that I had to do it. It hadn't been sleazy, demeaning, or dangerous, thank goodness.

I actually had fun with Yoshi. He didn't treat me weird at all, other than handing me a wad of cash at the end of our 24 hours together. It was still much better in my mind than having to perform naked in a strip club, or show people my butthole for money.

But I also knew that I'd never do it again.

I was the only person seated in my row on the plane, so I opened my purse and carefully counted the wad of money again, just to double check. I'd never had that much cash in my hand at once. I separated out Heidi's money from my own, which I tucked away in various places—mostly my bra. I didn't want to be bumbling around with a wad of extra cash in front of her.

As I flew back to LA, I found some peace with it. It was done and over with, and I could get my car fixed. It was a relief, a huge relief, actually.

Heidi had her girl pick me up at the airport. When we got to her house, she was all business. I handed over her cut of the money, not mentioning anything about my "bonus," and she asked if I'd be interested in seeing Yoshi again. He'd already called her to try to re-book me.

I was surprised, and a little creeped out. I'm not the type to push my luck. I told her I was one and done. Thanks, but no thanks. She looked skeptical, but was very polite.

She called me a week later to see if I could help her out with another client of hers. A famous actor. Again, I declined. I wasn't even curious. I didn't want to tempt the fates. I wasn't greedy. I wasn't open for business. I wasn't looking for a sugar daddy.

It was a really simple equation for me: I needed money to get my car fixed, an opportunity landed in my lap, and I gambled and took it. No loans. No paying anyone back. No asking anyone for help. I handled my own shit.

But just like my experience at the 7th Veil, I knew it wasn't for me. It had served my purpose, and that was that.

I didn't belong in that world. Just like I knew I could never be a stripper—I knew I could never be an escort. Whatever issues I had with men or with money could not be solved by selling myself, and it felt like a bigger act of rebellion to keep my clothes on—despite the potentially easy money I could make if I didn't.

Girls like me with daddy issues showed up in Los Angeles all the time and took off their clothes and were exploited, filmed, sold, abused, addicted, passed around and broken. The porn industry thrived here for a reason. People were desperate to be famous; people were desperate to make money.

I was damaged, but I didn't feel desperate. I wasn't broken. My car was broken, but I was not. A little sad, maybe, but not hopeless.

So, I had the Toyota transmission fixed at the cheapest place I could find—somewhere on Slauson, in South LA. They had me back on the road within a few days. I also bought myself a few new clothes, and a few thrift store splurges—my small wardrobe was quite literally starting to fall apart. I finally had a small buffer in my bank account.

That one night with Yoshi kept my head just above water for the next few months.

I went on with my life and didn't think a thing about it until many years later, when I'd see Heidi again, this time on the evening news.

Hollywood Madame, Heidi Fleiss.

13.0

[Power To The Music]

Early 1991

I was still working for Errol and living on Lanewood Avenue with Todd and Frenchie, Doreen and her boyfriend and his band, and my buddy Dale who shared my futon with me. I'd started dating Matt, my super cute boyfriend. My car was fixed, and life was generally fun and slightly chaotic living with so many people. My only refuge was my futon, where I would escape to read books and chill out.

Megadeth were still touring for the Rust in Peace album. The album debuted at #23 on the Billboard charts and was selling well, to rave reviews.

Tension was building in the country, it felt like, and in February of 1991, the United States invaded Kuwait. It was the first time a war was broadcast live on television. Errol had a small 13" TV at the office, and we turned it on and watched coverage of the first advances by our military as they deployed the full might and fury of the US Military. The burning oil fields, the exploding night-vision bombs they'd show us. It was all unsettling to me, Desert Storm. *Is it right? Is it wrong?* I became more curious about current events and politics. It was the first real military action of my adulthood.

The only person I could think of to talk to about it was my Dad, so I called him at home in Michigan for the first time ever. He was happy to hear from me, but sad about the war beginning. He said he hoped that the soldiers would make it out ok, and that he hoped the end goal would be worth the efforts and the casualties. He felt uneasy about it all, too, and didn't really have any answers, except that he didn't want to see another Vietnam—an endless war with a terrible outcome, leading to the deaths of millions in Southeast Asia.

It wasn't lost on me that *Rust in Peace* seemed to be the soundtrack to all of this. The album was intense, and really captured a snapshot of the mood in the country—serious, dark, questioning, with monster riffs that replicated the fury and precision of the United States military as we started bombing Kuwait. These times did not call for sappy power ballads by men in spandex and lipstick. Mustaine's snarl and irony were spot on.

When Errol found out that *Rust In Peace* was nominated for a Grammy, he did a little happy dance in the office and opened a bottle of champagne at the end of the work day. We drank it out of coffee mugs in his office, and chatted about all the possibilities and plans. Errol was a dreamer and a schemer and just a bit neurotic, but I loved when we had these idea sessions.

In addition to the good Grammy news, Mustaine was getting married soon to his girlfriend, Pamela. She was a stunning creature with willowy limbs and brand-new boobs, with the face of a supermodel. Mustaine had met his match. She was very friendly and soft-spoken the few times we met, and she was from Ohio, too. Errol advised them on where to get their custom wedding rings made, and he told them he had contacts in the diamond district. Errol even flew to Hawaii to deliver the rings and to attend the wedding in March of 1991.

We handled a lot of small details for Megadeth, and worked closely with their manager, Ron Laffitte, and his assistant, Sondra. Ron popped in and out of our office every couple of weeks. He was handsome, in his late 20's, with a strong jaw, brown eyes, and thick, long, light brown hair. Unsurprisingly, he was another earthy Virgo, like Mustaine, and Lord, was he cute. He reminded me of a long-haired Andy Gibb. He was always friendly and jokey with me, and I liked him a lot. Our conversations were easy and funny. I began to think it would be fun to work for him, but he already has a great assistant. Sondra was not only capable and energetic, she was also a huge sweetheart to me, always friendly and willing to help. I really clicked with both of them as we worked with Megadeth over those few months.

13.1

On a Friday afternoon in early April, Ron popped in for a quick meeting with Errol.

After 15 minutes or so, Errol called me in to his office, looking very serious. I looked between both of them, puzzled. "What's going on?" I asked.

"Hi sweetie, have a seat," said Errol. I looked at Ron, who was smiling. So handsome. He patted his knee and nodded at me with a raised eyebrow, openly flirting, daring me to sit there like a little girl.

"That's not usually where I prefer to sit on a man." I deadpanned, raising my eyebrow, daring him back.

Errol choked on his coffee and Ron hooted in laughter at my comeback. Only because it was Ron did I get feisty. Ron was too cute not to tease, even if I did want to work for him. But I thought it would also be super awesome if he asked me out. I had no idea of his romantic status, but I did wonder.

So, the reason they wanted to talk to me was that Brian Slagel over at Metal Blade Records was looking for an assistant. Ron's personal attorney, Bill, was one of Brian's oldest friends and shared office space with Metal Blade. He had acted as their legal counsel since Metal Blade's inception. In addition to helping Brian, Bill also needed a person to help him with his legal stuff.

Oh, WOW.

Bill and Brian were just starting the process of finding someone when Bill mentioned to Ron to keep his ears open for anyone who might be a fit.

And for whatever reason, Ron thought of me.

So, Ron scheduled a quick meeting that day as a professional courtesy to ask Errol if it would be OK if I interviewed elsewhere. He took time out of his busy day to come to Errol's office to offer me the chance of a lifetime.

After hearing the details and just about crapping myself and thinking *Brian fucking Slagel of Metal Blade Records, holy SHIT!!* Errol looked at me and said, "I'd hate to see you go, but I think it would be foolish of you not to interview. This is a great opportunity for you." He smiled at me with a kind look in his eyes.

"Ok, yes, of course I'll do it. I love Metal Blade! I've known about them for years. Thank you." I was stunned. I wanted to kiss the man, this Ron Laffitte, Megadeth's manager. I wanted to kiss Errol, too. I couldn't believe my luck.

From right there in Errol's office, Ron called Bill, and my interview with Metal Blade was set for the following Tuesday morning. Errol even gave me the time off to drive over to the Valley.

13.2

I made my way west down Ventura, looking for the low gray building next to the 405 where Metal Blade Records was based. I found the building and suite number and was greeted by a very sweet receptionist with a southern accent, Amanda. As I stood there for a minute in the small reception area, I noticed the poster for The River's Edge, and I thought of my old boyfriend Aaron and seeing that movie with him. I felt like I was having a moment of déjà vu.

Bill the Attorney came out and fetched me back to his office. In his early 30's, with dark hair and blue eyes and a moustache, he seemed nice enough, but was a tough read.

I was relieved that I hadn't under or over-dressed for the interview. I wore a pair of nice jeans, Payless boots with a low heel, and a pink, watercolor-patterned button-down shirt tucked in with a belt. Bill was dressed in an oxford with the sleeves rolled up, belted jeans, and loafers. When Brian came in, he greeted me warmly and with a firm handshake. He was wearing jeans, an Iron Maiden t-shirt, a baseball cap, and high tops. The building wasn't fancy, and neither were the offices, cubicles, or people. Everyone had jeans on. Most of the guys had on black band t-shirts, and the women I saw were dressed like me. I fit right in.

Brian had a handsome, pleasant face and a husky build, with a ring of frizzy reddish hair below the crown of his balding head, which he almost always kept covered with a baseball cap. It would be a few more years before he'd shave it off for good. He was easy going and polite, perceptive, direct, and I got a good vibe from him. Just a normal, down to earth metalhead. As I got to know him, I found out that he was also the only child of a single mom. I imagined that music had kind of been his parent, too.

Brian started Metal Blade at age 20 out of his mom's garage, after a stint working in a record store and publishing his own fanzine of the LA music scene. He was a huge fan of hard rock and metal, going to hundreds of shows, befriending the musicians, and writing reviews and interviews. He saw what was happening in the early 80s music scene and how popular it was becoming. This led him to think it was a shame that these artists weren't recorded, so he had an idea to showcase some of the bands on a compilation album, and Metal Blade was born. He was friends with Lars and James before Metallica even had their first gig. He had also offered them a slot on the upcoming metal compilation album he was putting together, and he was true to his word.

Those first *Metal Massacre* albums Brian released featured a Who's Who of later metal success: Metallica, Slayer, RATT, Armored Saint, and many others on the LA scene. He was passionate and self-taught, and by many accounts, already a legend by the time I met him. Of course, I knew all of this. I'd known who he was since high school, sitting in Aaron's basement and flipping through his albums.

Metal Blade was nine years old by the time I got there. It was turning a small profit, and Brian was good with numbers. He had assembled his core team, and had an ear for new music talent, an eye for picking up old album rights and re-releasing them on Metal Blade. He had organized an amazing body of work in nine short years—Metal Blade was always in production, signing new bands, churning out music, and keeping things in the black. It helped that he was a rock music savant. He had an encyclopedic knowledge of all things metal and built a life and a small empire around it, all from being a fan with a vision.

We settled into an easy conversation. I knew the Metal Blade catalog and artists, and I gushed a little about Armored Saint. He asked who my favorite new band in the last year or so was, and I enthusiastically said, *Alice in Chains*, and told him I'd seen them a few months ago at the Palace. He was also a huge fan.

The interview flowed well.

When Bill the Attorney talked salary, I didn't bother negotiating. It was a few hundred more a month than Errol paid me, and even though the drive to work would be longer, I'd be commuting against traffic from Hollywood to the Valley.

Brian and Bill exchanged a quick glance, and with no further discussion or drama or waiting around, Brian said, "So, I think this will work. When can you start?"

"How about Monday?" I asked. "That gives me time to wrap things up for Errol."

"Perfect," he said. "I'll see you at 10am Monday. We'll take it from there."

After letting Errol know, the first person I called when I got home that day was Sondra, Ron Laffitte's assistant. I told her I got the job, *Thank you guys so much, please let Ron know how much I appreciate it*. She was thrilled at the news and gave me a good pep talk. She told me to call her if I need anything at all, and that we should go out for drinks sometime soon. I was 19 years old, and I think everyone assumed I was older.

From my new desk the following week, I sent two promo copies of the new Armored Saint record to Ron and Sondra, along with quick handwritten note on Metal

Blade stationary to thank them again for the thoughtfulness in recommending me to Metal Blade.

My mom always taught me to send a thank you note, and Ron had done me a huge favor.

I didn't know if I could ever thank him enough.

13.3

A few weeks after I started at the label, I received a small bouquet of flowers delivered to my desk. The note said, *Congrats on the new position! Hope you're settling in. Love, Ron & Sondra.*

Attached in a separate envelope were four tickets and passes to the Clash of the Titans tour, coming up in a few weeks down at Irvine Meadows. Slayer. Megadeth. Anthrax. Alice in Chains. *Let us know if you need more*, the yellow sticky note said. I gasped in surprise at the good will and generosity of these people.

As luck would have it, later that very same day, Brian came out of his office and asked me to call a few of his contacts to get him set up with a couple of tickets and passes to the Clash of the Titans show. I reached in my desk drawer and handed him two of the tickets and passes that were sent to me, and told him that the Megadeth people had just sent them over.

"Wow! You're fast! This is great!" he said, smiling at me. He looked pleased and surprised, and he thanked me.

As I settled in those first few weeks, I got used to the drive over the hill from Hollywood to the Valley via Laurel Canyon Boulevard. I drove past Mario's place every day and wondered how he was doing. Would he even remember me if I stopped to say hello? It felt like a lifetime ago that I first arrived at his gate, though in reality it had only been 9 months prior.

Metal Blade was divided between two floors of the low gray building beside the 405 on Ventura. Most of the label operations and staff—art department, marketing, the mailroom—were on the second floor of the building, including Bill the Attorney, and Mike Faley, the president of Metal Blade.

Mike was from Buffalo, and it turned out, he was also the personal manager for Billy Sheehan, whom I'd seen in action a few years before when I was backstage in Columbus at the David Lee Roth show.

Brian's office was located on a different floor of the building. Only he and his operations manager, Tracy, worked there. My desk was in the front waiting area of this suite, where I sat next to a giant fax machine. I answered calls, took messages, screened drop-ins, and greeted people who came in for meetings. There was a central room lined with storage cabinets full of Metal Blade products and extra office equipment and supplies, and two offices located off that, where Brian and Tracy worked.

Brian had a big office with a panoramic window looking north toward the Sepulveda Basin, comfy chairs and a black leather sofa, a giant collection of audio equipment and speakers, and framed albums and awards. Tracy was in a smaller, functional office next to him, also with a big window. Her office was full of filing cabinets, art proofs, and posters.

Tracy was eight years older than me, and grew up on the east coast, in Connecticut. She had long, dark, straight hair, and a pretty, friendly, oval face with high cheekbones, and hazel eyes. She had the most beautiful hands with long elegant fingers, and she was an artist—a painter.

She was all business and no nonsense at first, but we warmed up quickly to each other after discovering that we were both Virgos. She had been at Metal Blade for about a year at this point, and was handling numerous duties of the label—production, coordinating the artwork and dealing with the nitty-gritty details of getting bands in studios, master tapes, and tour support. She also handled most of the daily financials of the label—payroll, budgets, bills.

Within a few weeks, I considered Tracy a good friend, a mentor, and I looked forward to seeing her every day. She was artistic, funny, and kind, and tolerated all my various questions with patience. She was the first vegetarian I had ever met. She had an east-coast work ethic, with a west-coast hippie worldview. She showed me the ropes at Metal Blade, and helped me understand key details that would have taken me months to figure out otherwise. After a bit, we were grabbing lunch together and while, technically, she was one of my bosses, she treated me like a friend, like a sister, almost.

***

Unfortunately, I didn't have a parking space in the parking garage at Metal Blade. The building was small, and the spaces were at a premium. Brian, Bill, Mike, and Tracy had their spaces, and that was it. The rest of us—15-plus on staff—had to park rough on the residential streets of Sherman Oaks, south of Ventura, with super-conveniently restricted two-hour parking signs on every street.

The City of Los Angeles Parking Mafia was always on the hunt for victims, chalking tires and then making rounds to see who still had chalk marks on the tires two hours later. There were a few of us who would gather up each other's keys and go move cars every few hours, but despite our best collective efforts, we all racked up parking tickets by the boatload.

Those $15 tickets were bittersweet. I kept up with the tickets as best I could on my $300 per week salary.

There were many times I shouted "FUCK YOU!!" to the smoggy wind in the neighborhood off the 405 when I'd get to my car and see yet another ticket flapping under my ratty wiper blade. I had to pay them down just enough to keep the dreaded boot-claw of shame off my car.

It was the price of working at Metal Blade and living in Los Angeles. It was a big fat dream-tax, and it took me years to pay off the parking tickets to the City of Los Angeles.

13.4

Things around Armored Saint were buzzing at the label as they finished up their latest album.

Early in their career, they had been on Metal Blade, but jumped to Chrysalis and put out a few albums. Then they were dropped by Chrysalis right as they got news that their guitar player, Dave Pritchard, had leukemia.

By the time he passed away, they had a few songs demoed, and a few songs finished. The band members were raw and in mourning at his loss, unsure of whether they could or should continue with the material they already had for another studio album. And, of course, now they had no label.

Brian, being one of their oldest friends and biggest fans, kept bugging them about the material, encouraging them to finish it. He eventually signed them back and put the album out on Metal Blade. It was a hard, bittersweet album for them to finish making. Because of this, there was a lot of buzz and interest in Armored Saint. Everyone wanted *Symbol of Salvation* to do well, not only for the band, but to honor the memory of Dave Pritchard.

By everyone's account, he was a great guy and well-loved, and the songs on *Symbol of Salvation* are a testament to his talent. The band ultimately decided to finish the album with guitarist Jeff Duncan, of Odin (another band featured in the *Decline of Western Civilization*), who stepped in to help finish some of the writing. The lineup of John Bush on vocals, Joey Vera on bass, Gonzo Sandoval on drums and his brother Phil Sandoval on guitar (who was in the band at some point previously), along with Jeff Duncan, was all set. This is the lineup that continues to record and tour even to this day.

But this was all new territory for everyone at Metal Blade: how to support a band that's been through a devastating loss of a band member and good friend, how to promote and market an album given the sadness surrounding it. Metallica had done it just a few years before when Cliff Burton was killed in a bus accident, and they moved forward successfully. In fact, it was Brian who had suggested their new bass player to them, Jason Newsted.

There was a lot of support in general from the metal community. The album had a great buzz and everyone was excited, but it was somber and muted.

There was an awareness that things would never be the same, along with a certain vulnerability and openness to this album. *Symbol of Salvation* was a true turning point for the band.

And so, the very first big project that fell to me as Brian's new assistant at Metal Blade Records was to arrange and coordinate the record-release party for the *Symbol of Salvation* album.

The album would drop in five weeks. Nothing had been planned. Time to get on it.

Holy Shit.

13.5

I gulped with uncertainty as Brian handed me his enormous list of contacts. I was to update the whole thing and make a new mailing list of invites for this party, which meant I'd need to check with a bunch of other people to make sure everyone who was supposed to be invited, was invited.

"Check with Tracy, each of the band members, Mike, Bill, Radio and Marketing," he rattled off.

I scrambled to take notes. I was still learning everyone's names, and where they sat upstairs. Armored Saint was one of Metal Blade's premier acts, and they were good friends of Brian's, so he wanted to do it up right. Brian told me that he wanted the party to be a big deal, and on the Hollywood side of the hill, not at some BFE supper club out in the Valley. Of course, we were on a budget. But he wanted to maximize the hype and keep the buzz going for this album.

I immediately started calling a few clubs to see what we could book on fairly short notice, and on our budget. I tried a club on Sunset, near El Compadre and The Guitar Center. It was cool enough, with a high-profile and historic location. Tracy and I took a field trip over the hill to make sure the club was what we wanted, and to deliver a deposit check.

Once we saw the stage area, we came up with the idea that it would be really cool if Armored Saint could do a live set for the party. Tracy was almost certain they'd agree, so she talked to Joey, who asked the band, while we told Brian. Everyone was on board.

Over the next few weeks, I got the mailing list compiled as I learned the Macintosh computer and software, which was all new to me. The club and band were booked, press releases done, artwork and invites printed and mailed. Tracy coached me through the entire thing.

Everyone was stoked for the album, and even more stoked that Armored Saint would be doing a set for the party. It was their first live performance as a band since Dave's passing.

It was a big deal.

13.6

One morning, during my first few weeks at Metal Blade, a long-haired guy in bike shorts opened the door to our suite and wrestled to get his large bike into the office. The pedal caught on the door jam, and the bike almost tipped over. My first thought at seeing his rather awkward struggle was, *who the fuck is this guy?*

I stood up to see if I could help him, hoping he wasn't a copier salesman. Maybe a courier?

I held the other door open for him, and he turned around to introduce himself.

"Hi, I'm John. I'm here to see Brian," he said. I'd seen his picture before, and patched him through to Brian when he called, but it was our first-time meeting in person.

"I didn't recognize you without your studded leather arm straps," I joked to him.

John Bush was easy to talk to, self-deprecating in his humor, and super perceptive. Not to mention, he was handsome, with a nice jaw of stubble coming in, and long curly brown hair pulled back in a ponytail holder. I buzzed Brian to let him know John was waiting, and Brian came out to greet him.

When he and Brian were done, he lingered a few minutes. He wasn't quite flirting with me, but was engaged and interested. I liked his energy.

He was newly single after a long relationship and still kind of bruised from it. We talked about how he missed Dave, his guitar player. By some random twist in our conversation, I found out he was a Virgo. We chatted about that for a minute and to myself I think—*Tracy is a Virgo! My boyfriend Matt is a Virgo! Dave Mustaine is a Virgo! Ron Laffitte is a Virgo! Mike Faley is a Virgo! All these goddamn Virgos!*

John and I said our goodbyes, knowing that we'd be seeing each other over the next few weeks as we got ready to launch his album.

***

Joey Vera, Armored Saint's bass player, also dropped by a few times, and was also friendly and handsome. He and John Bush had been friends since third grade, along with the Sandoval brothers since middle school. Armored Saint was a family and considered themselves brothers. Joey had a soothing, deep voice and a calm, peaceful vibe. We often chatted when he would call for Brian or Tracy, which was pretty often.

I didn't think anything of the calls. After all, Joey called for Tracy once or twice a day, at least. I was new, and we were in the middle of launching this album plus a few others, recording a video, planning a release party, and gearing up for media and tour support, so it didn't seem strange that he would call so often.

This was my first exposure to the mechanics of the label, and I learned there was a natural rhythm to an album cycle as they moved through the pipeline. Brian was hands on with his bands, dealing with them directly, or through Tracy or Mike. So, things would get busy for a while, with artists calling a lot, no big deal.

One morning, I entered the office suite to find Tracy and Joey standing in front of the giant fax machine near my desk. I caught a vibe as they moved away from each other. She was standing close to him, and his head was cocked toward her a little. The energy between them seemed to crackle.

Oh! Of course. There was no mistaking it.

"Hey Joey!" I put an armful of mail down on my desk and pretended to tidy up, grabbing a stack of albums.

Earlier in the day, Tracy had asked me to inventory how much vinyl we had on each of the old Armored Saint catalog titles, and to pull a few of each for something she was working on. I had the albums ready, on my desk, so I handed those to her along with a sheet of inventory numbers.

"You know," I said, smiling at them both as I handed her the pile, "I lost my virginity while listening to Armored Saint."

Tracy and Joey look at me with shocked smiles and raised eyebrows, "Really?" They both look intrigued.

"Yep. November 24, 1987. My first boyfriend, Aaron. I was 16. This album," I said, holding up *Raising Fear*. Tracy and Joey were floored. I told them the quick version, about Aaron and listening to all the Metal Blade bands when I was in high school in Ohio. Even though this one was on Chrysalis, they were still a Metal Blade band to me.

"I've been a fan for a while," I confessed. Joey looked genuinely touched by the story. "I don't go around just telling people how I lost my virginity," I said, "but I thought it was something you'd get a kick out of. Crazy, huh, that I ended up working at Metal Blade?"

"That's so cool! I'm honored!" said Joey. He was so gracious and funny. The moment of awkwardness was broken, and we all had a laugh at how life works out sometimes.

A few minutes later, after Joey left, Tracy came back out front to my desk.

"So...could you tell?" she asked.

"I could totally tell," I said, laughing. We talked, and she clued me in: She and Joey were a thing. They'd met at a GWAR show when she was still new at Metal Blade. Before the upcoming tour, they were taking their first getaway trip down to Mexico together. I nodded at her. "It's all good. I am thrilled for you guys and Joey is a real sweetheart."

They were in love, like the real deal.

But the catch was, Brian did not and could not know about it, or Tracy could lose her job. There was some precedent set by former employees, she told me, and Brian didn't want any hanky-panky going on between label staff and artists.

It wasn't that Brian was a prude or overly conservative, but he thought it could lead to messiness with business, which made sense, of course. Tracy explained it all, and our practical Virgo selves both agreed it was a sound, sensible policy.

It didn't change the fact that, here she was, involved hot and heavy with an artist on the label. Even from my few short weeks there, I could see that she was Brian's most trusted employee, handling the budgets, the nuts and bolts of label operations, and juggling many behind the scenes duties.

It could happen to anyone, meeting your soulmate under inconvenient circumstances.

But still, I'd wondered about that policy. Even though I was seeing Matt, I thought John Bush was pretty cute, but I certainly didn't want to lose my job over flirting or anything else, so at least this gave me a heads up. I didn't want Tracy to lose her job, either.

"My lips are sealed," I told her. I'd only known her a few weeks, and I knew that she was taking a chance trusting me with this, rather than letting me speculate. They did plan to tell Brian, eventually, but they wanted to get through this album and tour. They wanted some time for themselves before going public, she told me. I totally understood, and I was on board. The only other person to know at this point was John Bush, and his lips were sealed, too.

Over the next few months, a few of us would be the keeper of this secret, for a little while at least. In the meantime, there was an album release, a big party, a video shoot for their first single, *Reign of Fire* out at a venue called the Country Club in Reseda, and a tour to get ready for.

13.7

Tracy and I got over to the club early to find the manager and to put up posters and promo stuff. The crew and band were roaming about, setting up the stage. Soon, the sun set, and there was a line out the door to get in. I'd sent out 250 invites and had about 150 RSVP's, and I had budgeted for about 300 free drinks, with everyone getting two drink tickets at the door. However, we had more than 500 people show up, some with press credentials and no formal invite, or multiple people coming together on one invite. We managed to get everyone in, and the club continued to fill until we reached fire-code capacity.

We blew through the alcohol budget in about an hour. I found Brian and asked if he wanted to keep the tap on, or switch to a cash bar. To my surprise, he decided to leave the free booze flowing for another hour, until the band took the stage at 8pm. I mingled and socialized and played hostess. Everything was good and people were happy. By all accounts, the party was a roaring success, and the place was hopping, for sure. After an hour or so on my feet, I found an empty seat at the bar where I could sit for a few minutes to catch my breath.

Ron Laffitte found a seat next to me and gave me a hug and a warm greeting. Of course, I'd invited him and Sondra to the party, and they both showed up. I was so happy to see him. He looked great, tan and healthy. I thanked him again for everything he'd done for me.

He was happy that the party was going so well, and stoked to see Saint, too, as a long-time fan. I could tell he was already pretty buzzed, and we were both getting more so as we sipped our drinks together. We sat a little apart from the crowd of people, and I was super flattered at his undivided attention.

We were leaning in close to talk, when suddenly, he put his hand on my cheek and planted a sweet, passionate kiss on my lips. Surprised, I kissed him right back.

It was over too quickly, but it was awesome. I opened my eyes and he smiled as he slid off the barstool. I realized he was actually pretty drunk, but I didn't mind. It was just a kiss, an impulsive, sweet, awkward kiss by a stupidly handsome man. He lurched off to find the restroom, and I finished my cranberry vodka before heading back into the fray. I found Tracy and we made our way to the stage area.

I felt reenergized as Armored Saint opened their set. The crowd roared, and more than a few of us were a little weepy at the tributes to Dave, whose parents were there to support the band. I didn't know the guy, but I did care for these people. For Joey, and John. For Tracy, and for Brian. The emotion in the room was real, and strong.

I stood next to Tracy and saw a little wetness around her eyes, too. *I am a part of this moment.* I thought to myself. *I just pulled this whole thing off—an amazing party for an amazing band.* I moved here not even a year ago, not knowing a soul, and just look at me now.

Look the fuck at me now.

13.8

May, 1991.

A few weeks after the Armored Saint party was the Clash of the Titans show, down at Irvine Meadows Amphitheater, about 60 miles south of Los Angeles.

Although the Monsters of Rock a few years before had paved the way for a bigger, multi-artist rock tour like this, this was a historic in its own right—the first time a thrash metal tour had been packaged together for arenas and coliseums. Megadeth had been touring for almost nine months straight by this time. This was a co-headlining tour, and tonight, Slayer was on last. So, the lineup was Alice in Chains as the opener, then Anthrax, then Megadeth, then Slayer.

Matt was my date for the show. Although he was a rocker type with long hair, he wasn't too much into really heavy metal or thrash. He was a showman, and definitely leaned toward more commercial rock, like Bryan Adams and Bon Jovi. He didn't know what to expect, having never been to a show like this, and being a professional musician and performer with a healthy ego and strong musical opinions, he had an attitude for most of the show.

Alice in Chains was amazing, taking the stage just as the sun was stretching into long amber shadows. Layne had dreadlocked his hair and was wearing sunglasses. The seats were only about a quarter full at that point. *What a fucking shame*, I thought, so many people are missing out on this amazing band. It was my second time seeing them, and I loved them.

Anthrax came on next and did their typical stomp and mosh. An enormous pit erupted in the grass lawn above us. We were below, in the assigned seating. To look back and up on the giant swirl of humanity, moshing, was quite a sight to behold. With the angle of the hill so sharply slanted, it almost looked like a swirling galaxy of people up there, and not much different than the crowd at Buckeye Lake when I saw Anthrax open for the Crüe and lost my shoes in the mud.

Matt had looked bored, so far, though. My love of AIC and the joy and mayhem of Anthrax couldn't move him. He didn't get it. He didn't want to get it.

That, and sometimes he could be a jerk.

I knew what was coming, though. Megadeth exploded the stage with *Hanger 18,* and they felt about twenty-percent louder than the previous two bands. They were ferocious and focused, standing with feet planted on the stage, no "moshing" antics or theatrics or gimmicky showmanship. Just straight, punch-to-the-face headbanging metal, delivered with Dave Mustaine's curled lip and attitude.

This is what finally got Matt's attention. He sat bolt upright, then joined me in standing. He looked at me with eyes wide open and said, *HOLY SHIT—that's tight!!* The look on his face was priceless as he tried to process what he was hearing.

He was totally blown away by Megadeth. He shook his head in disbelief at the guitar playing, and the velocity of the melody. He loved that Mustaine was dressed in a plain white oxford shirt tucked into jeans, with sleeves rolled up and white sweatbands around his wrists as he shredded on his flying v shaped guitar. Mustaine had the music and audience at his command, and as a fellow performer, Matt was impressed, and maybe a little envious. No spandex, no hairspray, no prancing. Just tight, commanding musicianship and a brutal, snarling delivery of the songs. Afterward, Matt gave nothing but praise to Megadeth. Even after touring constantly for the past nine months or so, they were still in top form.

Matt didn't want to stay for Slayer, but I made him watch four songs anyway. Then, I headed backstage to say hello to Ron and Sondra and to thank them for the tickets and passes. Matt waited near the catering area while I went to the production trailer. I found Sondra and Julie Foley, and we talked for a few minutes. Ron wasn't around at the moment—he was in the dressing room with the band right now, which was fine with me. I wasn't sure if I would feel awkward seeing him after the kiss he'd planted on me a few weeks before at the Armored Saint party, or if he'd even remember.

I stayed about 10 minutes before telling the girls that my boyfriend was waiting on me in catering. As we said our goodbyes, we bumped into Rick Sales, Slayer's manager, and Julie briefly introduced me. He was cute, in his late 30's or so, with dark eyes, a goatee, and slicked back black hair in a ponytail with a widow's peak. He was nice, but didn't stay and chat. He'd called the office a few times for Brian, and now I could put a face to his name.

I found Matt and we drove back to LA, listening to Megadeth and Alice in Chains the whole way home.

It had been an amazing couple of weeks.

14.0

[Dragstrip Superstar]

Life with Todd and Doreen at Lanewood Avenue was stressful and chaotic, with sometimes a dozen people sleeping in the apartment. Mercifully, the lease would be up June 1st. Despite looking desperately for an apartment I could afford on my own, I had no luck. After giving up on Hollywood, I started looking in the Valley to be closer to work, but I was running out of time.

Doreen got a place with her boyfriend, and Dale started sleeping for free at the place he worked with Kevin. Matt suggested that I move in with him for a little bit, at least until I could get a plan together and find another roommate. I was grateful and happy that he suggested it, and I moved into his apartment at a complex called Club California, on the corner of Burbank and Colfax, wedged right up against the exit to the 170 freeway in North Hollywood. Everything I owned still fit into the blue Toyota, so I was moved in, all in one trip.

Born in 1962, Matt grew up in a small town in Ohio, fifth amongst 10 kids and raised Catholic. He was obsessed with KISS, and by the time his dad passed when he was 16, he had decided that he wanted to be a musician. He moved over to Columbus and played on the scene regularly. His good friend, Evan, had started a band called Scarlet—full androgynous makeup, a cross between Rocky Horror and Ziggy Stardust, and Matt joined them as they built a huge following and reputation in Columbus and the Midwest.

Ever ambitious, and quite talented, Matt moved to LA in the mid-1980s and started working as a musician. He toured as the guitarist with the pop artist Tiffany, and his own band, The Touch, had won Star Search in 1990. By the time I met him in early 1991, he had two or three different band projects, was doing studio work, and played out on weekends. He had an encyclopedic knowledge of popular music and was very talented as the lead singer and front man. He was funny, sharp, dirty, and engaging with the audience, always playing the part of the Rock Star and a true professional. He took shit from no one when he was on stage. It helped that he was a walking human jukebox.

Still, despite these successes and his obvious talent, he was living in an apartment in North Hollywood with three other guys, and working as a drywall finisher during the day, physical and dirty work. He drove an old red Chevy Blazer, permanently covered in a layer of drywall dust from all his tools and equipment in the back. Almost always, he hauled his four-track recording machine and his acoustic guitar around, as well, stored in garbage bags to protect them from drywall dust. He was constantly writing and demoing songs.

Matt shared the apartment with three other roommates, one of whom moved out when I moved in, and another—my old boyfriend, Johnny. He had been out here a few months longer than me, trying to make it as a front man. It was great to see him and catch up, but now I was living with my new boyfriend, plus an ex-boyfriend. *Good Grief, Anna-Marie.*

Matt and I shared one bedroom and bathroom, and Johnny and the other guy shared the other bed and bath. The apartment was definitely a bachelor pad, but Matt was a fairly clean person and a considerate roommate. There were a lot of tall trees and barbecue pits, and a large clean pool at the complex. I got a spot in the parking garage.

The place was crawling with long hair rocker-types. Strippers and other adult entertainers lounged by the pool in their tiny bikinis, and a good number of augmented breasts were on display, as well as tattoos. I didn't mind, though. I actually felt proud of my natural body compared to the women who'd had theirs altered.

I was 19 years old, 5'6", 118 lbs, size 6, and a size 34B bust. I had a flat belly and a decent bum, narrow hips and broader shoulders, long arms. My hair was wavy, thick and dark brown, almost to my elbows. Matt thought I look like a cross between Linda Ronstadt, Joan Jett, and Susannah Hoffs from the Bangles, and he told me I was beautiful all the time. He praised my body, my breasts, my skin and hair, and was really the first man to tell me any of this, ever, on a regular basis—that I was pretty. It startled me at first, and then I began to understand, to appreciate myself more. I always thought I pretty plain, with a few advantages, and with an enthusiastic commitment to good grooming and mascara, always. I tried to make the most of what I had, but not to the point of silliness.

Matt didn't mind. He loved women, loved my rebelliousness. All his life, Matt had been a notorious womanizer and attention-seeker. He'd slept with multitudes of women, and been in some of the dirtiest rock-star sex scenarios I'd ever heard. He literally had a wall of women—pictures of all the women he'd been with—tacked up on his wall. It seemed he could nail all the women he didn't care about in the dirtiest of ways. It was about the chase, the conquest, the moment.

The women he did care about, though, he couldn't. He couldn't get too close or allow himself to feel those feelings. So, although he gave me lots of attention, and the praise and support I really needed, he couldn't love me in the most basic of ways. He never wanted to be intimate. He held himself back from me. It took me many, many months to realize it, and it crushed me.

But I was still young and always hopeful that he'd change, that he'd be overcome with emotion and pledge his undying love for me, that I'd be the one to settle him down.

So, I moved into his apartment for a bit, and we enjoyed each other's company. I bought myself a few bikinis at Kmart, we sat at the pool on the weekends, and I developed a healthy golden tan. We'd get up in the mornings and walk to 7-11 for coffee. We spent every free moment together, and I attended his rehearsals and shows. We were a couple, and I loved him dearly. He was my closest friend, but something wasn't quite right, and I was still figuring it out.

It was all fine for now, though. I was safe and cozy, but I still needed to find a place to live.

14.1

The Toyota transmission that I paid for with my soul lasted until exactly four days after the 90-day warranty expired. It busted again just as I was turning onto Colfax, right near Matt's, and I had just enough power to do a U-turn and park on the street in front of the apartment complex. I didn't want to garage it. I knew the drill. I knew I was going to have to tow it somewhere. I cursed those transmission guys down on Slauson. Those motherfuckers.

Matt drove me to work at Metal Blade for two days, and co-workers drove me home. I couldn't take it. I hated not having a car. One Saturday afternoon, I asked Matt to drop me off at a used car dealership on Lankershim. There were a few others within walking distance if I couldn't find something at this place.

I found my car right away: a dark blue 1984 Honda Prelude, with a sunroof. It only had 67k miles on it and was in great shape, other than needing a new set of tires. It was priced at $5900.

I filled out the finance application, knowing full well that my dubious credit, maxed out Discover card, and small salary wasn't going to do much for me. I lied outright about the salary on the application, almost tripling it. They told me they'd give me $500 for the Toyota, and I told them they could run my Discover card for up to $500 as well.

I was approved for a $4500 loan, and with $500 down and $500 on trade, I was really close on the price. The sales guy, a greasy-haired, red-nosed alcoholic in his mid-40's who reminded me of the principal from Ferris Bueller, looked desperate for a sale.

"I can't buy the car at $5900," I told him. "The car needs new tires. You can sell me the car for less, and swap me out for a newer set of tires, or I can walk down the road and find another car to buy. It doesn't matter either way because I'm buying a car today."

He left the desk and came back 90 seconds later, done. They pulled my new Honda around to the garage and put on a newer set of tires with better tread while we did paperwork. I handed the guy my Discover card, which he ran over the old-fashioned card-rub machine, with a carbon. It would take them a few days to figure out that I was over my limit, at least. I planned to make a call to Discover the next day, to see if I could get the charge to go through.

I drove away with my new-to-me 1984 Honda Prelude. My payments were $176 a month for three years. I also had to buy insurance for the thing, something I had skated on with the Toyota. It added another $40 to my monthly bills, and my Discover card was maxed out. But still—I just went and bought a car! A really cute car that I loved. Plus, it had air conditioning—a luxury I'd never had in a car I owned.

To celebrate, I drove Matt and I to our favorite Sushi restaurant called Tokyo Delves. We stuffed ourselves silly, did sake bombs and maxed out his credit card, too.

***

The following Monday morning, the dealership called to tell me that I needed to provide proof of income. I panicked for a second, but took their number and told them I'd fax everything over in a bit. No problem, they said.

So, I went to work. I took a few blank Metal Blade check and payroll statements and photocopied them, careful to replace them back in correct sequences. I created a new, current paycheck, and a series of payroll statements with false information, tripling my income and calculating taxes, right from my Macintosh computer. I loaded the printer carefully, using the photocopied checks, making sure everything lined up and that statement numbers and check numbers all made sense.

Then, I faxed the whole packet of false paystubs to the dealership. I told Tracy that she might get a call from the dealership to verify employment and income, and she was great about it. When they did call, she verified everything with the false information for me. She wanted me to keep the car, too.

Finally, the loan was fully approved and Discover didn't reject the charge. The tow truck showed up for the Toyota and I felt nothing but relief that it was finally gone—the car that had plagued me at every turn. My last bit of baggage from Ohio.

Good riddance, you piece of shit.

The new Van Halen record was out, and it cranked up nicely in my new hot little Prelude.

Van Halen. Sunroof. California. It was great to be alive, even if I could barely afford the cost of being there.

14.2

As 1991 unfolded, the LA music scene was ripe with potential, and it felt like the ground was moving beneath us, and not from the few real earthquakes that shook me awake while living at Matt's. Alternative music was bubbling up. Jane's Addiction and the Red Hot Chili Peppers were already on the radio, but hair metal was still relatively popular, with Poison, Slaughter, Bon Jovi and Warrant all selling well.

There was a thriving underground movement in LA with echoes coming down from Seattle. Soundgarden had really started the buzz a couple of years before, and with the success of Alice in Chains, things started turning away from the hair metal, power-ballad formula that LA had been churning out for years. Hair metal and glam, bands that had been the life blood of the Sunset Strip and selling well for a decade, were losing steam. Interest in finding the next Poison shifted into finding the next thing in the pipeline from Seattle. Within a few very short months, hair metal would become irrelevant. Within the year, all but dead, as a genre.

The promiscuous glorification of casual sex went underground, too. The sexism and party-girl "groupie" culture represented in Mötley Crüe's *Girls Girls Girls* became passé, at least on the surface. Within a couple of months, the music industry quickly went from promoting singles like Warrant's *Cherry Pie*, to promoting Alice in Chains' *Man in the Box*.

Bobbi Brown, the model who appeared in the *Cherry Pie* video, was an all-American, girl-next-door representation of womanhood. But with the underground and grunge scene churning, deconstructed women, like Courtney Love, became the new ideal. Sloppy, rebellious, punk, dirty. It was a different mindset, a different aesthetic for my generation of women, and a new way that definitely felt more organic and less plastic.

Meanwhile, the LA scene was brewing up early versions of Nine Inch Nails, Rage Against the Machine, and TOOL. Smashing Pumpkins were a new "buzz" band. Piercings, tattoos, goth, tribal, and fetish dressing all became the norm.

Seattle came roaring, with albums by Soundgarden, Pearl Jam, and Nirvana all in the pipeline on major labels, and all of them gigging around LA while in various stages of recording, production or promotion. LA was crawling with goth bands and punk bands and a few shockers, too, like Green Jelly, Duchess Du Sade, and Haunted Garage. The LA scene was a magnificent stew of metal, punk, alternative, and now this "grunge" that seemed to blend all of it together with a touch of folk—it was an amazing mix of bands, so many on the verge of hugeness. It was evolving quickly into a new underground, more authentic, more dangerous, less concerned about image than the hair band era.

And the Seattle influence was largely responsible for it. We just thought Seattle was filled with a bunch of depressed metalheads making interesting music, and I imagined the movie *The Rivers Edge* as what it was like up there. We didn't imagine the sea-change that was coming.

14.3

Brian, already having signed a few bands with very questionable gore content, like Cannibal Corpse and GWAR, went ahead and signed Haunted Garage. They released their record, *Possession Park*, on August 1, 1991. The guys in the band were a cross between geek-normal to full cross-dressing drag. The lead singer, Dukey Flyswatter, well known for his B-movie acting roles and scripts, often attached mousetraps to his face and stuck himself with safety pins and rubbed himself down with blood and whatever else he could find. He donned a G-string and mounted a fat-vibrating machine onstage, splattering the audience with slime, blood, and mannequin parts while faking orgasms.

Not quite as silly as GWAR with their monster costumes, or as hardcore as GG Allin—no pooping on stage—Haunted Garage was notorious for the gore and silly horror movie style shows and bizarre humor and sex. Lots of sex. Two dancers—the Gore-Gore Girls—

in bondage with electrical tape on their nipples, were a regular feature at their shows. One of the dancers was Mistress Barb, front woman for her own sex-shock band, Duchess De Sade. She and Dukey were in a relationship, and they reminded me of the Addams Family.

Going to a Haunted Garage show was an experience in itself, but it was Duchess De Sade that really impressed me. I'd never seen anything like it. Part rock show, part performance art, part public sex acts, part strip tease, Mistress Barb was a master at commanding an audience with her dominatrix-style show. Blow up dolls, dildos, strap-ons, domination, submission, bondage, and whips—all part of the lineup.

This open display of tongue-in-cheek sexuality and vulgar sex acts didn't bother me nearly as much as what I had witnessed my two nights serving drinks at the 7th Veil the previous year. The Duchess Du Sade was shocking, and empowering, and super funny, even. The women were in charge on stage, half naked and ordering men around and whipping them into submission, penetrating them. It was hilarious and shocking. The strippers at the 7th Veil were not like this, not this empowered. They were desperate and drugged out. There was nothing funny or silly about their situation. Nothing funny about them at all.

14.4

While hair metal withered on the vine and Grunge didn't have a name yet and Gun's N Roses were still huge, thrash metal was doing pretty well, carving out its own meaty genre. It was going mainstream. Albums by Megadeth, Anthrax, and Slayer were all selling well, and there was huge hype and a lot of anticipation regarding the newest Metallica record.

They recorded the album in North Hollywood, on Lankershim near my favorite sushi restaurant, Tokyo Delves. Brian visited the studio a few times to hang with the guys and hear the new material. He hinted that it had been a difficult album to make, and that there was major friction going on with the band. When he got the advance copy by courier, he took it straight to his office and closed the door. A few minutes later, he called Tracy and I in to join him and we sat on the black leather sofa in his office and listened to most of it through his premium sound system and big speakers. It shook all of the framed albums hanging on the walls.

It was a great album, heavy and melodic, but I had mixed emotions about it. It was definitely Metallica, but playing more radio-friendly music. The songs were solid, and so polished. It felt like the rounded edge of a sharp corner, a little safer than their previous albums. The production was large and warmer than I'd heard before. I liked it. Mostly.

Brian kept saying it: "This album is going to be huge."

It would be known as the Black Album. We had no idea.

14.5

Things were going well for me at Metal Blade as the summer progressed. Brian was a good boss, friendly and not too picky on things. The only quirk he had was that he hated using anything but black pens. So, I made sure to only order black pens for him. I got to know his routines and expectations, and I was learning about record deals and publishing rights and budgets and contracts with artists.

While Brian was pretty easy to work with, Bill the Attorney was a little more challenging. He kept me on my toes as he handed me corrected contracts to retype on the MacIntosh. Although I practiced, I was still a timid, peckish typist at best, and he reminded me of that often. Plus, my hands shook from nerves when he'd stand there, supervising my mediocrity.

He wasn't cruel, but he wasn't ever overly kind to me, either. He often said things that would complement my intellect on one hand, and then insult my abilities with the other.

"You're a smart girl. Did you fail typing?" he asked me one day. He was always very direct. I appreciated that about a person, but sometimes it stung.

"Actually," I said, "I received a D. I barely graduated high school," I confessed. It didn't seem right to tell him why I almost didn't graduate. It is what it is. I'd been a shitty student, and I was a shitty typist and that was that.

He looked at me with a straight deadpan gaze and said, "Well, that's hard to believe. You'll need to know how to type well if you ever want to go to college. You'll have to write papers, and they'll need to be typed."

"Yeah, I know," I said. "I'm not really sure if I could make it in college. I've thought about community college, but I don't know."

"Look, you're smart enough to go to college. To a real college. You could go to USC, or UCLA. You'd be fine. You just need to type faster. And the only way to learn to type faster is to actually type. So, I need to get these contracts revised and back out by courier later today."

"OK, got it. I'll go as fast as I can," I said to him.

College. I hadn't thought about college in a while. That he even thought I was smart enough to go to "real" college made me stop and think. Maybe he was right. Maybe I should look into going to college. To do something with myself. I was a 19-year old receptionist, and I had no plan. I didn't even know what I would study.

As the weeks wore on at Metal Blade, I would type out letters and send them to my friends and to my mom, so that I could practice my typing. My mom loved getting my letters and notes, and our correspondence picked up quite a bit once I made the effort.

One letter to my mom described an amazing dream I had about a beautiful blonde-haired, brown-eyed baby girl. It was such a vivid, loving dream, I knew it was my future daughter. I hoped I would be a good mom, someday. I wanted a husband, an education, a happy life. I wanted to feel "normal" whatever that meant. I didn't want to struggle like my mom had struggled. I didn't want to keep struggling, at all.

And somehow, through sheer force of will and having Bill the Attorney literally breathing down my neck for months on end to type faster—I started typing much, much faster.

14.6

August of 1991 wore on, and Armored Saint was on the road. Fates Warning was in the studio, recording their next album, and I was busy helping Brian and Tracy do whatever it was they needed to do. I went to a lot of shows, did a lot of errands, drove band members around town, picked up lunches, booked hotels and flights for Brian on his many travels.

It was nice to finally have a decent little car to buzz around in, although I was still living at Matt's apartment, sharing the place with 3 men. I was starting to get antsy and annoyed at the whole situation, especially when I found out that Matt was still talking to his ex-girlfriend. I needed to find a way out of the situation.

Brian and I were chatting one afternoon and I mentioned that I was looking for a roommate. He paused and looked at me, "Oh, really? You should talk to my girlfriend, Karen. She wants to move to the Valley, and she's super-cool." I was flattered that he'd suggest it, and it was the first real lead I'd had on a potential roommate, so I took him up on his offer.

I already knew Karen's voice because she called in for Brian on occasion, and we were always friendly on the phone. Brian gave her a heads up, so when I called her about the possible roommate situation, it wasn't completely awkward.

We agreed to meet at Jerry's Deli, in Tarzana, on a Saturday afternoon.

She was tiny and blonde with big brown eyes and a great smile. We hit it off immediately and slid into a booth to get to know each other a bit. I liked her, instantly.

She was currently working at DHL, the shipping company, but had been interviewing for jobs in the music business, she told me. Raised mostly in Colorado, she'd come to LA a few years prior. Like me, she was also a shy singer with a great voice who loved heavy metal. And, like me, she'd discovered quickly that she was not a performer.

Ironically, just after high school, she had attended The Recording Workshop, of all the backwoods places to know about in Ohio. I'd gone there a few times with my first boyfriend to record his demo tapes. While she was there, she'd met and become good friends with a guy named John Marshall. He was in a band called Metal Church, and was a roadie for Metallica. He would go on to fill in on guitar for James Hetfield on the Master of Puppets tour, when James broke his arm skateboarding. He was on the bus when it crashed in Sweden and Cliff Burton died.

She was a huge metalhead, and she knew her stuff. She and Brian seemed like a perfect match to me. They'd been dating for about a year, meeting at a Faith No More show at a music industry event. She was able to keep up with Brian through her love of Slayer, Iron Maiden, Metallica, and, surprisingly, Kings X—a favorite of Brian's, and a band I also loved. She was also a huge Armored Saint fan.

Karen was looking to move to the Valley as she was currently commuting over the hill, from Hollywood to Burbank, for her job. As we continued the conversation, we both agreed on what we were looking for: a two-bed/two-bath apartment in an OK area somewhere in the Valley for as little money as possible.

I order a $9 baked potato, which seemed obscene to me, but it was just about the cheapest thing on the menu, and it came loaded with bacon and veggies, so I went for it. Jerry's Deli was known for its enormous portions; the potato was so monstrous I took half of it home and ate it for breakfast the next day.

I mentioned something about being a frugal Virgo, and she said, "Yeah, I'm a Virgo, too! I'm the 14th, when are you?"

Shocked, I look at her in astonishment. "No way!" I pulled out my driver's license and showed her.

She was four years older than me, but we were both born on September 14. I'd never in my life met my birthday twin, and neither had she. We knew it was meant to be, a cosmic sign from the Universe. We agreed on that fact, immediately.

It was all set. We liked each other. We were going to be roommates. I had just met a soul-sister, who happened to be my birthday twin, and who would end up being one of my very best friends, ever.

Karen and I started searching for an apartment that weekend, and after tromping all over Studio City and Van Nuys looking at shitty, expensive apartments, we found a moderately OK shitty apartment that we could afford in North Hollywood, just north of Victory, between Laurel Canyon and Lankershim, at 6545 N Simpson. It was right near the FM Station, the famous Valley metal club, and it was only blocks away from where I had worked for the Armenians the summer before, which seemed like a lifetime ago.

It was an upstairs apartment in a courtyard-style complex, with a pool at one end. The apartment we looked at had been recently renovated—all new carpet, paint, and blinds. Both bedrooms were a decent size, one with a small bathroom attached. It was bright, airy, and very clean, and only $650/month. There were trees all around, and it was an easy commute for both of us. The neighborhood wasn't great, but it wasn't awful, either.

It was good enough.

The landlord was an older lady named Flora. She had some kind of Germanic accent, bleached blond hair, a bad tan, and wore flowered caftans, almost like Mrs. Roper from Three's Company, with a little Green Acres thrown in. She smoked brown cigarettes, and her own small apartment was a yellowing, dank mess of paperwork and overflowing ashtrays and macramé art.

It was all pretty casual, getting the apartment. She took our deposit and first month's checks, got us all hooked up with a one-year lease, gave us the clickers and the keys and it was done. I don't know if she even checked our credit. Karen and I moved in around September 1st, and Brian and Matt both helped us carry the heavy stuff up our stairs.

I finally had a place with my own room. It had taken me more than a year of bad roommates and couch surfing, but I finally had my own room. I was so grateful for my own space. I had a nice small closet with a mirrored door, and a bathroom in the hallway, just steps away. My bedroom window looked out into trees, and sunlight dappled everything and the birds chirped me awake in the morning. It was very peaceful. Aside from a few midnight police helicopters, the complex was fairly quiet, and I had gated parking for my Honda.

Karen found a used fridge, and then splurged and bought a sofa and loveseat. We hardly had anything between the two of us, but she was making a bit more money since starting at Caroline Records, and she had a small savings account. She also had an old TV that I rigged up with paperclips and tin foil, just like I did when I was a kid on our old TVs. Once in a while, we'd actually turn it on and watch a show.

Karen and I became great friends. We had a similar sense of humor and we made each other laugh. There was no such thing as too much information with us—we talk about every damn thing. When she wasn't with Brian and I wasn't with Matt, we hung out and got to know each other really well. She was easy to live with, and a lot of fun. A person of substance and ethics, of her own mind, with her own quirks and preferences. To this day, she is one of the deepest, funniest people I've ever met.

I had my futon and some milk crates for my bedroom. I found an old upholstered chair and a small wooden dresser at a Goodwill, and I put up a few free posters on the wall. I bought a cut glass Victorian lamp at Kmart for my bedside, along with some new sheets, pillows, and a quilt. It was a cozy, pretty little bedroom. It had taken me more than a year of living rough with multiple people, and in dubious situations, but I finally had my own little place with a friend. Our own little North Hollywood girl-nest, up in the trees.

15.0

[Danger]

September 5, 1991

Karen had started a new job at Caroline Records just a couple of weeks before, and had scored a single ticket to the MTV Video Music Awards up at the Universal Amphitheater. Brian had two tickets as well, so they asked if I wanted to tag along and use the extra seat. Brian's tickets were down on the floor; Karen's ticket was up in the balcony. It sounded like a cool thing to check out and I was glad they asked me. I didn't mind being the third wheel with my boss and my roommate.

We inched our way through traffic up to the parking garage and made it into the venue. We agreed to meet up back at the same spot in the lobby after the show, and I climbed the stairs to the balcony.

I picked my way over to my seat and settled in. The view of the stage wasn't too bad. A man approached and sat in the seat next to me, and upon looking him full in the face, I realized that I was sitting next to the infamous Dr. Frankenfurter, Tim Curry, from *The Rocky Horror Picture Show*. I couldn't believe my luck.

I smiled and said hello in a non-weirdo way—at least I tried. He looked at me and smiled thinly and didn't return the greeting. He ignored me for the rest of the show while I side-glanced his profile from time to time.

It was Dr. Frankenfurter! I'd seen the Rocky Horror Picture Show dozens of times.

The VMA's went long, and were being hosted by Arsenio Hall. Some of my favorite bands were performing—Metallica, Queensrÿche, Van Halen. I was super stoked for Prince since I'd always been a fan. Even Guns N' Roses were broadcasting a song from Wembly Arena, in London. All of these acts and artists were monuments of talent.

And then, there was Poison. I'll admit to a very brief infatuation with them when they first came out in the mid-80s, when I was 14 or so. A real novelty. They were SO pretty and had catchy, teeny-bop rock—a little more dangerous than Duran Duran—just as I was making the transition into loving metal, before hearing Motorhead, Mötley Crüe, and Metallica.

Poison had a slot at the awards show, which turned into a debacle when C.C. DeVille forgot which song they were supposed to play, and played *Talk Dirty to Me*, instead. To top it off, C.C. played as shitty as I've ever heard anyone play a guitar in my life. At first, I thought there was something wrong with the sound system, but then I realized C.C. DeVille was just playing out of tune, and wildly sloppy.

His guitar even came unplugged, of all the rookie mistakes to make at a big awards show. To their credit, the other three members of Poison managed to pull it off and finish the song, but you could sense the tension as they faked their way through having a good time.

They were professional about it, but I felt embarrassed for them. They had always come across as nice people, with a good work ethic. But times were changing for music. Things were going darker, harder.

In my mind, I'd just witnessed the death of hair metal. Right there, on that stage at the VMA's, at that moment, hair metal was dead. Irrelevant. Not worthy of any more attention.

Without meaning to, and in a flash, C.C. DeVille's mistake seemed to change everything. All the other acts that night were performing their hits off recent successful albums—Van Halen played *Poundcake*, Metallica, *Enter Sandman,* Queensrÿche, *Silent Lucidity*. Poison played a weak, thin, five-year old song—like they were already a nostalgia act.

And right there, that night, they became one.

Poison bumbled themselves off stage, and were followed immediately by Van Halen, who sounded tight and bright and heavy, as a real band should, and with Eddie's amazing playing. It was my first time ever seeing them in a live setting, and I was stoked. One song, they were great. They made Poison look all the worse.

Metallica was a real punch in the face with *Enter Sandman*—you could feel the fire in their belly. Arsenio Hall looked a little stunned after their performance.

But the thing that really stood out—aside from sitting next to Dr. Frankenfurter and watching Poison blow it for a whole genre of music—was Prince's appearance. He gave a sexy, homo-erotic performance in a yellow, lacey, ass-less suit. It was an amazing set. He pushed the envelope with his outfit and his performance. His perfect little butt was beautiful onstage.

I stood on my feet and cheered for Prince, and then I accidentally stepped on Dr. Frankenfurter's foot as he stood up and cheered for Prince, too.

15.1

After moving out of Matt's and into my new little place with Karen, Matt and I were still seeing each other, but a little less frequently because of his schedule. In addition to working his day job, he was playing in a few different bands and gigging a lot.

Our birthdays were approaching, with Matt's birthday the same weekend. When I assumed that we'd be going out to celebrate together, he became a bit evasive and told me he'd already made plans with friends a few months ago. He was sorry we couldn't spend our birthday weekend together.

I was surprised and hurt, although I had no logical reason to be.

A day later, he told me the truth of it: he was taking his ex-girlfriend to a Don Henley concert. Not only that, but the show was up north, and he was driving to Santa Barbara with her and spending the weekend there at a bed n' breakfast.

I was stunned. I appreciated him telling me the truth, and told him that I understood, even though I was deeply hurt. He couldn't even have sex with me, how was he able to do it with her? But the truth was that he still had feelings for her. He still loved her very much.

I felt not good enough, like I was a failure. Would I ever be good enough? No man had ever put me first. It was always other women, music, their own interests—everything else first.

I tried to play it cool, though. I didn't want to bust his balls over it—there was some part of me that tried to keep my dignity. I didn't need to know why. He was human and not perfect. I did love him as a person, and I knew he loved me as a person and maybe that was the best we could do. He still had an obvious, deep connection to his ex-girlfriend. I didn't need to hear a big explanation. Just as my mom always, always told me: *Actions speak louder than words.* I felt a little foolish being so attached to him.

Karen was going out of town with Brian for her (our shared) birthday, on a trip to go see a hockey game, which Karen wasn't thrilled with—Brian thought it was the perfect gift, Karen did not, but was too polite to tell him going to a hockey game for her birthday wasn't all that special. They went to hockey games all the time. But off to Sacramento they went.

So, I had the apartment to myself. The nights were cooling off, and I was on my own in the city for my birthday weekend. I was looking forward to the alone time—true alone time, nesting in my own space. I'd done it since I was a kid, to snuggle in and read books and relax.

It's like a holiday! I told Tracy at work on Friday, and once she realized that I was going to spend my birthday all alone, she insisted on taking me out to dinner on Saturday, my actual birthday. I'd been at Metal Blade for almost six months by now, and Tracy always looked out for me and treated me like family. She and Joey included me in a lot of stuff, and it was fun to hang out and go to shows with them.

Tracy and Joey picked me up and we drove over to El Compadre on Sunset, where I ordered a plate of chicken enchiladas rancheros style. My very favorite.

I ordered a margarita, too. On the rocks, extra salt. The margaritas at El Compadre were set ablaze and arrived at the table with a flame on a little slice of lime that held a few drops of Tequila as fuel. It's quite the fun spectacle, A strong devil's brew, and absolutely delicious.

Tracy and Joey smiled and said, "Make a wish!" when it arrived.

"Thank you, guys. I hope my 20th year is as awesome as my 19th," I said.

I blew out the flame. Tracy and Joey clapped and wish me *Happy Birthday!* The mariachi band was playing a jovial tune in the other part of the restaurant.

The flame died and I licked the rim of the glass to get some extra salt on my tongue. I raised the glass and took two big, delicious gulps of the margarita. It was super sweet, sour, salty—the tequila almost choking me, the sexy tingle hitting my belly immediately.

Hello, 20! I thought, as I swallowed the warmth, the delicious fire. It burned my throat all the way down, and I liked it.

15.2

Early October, 1991

October was often warmer than June in Los Angeles, and the hot devil winds had started to blow. The light had changed, shadows were longer. It felt like autumn, but the Santa Ana's made it feel like summer again, even down near the airport, right next to the ocean.

Metal Blade was one of the co-sponsors for the Foundations Forum, a trade conference specifically geared toward heavy metal music. Industry professionals, bands, managers, marketers, gear companies—everyone converged upon the Airport Marriot near LAX to network, share, listen, commiserate, and to do business.

It really was an amazing concept, all these metalheads uniting.

The Foundations Forum conference was like some kind of Mothership, calling the metalheads home. Everyone was there.

Me and a bunch of other Metal Blade staff set up a booth and transported merchandise. The Metal Blade office was on a skeleton crew while everyone attended the conference on various days. I was at the conference all three days and got to see a bunch of live performances and was able to sit in and listen to a few of the panel discussions. There was a lot to learn about the music industry.

We all took turns staffing the booth, and we had arranged for various Metal Blade bands to be there to sell albums and sign autographs. One of the bands had a new album out and the singer and I started flirting a bit. His name was Tony.

Later, he and I met up for drinks in the lobby of the hotel. As we were sitting there, Brian came up to the lounge area and joined us. He plopped down in one of the big comfy seats and started talking to Tony, totally not noticing our vibe at all, which was a really good thing. He chatted our ear off about the day. We touched base about a few things that needed done at the office.

Brian heard that Pantera was over in a private area of the bar and asked us if we wanted to go say hi to them. Tony knew the guys from his Texas days, so I tagged along and got to meet Phil and Dime. I was the only girl there, and sat for about 15 minutes as I listened to them shoot the shit.

Even though no one said it, I was definitely the third wheel after a bit. As soon as the talk veered off toward pussy and tits, I stood up and made as graceful an exit as possible. I could tell Brian was embarrassed, but there was nothing to do about it.

"Guy talk! I'll see you guys later," I said to Brian and Tony. No one was trying to be a dick, and I wasn't offended. They were just a bunch of drunk Texas boys, doing shots and having fun. Brian was a good guy to me, and didn't ever talk that way at all. Brian was always respectful.

I left the rockers to schmooze amongst themselves.

It had been a long, long day, getting down to the hotel at 8am to set up and haul boxes, walking around. By 4pm we'd all started having drinks because we still had to get through the evening of shows, dinner, parties, and socializing. By this time, 9pm, we were all pretty hammered. I wandered off and found Tracy and Joey and a few other Metal Blade people out at the pool.

Tracy and Joey were actually in the pool floating around and drinking beer. They had booked a room at the hotel so they wouldn't have to do all the driving across town. They had finally come out to Brian about their romance, and the people who knew were super happy for them.

After a minute of chatting, with my boots off and my feet in the water on the edge of the pool, they urged me to join them.

"Get in! It feels great! There are extra towels!" they said. It looked so peaceful. The water was warm. The air was warm. The palm trees above us were being blown sideways by the devil wind, but down here surrounded by the hotel, the pool was calm and serene and balmy.

I'd worn black underwear that day so it didn't look much different than a bathing suit, especially in the darkness. So what if I had to drive all the way back to the

Valley without any panties or bra? I'd still have a dry shirt and jeans. I piled my hair on top of my head and fixed it with the pony-tail holder that was always around my wrist.

I stripped down to my underwear in front of my friends and got in the pool. We floated and talked, moved over to the bubbling hot tub for a bit, and we were joined by a few others, including Tony, who I sat next to and flirted with as I drank my last Corona.

I drove home, exhausted and slightly buzzed, after midnight, warm, damp, and naked under my dry clothes. I rolled the windows down to feel the Santa Anas on my body as I made my way north on the 405. There is something wild and primitive about that hot devil wind from the desert. It was exotic and relaxing on my bones.

I'd never felt anything like it before, and it felt divine. Holy, even.

15.3

At the conference the next day, Tony asked me out on a date. He had tickets for RIP Magazine's fifth anniversary party, and it was happening just a few days later. I was super-stoked to go with him. An actual date with a cute singer in a respected band.

I told Brian that Tony had invited me to go to the party, but that it was just as friends, of course. I didn't want it to be weird if he found out, or if we ran into him there. He understood—Tony was in town, had tickets, needed someone to go with, didn't know a lot of people. I had a car and could drive him. It was no big deal and we were just friends. Plus, I was technically still calling Matt my boyfriend, which he still kind of was.

First though, Tony and I had dinner at El Compadre, no surprise. It was the go-to place if you were in Hollywood and wanted a cool, low-key scene, and good heavy Mexican food. The place was crawling with rockers and other famous people.

We made our way to the Hollywood Palladium. I drank my typical cranberry vodka, and then Spinal Tap (the actual Spinal Tap!) came out and did a song. I'm pretty sure I spotted Angelyne in the crowd, standing out like a hot pink angel in the darkness and gloom of the grunge crowd. Angelyne. The beautiful mystery girl who was famous for nothing but her suggestive billboards and her pink corvette spotted driving around town, like she was bestowing blessings on the city, a saint of LA.

Alice in Chains, Soundgarden, Pearl Jam, and Temple of the Dog were on the bill that night. It was a big Seattle meteor that streaked across Los Angeles that night, and killed the Hair metal dinosaurs dead in their faux-cowboy boots and femme-masculinity and power-ballad mediocrity.

15.4

The night of RIP Magazine's 5th Anniversary party and show, everything changed. This was a new scene, and it was powerful.

There was an authenticity to the music that appealed directly to my sensibility. We were witnessing the birth of Grunge. It had been brewing in Seattle for a few years, and there was a buzz on certain bands for sure—but we had no idea what we were seeing or what was to come. We got a big taste of it that night.

I'd been into Alice in Chains for a year now, since Frank at Top Rock had given me the tape. I was a huge fan of this darker, tuned down, flannel music. Metalheads from Seattle—that is what it all seemed like to me.

During most of the 80s, metal was considered metal and it was a big umbrella. RATT was metal, Mötley Crüe was metal, Posion was metal, just like Iron Maiden, Black Sabbath, or Motorhead were considered metal.

The heavier stuff—thrash metal—had its own, more underground scene, but really came into its own success with what would be known in the future as the "Big Four" (Metallica, Megadeth, Slayer, Anthrax), all releasing commercially successful albums in 1990-1991. Although still selling records, the spandex and hairspray bands seemed frivolous. The free-spirited, worry-free 1980s were over, the good times gone.

Just a month after the RIP party, Magic Johnson would announce that he had HIV, and Freddy Mercury of Queen would die of AIDS. We were at war in Iraq, and in a recession. Combat boots and flannel matched the mood of the country.

By late 1991 the Los Angeles music scene was much different than the spandex and hairspray Sunset Strip crowd of even the year before, when I'd first arrived. It shifted so quickly. This was when what we know as "hair metal" split off and died a bloody death on a power ballad sword.

No pretty boys here, except for maybe Chris Cornell of Soundgarden, who was one of the handsomest men I'd ever seen. I just stared at him in wonderment. His physique. His face. The hair. THAT VOICE. He was an amazing performer.

And then there was Tony. He was pretty damn cute, too. I don't think my boyfriend or my boss would imagine that I'd take Tony home and sleep with him that night, but I did. It was great—tender, sweet, awkward, intimate. We made love to candles in front of my mirrored closet doors and slept with our long hair entwined on my granny pillows until the birds woke us at dawn.

15.5

Christmas approached, and my parents had sent me a plane ticket to visit Ohio. After attending the Metal Blade Christmas party at a bowling alley on Ventura, Brian drove me down to LAX himself. I flew home on a red-eye, and missed LA for the entire six days I was gone.

Matt was with his ex-girlfriend again, so Tracy and Joey invited me to spend New Year's Eve with them. Tracy was still living in Hollywood, right near El Compadre, and her roommate was out of town. Spending a night in, with friends, sounded perfect.

They had also invited John Bush, and it would be the four of us. They both pleaded innocent to a setup, but did mention that they thought John and I should get to know each other. I was a little nervous, but once the alcohol started flowing, all bets were off.

We made a huge batch of homemade guacamole and other appetizers, and we ate and drank and laughed the night away. We turned on the TV to watch the ball fall in Times Square, and we kissed all around when it hit midnight. We stayed up and drank and talked for the first two hours of 1992.

Finally—there wasn't much discussion—there was no way I could drive home. I was pretty hammered—we all were. Tracy and Joey went to her room to crash, so John and I found our way to her roommate's bed, where we both took our pants off and crawled under someone else's sheets. We were too drunk to care. We made out for a few minutes, and then we passed out, and slept until 9am.

John didn't live far from me in the Valley, so I drove him home straight over the hill on New Year's day, and we stopped and had breakfast at a diner on Laurel Canyon. We were both rough from the night before, but it was good to hang out, sober, one on one for a little bit longer. I really liked John, but I didn't want to lose my job at Metal Blade.

We stayed friends for many, many more years after that, and he was always a decent and fun guy to hang out with.

15.6

Life at our apartment in the Valley was cozy and homey, and Karen often travelled with Brian on the weekends, so I had the place to myself much of the time. Our complex was quiet, and there was a nice male kitty that roamed freely and said hello to me almost every day.

I'd even bought a small bag of cat chow for him, for when he'd come up our stairs to visit. He'd meow, I'd let him in, we'd cuddle up and hang out for an hour or two. He'd rub on me and purr, have a meal, then he'd go back to the door and ask to be let out. It was great having a part-time cat. I didn't mind if he was using me.

He had great social skills. Karen wasn't a huge cat person, so I'd only let him in if she wasn't there.

Mr. Kitty greeted me at the laundry room early one cloudy Saturday morning as I was getting my two loads into the machines before the Saturday laundry rush.

I noticed a commotion going on at an upstairs apartment, one that overlooked the pool. As I walked back to my apartment, I ran into Flora the landlord, who looked a little flustered.

"Hey Flora, what's going on?" I asked her.

"She didn't pay rent and has disappeared," she said with her accent, gesturing with her hands. "The police have already been here to take report. We cleaning out her apartment so I can rent again. You come up and look? Maybe something you want?"

Curious, I went up with my empty laundry basket to have a look-see around the apartment. In speaking with Flora further, I realized that this apartment belonged to the tiny chick with the spiky blonde hair, whom I'd said hello to a few times in passing at the complex. I knew she was a dancer or stripper of some kind, or maybe a prostitute, just by her outfits—big boobs, spandex, platform heels, glitter makeup. But she was always genuinely friendly the few times we'd exchanged greetings. She drove a little blue Nissan Pulsar, and it was still parked in her parking spot, gathering dust a few spaces away from my Honda.

Her apartment was musty and stale. Messy, a crash pad, with clothes strewn everywhere. It had been six weeks, and two missed rent payments, since Flora had seen her. Dirty dishes in the kitchen sink, the small window above it slightly open. I saw an empty cat dish, filled with dust, and then I noticed Mr. Kitty had followed me into the apartment. I wondered if he was her cat? He sure seemed comfortable here. I noticed that the small kitchen window was propped open just wide enough for him to squeeze through. Maybe he had been coming and going, waiting for her to return.

I was looking for practical treasure—antiques, heirlooms, jewelry, kitchen equipment, even bedding and towels in decent shape, all of these I would have taken. I was also kind of looking for clues. Why had she disappeared?

Unfortunately, her apartment had been picked over already, and what was left wasn't much. I poked through a few things and found nothing I felt comfortable taking. Tiny spandex outfits hanging on old bent hangers. Scuffed stripper stiletto's, size 6, too small for me. Rusty razors in the shower. A stained and sagging mattress. She hadn't been a rich woman. Even the canned food in her cupboard was not worth taking.

I turned around to leave, and then my eyes fell upon a bookshelf in the corner. A wicker bookshelf with an arched top and rosette curlicues, circa 1974. It stood there like an old soldier, leaning slightly to the right under the weight of the all the treasure. Row after row of astrology books, spiritual books, pagans, witchcraft, all kinds of esoterica. An Aleister Crowley book. My heart skipped a beat. *Look at all the books!* Holy shit.

"Flora! I want all of these books. I'm going to take them!" I called to her.

"Take them!" she said. "Otherwise they go in dumpster. Take them all!"

So, I hustled. I didn't do any sorting. I just piled the books in my clothes basket, and hoofed them down the stairs, around the pool, all the way down to our apartment, up our stairs, and into my bedroom.

I humped over four laundry baskets of books to my bedroom, and then I went back for the bookshelf. I piled all the books up on the floor in my room. It was a huge pile. I wanted to go through them, and they needed dusted off. I couldn't believe my good fortune—I had an instant library of esoteric books, on subjects I'd been fascinated with since I was a child.

I fought the urge to roll in them, like a pig in the mud.

I spent the next few days going through all of these magical books. I found her name inscribed in most of them:

Claire Elizabeth Bolton, scrawled in cursive—loopy, old fashioned, and somewhat childlike. It sounded so classical, a writer's name, or a name that sounded like it belonged in English literature. It didn't sound like a stripper's name.

Regardless, she had been a reader, for sure. A curious reader with an open mind that pondered the mysteries. Just like me.

Where are you, Claire? I thought to myself as I paged through the collection.

I found receipts in the various books. Most of them had been bought new from the same bookstore in Portland, Maine, many years ago. Whoever she was, she was a long way from home.

Those first few nights with the books beside my bed, I slept an uneasy sleep. I started dreaming a stunningly visual dream about Claire Elizabeth Bolton. I woke up sweating and upset, feeling that she had been murdered, and that her body was laying on concrete, somewhere near a freeway and the LA River. The dream was like some kind of alternate reality, like I had been there and seen it.

This thought bugged me so much for a few days that I went and talked to Flora to get the name of the detective she'd talked to. It was she who had filed the police report. Flora suspected foul play right away—that something wasn't right with Claire just disappearing and not paying rent. She'd been living there for years.

I called the detective and explained that I had these receipts from these books, and they all indicated that she was from Maine. He sounded very interested and said he'd follow up to see if they could find her, or any family in that area. He took my name and phone number and said he'd be in touch if he needed more information.

A few days after that, I got home to my apartment to a voicemail to call the detective. I dialed the number and got him directly.

He said, "I wanted you to know that we found Claire."

I asked if she was OK?

He said, "No, she is deceased. They found her body near the LA river a few weeks ago, and she had been waiting at the morgue for an ID. But we were able to find her family in Maine."

My skin tingled and I got teary. I was really sorry to hear it. *That poor woman.* It was a punch in the gut, knowing that I had already dreamed this outcome. I thought of the Black Dahlia, laying in a field, mutilated.

People—young women—came to this city from everywhere, and sometimes they went missing. Sometimes the price of living here would actually cost you your life. This city did not fuck around.

Los Angeles felt heavy to me then, dangerous, like a burden I almost couldn't bear.

I've kept her books with me since then. They came to me for protection, I feel. They move where I move. I will always be connected to those books. In some strange way, Claire and I know each other, and have some kind of soul contract.

She gave me her library, and she seeded an idea about books, and it was she who made me aware that I might have this ability to know things. It explained a lot about my childhood, always feeling different, my fascination with the supernatural, magic, psychics, mysteries. My visions and dreams have happened my whole life, and they still happen on a regular basis.

Claire. Her very name means light, clarity, and it's exactly what she did for me.

Somehow, through this dead woman's library, I found a life line to my future.

16.0
[FAKE]

February 14, 1992.

It was the rainiest February in 50 years in Los Angeles.

My little Honda sat low, and the flooded streets of Los Angeles crept up right to the pop-up headlights. I drove to work slowly down Ventura in awful traffic, absolutely sure I was going to stall the engine in high water, and that I'd have walk to work in the rain. I'd brought dry clothes in a plastic bag, just in case. Helicopters were rescuing people stranded in the flood waters, and the Metal Blade offices were about a mile away from the Sepulveda Basin where this was all happening.

It was also Valentine's Day, and Brian's birthday. I managed to swing by a Ralph's on the way in to work to buy a birthday cake for him from the office, and a few supplies for his surprise birthday party, happening later that night.

In addition to planning for the surprise party, it was a busy couple of days for everyone. Metallica was playing the Forum, and the guys in Cannibal Corpse were stopping by the office for a few hours before heading out to their show in Riverside.

It was Karen's idea to throw a surprise party for Brian. She truly wanted to show him how many people appreciated and loved him, and when she asked me to help plan it, I didn't hesitate to jump in. We both worked for weeks contacting people, aligning schedules, and pulling it all together for this party. Karen had even travelled to a Metallica show in Sacramento the month before, and with a little help from Byron at Capitol Records, she was able to get backstage to ask James and Lars in person if they would come to the birthday party while they were in town for their shows at the LA Forum.

Of course, they agreed. Lars was one of his oldest friends, and James, too. They wouldn't miss it, they said. By this time, they had been on a continuous tour in support of the Black Album since August. Just like Brian predicted, it was a huge success. The tour would continue for another year, including the upcoming stadium tour with Guns N' Roses.

So, with all that happening later, first I had to get through the crazy rainy day. I made it to the office and parked my car on a flooded street, making a mental note of the time so that I'd remember to come out and move my car in two hours, just in case. I hauled the cake and a bag full of party supplies a couple of blocks through the rain to the office building. I was drenched. I cleaned myself up as best I could and fixed my makeup. It was going to be a long day, and I'd be meeting rock stars.

I set up the conference room for lunch, set out the cake and drinks and utensils, and when the Corpse guys arrived, I took everyone's lunch order and had it delivered while they met with Brian and got to visit with everyone in the Metal Blade office.

Although I met all the Corpse guys, I really only remember Chris Barnes. He had deep blue eyes, nice teeth and an angular jaw. A thick head of dark hair. He was pretty cute, even if his music scared the shit out of me, and I couldn't quite reconcile it within myself. I was working for a label that was promoting a type of art that I couldn't even pretend to like. Still, they were all very nice, normal guys, and my personal feelings weren't part of the deal. This was just business.

We all ate lunch together, the staff and the band, and I don't remember much about the lunch other than it involved pita bread. What was most memorable was the birthday cake I'd hauled through the rain.

We sang happy birthday to Brian, and Chris Barnes sang it "normal style" and didn't growl. When I went to cut the cake, my fingers slipped and I ended up with cake icing all over my thumb and two fingers and knuckles as I tried to get a slice of it onto a paper plate.

Chris Barnes was standing right next to me. He grabbed my hand and inspected it for a moment, smiling. Then he raised my hand to his lips and sucked the icing off. He wiggled his tongue on the webbing between my fingers, and licked my knuckles clean. He stared at me the whole time he did it.

Whoa, I thought. *That was fucking sexy.* And in front of my boss and coworkers, even. I felt a little tingle in my nether parts. My goodness, Chris Barnes.

He pronounced me delicious and asked Brian if he could have a bigger piece.

The double innuendo made us all laugh, me a little nervously. I joked around the best I could—*my fingers aren't very meaty, especially to a cannibal.* Or something like that.

I didn't know if he was boyfriend material or not, but after that interaction, he would call into the office and we'd talk for 15 minutes before I'd patch him through to Brian. We kept in touch for a while, even later into the year, but getting to know him a bit, I couldn't reconcile it in my heart. Even just the thought of sleeping with him—sleeping with a guy who sang about raping dead babies and eviscerating live women—I just couldn't get past it. I don't think I can get vulnerable with a person who even *thinks* those things, much less makes music about it.

But that momentary human to human tingle? Looking into his eyes as he tongued my fingers? That momentary sexual spark? That's a feeling I'll always treasure.

16.1

Karen had come up with a plan to get Brian to leave the office a little early so we could launch the surprise party plan. So, I left a little early, too—made it home to change again and fix myself up. I loaded up coolers and went to another Ralph's to buy ice, beer, and water. Had either of us had any kind of budget we would have had a proper bar, but we were catering it ourselves, and we managed to get a couple of platters of Subway subs, soda, water, beer, and big bowls of potato chips.

She had booked a recording studio in Burbank, of all things. The story she came up with, as they made their way through her false evening plans, was that she told him the Mighty Mighty Bosstones were recording at this studio, and that she had been invited to stop by. Brian balked a little at first, but loved the Bosstones, so he relented and walked into the studio right on time and just as planned.

It was like a Who's Who of Metal Blade artists and friends—a great big reunion. Lizzy Borden, Betsy Bitch, Armored Saint, Metallica; Rick Sales, Slayer's manager; Bill Metoyer, the legendary record producer and an overall awesome guy, and a bunch of others. As all these people started to arrive, I made sure to have everyone "hide" in one part of the studio. We had a good crowd going when Karen and Brian showed up; when I hit the lights, everyone jumped out and yelled surprise, just like an old-fashioned surprise party should be.

Brian was completely floored and genuinely shocked. He kept thanking me, throughout the whole night. I couldn't believe that we pulled it off.

We all mixed and mingled, and at one point, as we were standing around talking with about four people, James Hetfield walked up and joined us. He introduced himself to me directly, and shook my hand, and was just charming and sweet, a gentleman. His Leo light shone bright—he seemed to radiate warmth and humanity. We had a few laughs, making me all warm and fuzzy from our relaxing and enjoyable 10 minutes of conversation. He was tall, earnest, and he was actually handsome—something I had never noticed as a fan, from afar. He had the kindest, sparkly eyes and a genuine smile.

Jason Newsted, on the other hand, must have had a bad night, because he treated me like the hired help (which, in actuality, I was) when we ran out of bottled water. He was intense, and just a little bit sharp with me. But I didn't hold it against him; I'm sure he was tired from touring on the Black album almost nonstop for six months. I know it's mentally taxing. I get it. It had been Brian who recommended Jason to the guys in Metallica. I wasn't about to take any grumpiness from him too personally and get myself in trouble.

Lars was his usual self, the life of the party, the gift of gab and humor and story, all energy, in the center of things. Kirk Hammett was more reserved, lurking in corners and having personal conversations, kind of how

I remembered him from the time I saw him chatting with Glenn Danzig at a Hollywood club when I had first moved to LA.

As the party continued, I met Rick again, Slayer's manager, and we hit it off right away once we started really chatting at the party. By the end of the evening, he told me that I absolutely *had* to go out to dinner with him, and I agreed. Although he was an attractive man and financially secure, I liked him because there was no bullshit. He liked me, I liked him, we were going to go out on a proper date, and that was that. He was almost 40, I was 20.

I invited him back to my apartment in North Hollywood after Brian's party, where we rolled around and made out for a while. I wouldn't sleep with him though. I told him he'd at least have to buy me dinner, first.

A couple of nights later, he did.

16.2

Right before I started seeing Rick, I had also been getting friendly with a guy who did contract work for the label. Troy was based out of New York. After months of talking to him on the phone and faxing each other stupid jokes, he finally came out and told me he really wanted to meet me.

He sent me a plane ticket to NYC so I could fly to him for a long weekend. He picked me up at LaGuardia in person, and we spent time being tourists. We ate dim sum in Chinatown, sushi uptown, went to the World Trade Center to go the observation deck, took a horse-drawn carriage through Central Park. It was my first time in NYC, and it was magnificent and overwhelming. We took the train to and from his place in Queens, and I thought that there was just no way I could live in a city like New York. I loved a lot of things about it, for sure, but it was far too crowded for me. I loved wide-open spaces and big sky. Even LA was beginning to feel too crowded.

Troy told me he loved me after that weekend. He was arranging to be transferred to Los Angeles so that we could start really seeing each other. I really liked him—he was tall, educated, funny, and very considerate. We made love twice that weekend, and he literally had the largest penis of any man I'd ever met in my life

Because of this, the sex was awkward and painful. I thought to myself, *could I ever get used to this?* I mean, good lord—what a penis. I wasn't sure if it was a reward or a curse. Is it weird to reject a man because his penis is too big? Did we have real chemistry, or was I just flattered at the attention? I wasn't quite sure about any of it, except for the fact that our bodies did not fit together comfortably.

But he told me he loved me. He told me he was IN love with me. *We will figure it out when I get to LA,* he said. After the trip, of course, our contact dwindled down, until it was purely professional again.

I can only wonder. I met Rick a few weeks later, so it didn't really matter.

By the time Troy did move to LA, two months later, I found out that he'd been having a romance with another chick at Metal Blade the entire time that he and I were in contact, including during my trip to NYC.

He'd been playing both of us. I was a little creeped out by the whole thing, but somehow, I wasn't surprised. He was a world-class bullshitter. I should've known.

It had been a great first trip to New York City, anyway.

I'd never had dim-sum before.

16.3

Dating Rick for a few months really spoiled me in some ways. He was a gentleman, a conversationalist, and very worldly. He drove a gold Corvette and lived in West LA, and was always in pursuit of a good bottle of wine. He fretted about his weight, although I thought he looked great—he wasn't heavy at all, a solid guy just on the brink of middle age. I loved his goatee and his ponytail. We made a cute couple, despite the age difference.

Matt and I were still close, and we still went out, although I was beginning to understand that I was never going to be the one. My interest in other men was fueled mostly by feeling rejected, emotionally and sexually, by Matt. I still called him my boyfriend, but I knew something wasn't right. I knew he loved me, but only as much as he could love me.

Rick treated me like a precious thing—he always made sure I was comfortable and we would talk, really talk. I broke out with a couple of pimples on my face, and he was so concerned after hearing my cheap regime of Dove soap and Oil of Olay lotion, that he took me to Nordstrom to buy me a new, expensive routine. He wanted to get me the good stuff. He told me to shop while we were there, *spend some of my money!* he urged. He wasn't filthy rich, but he could support himself in style. A few hundred bucks wasn't a big deal to him.

It was hard for me to accept his generosity. It was fine if he paid for meals and shows and travel—those felt ok to me. Much of it was related to his business as a band manager. But having him buy me makeup and clothes made me feel weird.

Despite feeling weird, this one time, I let him buy me the skincare stuff, plus a new expensive lip gloss. My one pair of good jeans were getting threadbare, so I picked out a new pair of Levi's. Then a pretty white, ruffled blouse to go with it. That was it, about $150 total. It was about what I would have spent on myself in one trip, had I had any money to indulge.

I think he was surprised that I didn't go hog wild. I was super grateful that he wanted to take care of me, to indulge me, but I'd never not paid my own way.

I'd never in my life just "gone shopping" and not worried about the price of things or had a budget. I bought much of my wardrobe from Kmart and the used clothing stores down on Melrose. I honestly couldn't remember the last brand-new pair of jeans I had. I could get them in good shape for $6-8, used. To pay $40 for a brand-new pair of Levi's at full retail price was obscene to me, a complete indulgence.

Of course, I told him all of this as we were finishing up at the register.

Rick didn't bat an eye. He pulled out his Gold AMEX card and handed it to the clerk, smiling at me, shaking his head.

"Relax, sweetie, this is no big deal. Just enjoy it for a minute, OK? It really is my pleasure." He patted my hand. "Now, should we do Italian or Thai tonight? Let's go down to the Promenade and shop some more. We'll get dinner down there."

More than any other thing, I always loved a man who would feed me.

16.4

There had been historic rains for weeks and weeks, on into March of 1992. It seemed like it lasted forever, the gloom and flooding in Los Angeles. The recession continued, and the music industry was in turmoil. All of a sudden, Grunge was it, and labels were dropping metal acts, reorganizing departments and looking for the next Nirvana.

Metal Blade had a contract with Warner Brothers Records to promote and distribute four bands: GWAR, the Goo Goo Dolls, Armored Saint, and Fates Warning, but there were meetings and no one was sure what would happen if the agreement wasn't renewed.

Brian's door had been closed more, and I knew that if the Warner contract was ending, there would be some financial implications for Metal Blade. Warner had wanted GWAR to tone down some of their act, and Brian wasn't about to go along with it.

Everything was moving toward something other than the metal we had known up to this point. Labels were nervous about metal. While smaller labels like Metal Blade, Megaforce, Earache, and Roadrunner handled the more extreme metal niches, the big labels had fat rosters of hair metal bands, which were more commercially viable. But as soon as grunge started taking off, the big labels pivoted hard and pruned those rosters ruthlessly. Some really great bands got thrown in the dustbin.

The underground LA scene was bubbling over with talent and breaking out, too, almost paving the way for the Seattle scene. Janes Addiction and The Red Hot Chili Peppers were starting to enjoy mainstream success. A band called Stone Temple Pilots was causing a buzz with their upcoming record. Rage Against the Machine was in the studio. TOOL had just been signed.

My friend Kevin Amici's band, Bad Reputation, had all kinds of label interest, especially at Warner, but were passed over for Green Day, instead. Rick was managing an awesome band called The Electric Love Hogs, whom I loved.

I tried to ignore Nirvana, but I heard *Nevermind* while driving with Tracy and Joey to a show, and then I understood. They gained big steam in early 1992. Soundgarden was amazing, and the Smashing Pumpkins were also pushing this new alternative/grunge wave.

Warner Brothers had signed a band called LSD—Life, Sex, Death—who had a singer named Homeless Stanley. No one was sure that he was really homeless and mentally ill, but he really did seem like it.

If he was faking it, he was "in character" the whole time, complete with abhorrent body odor and filthy clothes, natty gross hair, rotting teeth, stories of pooping or masturbating in public. He would wander the audience before their shows and make people uncomfortable—because they thought it was a stinky homeless guy and didn't know it was the singer of the band they were there to see.

I'm pretty sure he was faking it, though, because once you saw the band perform live, he was absolutely brilliant as a front man. I was totally blown away. The band had some great songs.

There was rumor that he came from old Chicago money and chose to live this way and that "Stanley" was performance art, a social experiment, and a purposeful gimmick. He came to the Metal Blade office one day with some Warner executives to meet Brian, and he communicated in grunts.

As if Cannibal Corpse weren't extreme enough, only in Los Angeles would a record label sign a homeless person—fake or not—in order to make money.

17.0

[Don't Go Away Mad]

As the music industry made this momentous shift during a nasty recession, we were all keeping up with the Rodney King police trial. It was coming to a conclusion, and speculation of civil unrest was all over the news.

Understanding what happened to Rodney King, and why these policemen were on trial, made me kind of sick to my stomach. I'd never really paid attention to how black folks were treated. I didn't realize that people were still racist, or that cops might be quicker to use force on black men. I didn't understand any of it because I never saw it. I was in a bubble of whiteness, I guess. I had watched *Good Times* and *The Jeffersons* and *The Cosby Show* at various times as a kid and black folks didn't seem any different than me or my mom. My mom had always mixed and mingled with black people. My old boss, Earlene, had been like a second mother to me, a huge role model. She'd never let on to me that things were different for her as a black woman.

I had never perceived that, despite our Constitution and the Civil Rights movement, some people were still viewed as less equal than others. How the law was applied was different for people of color, it seemed. As I learned about the Rodney King trial, I began to understand. There was absolutely no denying the power of that video, that what happened to him was so, so wrong.

Listening to news updates one morning on the way to work, I flipped the channel to Howard Stern as he announced that Sam Kinison had died in a car accident out in the desert. I remembered my first night in LA, sitting in The Rainbow across from him watching him hold court and do a mini-performance. It was a painful death on a lonely desert road.

Stern dedicated a good part of the show to talking about and remembering Kinison, playing his interviews and bits, talking to his friends. He'd been a fixture on the Strip for years, and was friends with all the rockers on the scene.

His death felt like it marked the end of an era. The age of the "Wild Thing" video was gone. There was a turning away from what we had known. Some kind of reckoning. The City of Los Angeles was on edge. A collective sadness at the news of his death, and tense with the speculation about the Rodney King police trial.

You could feel it in the air, all the heaviness.

17.1

Friday, April 24th, 1992.

I had a weird feeling when I arrived to work at the Metal Blade office that day. Around 10am, I was called upstairs and into Mike Faley's office. He told me he was really sorry, but they had to let me go, that things took a turn for the worst with the Warner deal, and the label had to cut non-essential positions in order to survive.

I'd seen some of the budgets and numbers at times. I knew the label had to lean up. The entire industry was in upheaval, and we all knew it. Mike handed me my last paycheck, plus a one-month severance. I really wished Brian had been the one to tell me, but I also understood—despite whatever personal affection he might have felt for me, this was just business. The whole thing was awkward because I was still roommates with Karen and they were still dating.

Three other people were let go at Metal Blade that day, too. I wasn't surprised. I'm sure Brian was super-bummed that he had to lay people off. No business person wants to do that.

It had been an amazing experience, and an honor.

As I packed my boxes of things, Tracy came out of her office to ask if we were still on for dinner and drinks that night.

Of course. It was Joey's 29th birthday. I wouldn't miss it. We were on for a date at El Compadre, where I proceeded to get drunk on shots of Tequila and a couple of flaming margaritas.

Tracy and Joey bought my dinner, consoled me as best they could, and got me home safely that night. I was now, officially, unemployed.

Tracy had explained that it was nothing that I did—that I had been a great employee and that it was really hard for Brian, that it was purely a cutback to survive. Karen confirmed it all, and she was crushed that she had known and couldn't warn me out of loyalty to Brian, but I understood. I knew it was hard for her. It hurt, but I got it. I loved her like a sister. It seemed that this was a "Black Friday" type of day across the music industry—we all knew of others at different labels that were now looking for jobs. One of the trade magazines mentioned it as a shift in the music industry.

Still, I was optimistic about finding something else. I knew a few people who had leads. I was going to call

Errol. Rick needed to talk to an accountant buddy of his, and also told me to call Lonn Friend over at RIP Magazine—maybe he'd know of some leads. I had enough money to float for a month. I decided I was going to go get a few applications and do retail again, or to temp around if I had to.

17.2

Five days later, on Wednesday, April 29, the Rodney King Police trial verdict was announced to pandemonium: NOT Guilty.

As news of the verdict spread, the City erupted in riots. Although we felt relatively safe out in North Hollywood, we were sticking close to home and not venturing far. Curfew was declared as fires raged on for days over the hill. Mobs of angry people took to the streets, smashing and looting and marauding. I was in shock as I watched the news coverage. I'd had no idea that people were this angry—that they'd sacrifice their own neighborhoods and communities and their own basic humanity to show their outrage. It was stunning to me.

Watching the footage of poor Reginald Denny getting his head bashed in—it was the sickest feeling I've ever felt, the ugliness of what was happening. I suppressed the crazy urge to get in my car and go try to rescue that poor man, but from the looks of it, I'd die trying. He had suffered such a grievous injury, and it was in real time, it was raw and unedited and happening just a few miles away over the hill, and I felt powerless and trapped. I was unemployed, and trapped in a city that no longer felt safe.

Watching people loot stores made me realize that I had no food in the apartment, so I prayed the news reports were correct—that there were no signs of rioting in the Valley—and I made a quick dash over to the grocery store on Laurel Canyon. I bought just a few things: milk, coffee, bread, butter, apples, a couple of frozen dinners. Just enough to get through the weekend as the City was going into a lockdown mode. As I went to check out, a black lady arrived just behind me in line. She had a small child with her, and had just two things: Bread and milk.

"Hey, you go," I nodded to her. "You've only got a couple of things."

She looked me in the eye and smiled. "Thank you. I really appreciate it."

The little boy smiled at me, and I winked at him. He might have been four or five, so tiny and innocent. I wanted to hug him, but I didn't.

They stepped ahead of me and the transaction was quick. As she finished paying, she turned and made it a point to say to me, "You take care, now." She smiled at me as she said it. No animosity, no hatred. Just one human to another, one small moment of understanding.

"Thank you, I will. You too."

I got back to my apartment to turn on our old TV for more updates on the riots.

I saw the Reginald Denny footage again, and then I broke down and cried.

17.3

Saturday, May 2nd, 1992

A few days later, in a fit of rebellious cabin fever, Karen and I broke the city-wide curfew and drove ourselves in her little white Honda CR-X down Laurel Canyon all the way from our apartment up at Victory, over the hill, past Mario's, down to Sunset, and across to The Rainbow Bar & Grill. We'd been cooped up all day, trying to lay low while the City simmered around us. But now, jailbreak. It had been a while since I'd been to The Rainbow, and when Karen suggested an adventure, I was in.

The traffic was sparse the whole way over, and I felt conspicuous—there were no people on the roads. Sunset Blvd. was completely dead—shocking for a Saturday night. We traveled slow and steady, and amazingly, we didn't see one cop. We weren't even sure if The Rainbow would be open, but the signs were on and everything was lit up. We parked ourselves on Sunset, right in front the restaurant. It was surreal, the city feeling deserted, like a ghost town.

Pops was at the door, and he greeted us warmly. I was pretty sure he didn't remember me, and I left it like that. He told us they had a table available, no waiting, which was a first, and he walked us to the table and sat us himself. He looked happy to have customers.

We were surrounded by a small tribe of famous musicians and executives. It was not packed like all the other times I had been there. The mood was low key, but jovial. The waitresses were lively and the drinks were flowing, and I ordered my typical cranberry vodka. I spotted Lemmy in a booth. A guy who looked like Slash was sitting nearby, but I couldn't confirm if it was him or not. Byron Hontas. from Capital Records was there, and he sat with us for a drink while we caught up. I'd first met him when I worked for Errol, and he had helped us out with Brian's birthday party. I told him I was looking for work, and he said it was tough out there, but that he'd keep his ears open for me.

Karen and I nestled into the warm booth, into the pink lights and shadows, and marveled at the luck of finding The Rainbow open, and getting a table so quickly—it was a real treat not having to deal with the crowds of people. I sipped my favorite drink, and ordered my favorite dinner: the house salad with red wine vinaigrette, and the fluffy cheese ravioli in a light, rich marinara, dusted with parmesan cheese. It was absolutely delicious, and I sopped up the sauce with a piece of bread.

After dinner, Karen and I drank our cinnamon coffee and sat in a bubble of peace and comfort. While the city Los Angeles burned around us, we felt like we were in a different world, our own special mellow moment in time at The Rainbow, during a very, very strange time, indeed.

17.4

Over the next two weeks, the city reeled from the riots and tried to recover, and all my job prospects seemed to dry up. Retail was in a dismal state. I couldn't even get an interview at Tower Records. No mall jobs. I put my name in at a temp agency, but they had nothing worth the effort—a receptionist job in Huntington Beach wasn't going to cut it. I'd lose money by commuting. Fast food was beginning to look like a reality. I wasn't sure I could survive on minimum wage. My money was dwindling, and so were my options. The city was burning, and I was wracked with worry.

And, finally, I realized that I was also heartbroken. Los Angeles was a lover that seemed to fail me at every turn. It was heavy and sad and I felt a certain sense of betrayal. Maybe I didn't really belong here. Trying to scratch out a living and the indignities and challenges and dealing with the damned Parking Mafia.

For all the awesome things that had happened to me, it came at a price, a price I wasn't sure I could pay anymore.

As I came to terms with all of these things, I knew in my heart what I had to do, how to end the struggle. The thought of it, although sad, was also sweet relief.

It was time to leave.

I needed to get away from LA. I decided to drive home to Ohio. I called my mom, talked to Karen, said goodbye to Matt, and talked to Rick. Two days later, I packed up my little Prelude and pointed it east.

I was done here. I was done with worry. I was done with men. I was done struggling to survive in a City that broke my heart.

I was done with Los Angeles, and I was pretty sure that Los Angeles was done with me.

18.0

[Kickstart My Heart]

Eleven Years Later...

May 2003, Los Angeles

I was as nervous as I had ever been in my life.

I was standing in a low, gray classroom on the north side of UCLA's campus, getting ready to present my graduate-school portfolio to an audience of my professors and peers. I was at the front of the room, waiting to begin, fidgeting with my outline, making sure the projector was hooked up correctly. Cotton-mouthed and clammy, I'd always had stage fright and today was no different.

Soon after leaving LA the first time, broke and brokenhearted, I had moved back to Ohio and met my husband—the first short-haired guy I'd ever dated. West was where my heart was, so we moved to Arizona in 1995. After working several crappy sales and customer-service jobs—and even with my bad high-school transcripts—I managed to get accepted to Arizona State University at the age of 25 on academic probation. I graduated four years later with honors.

It was my husband who suggested going to library school, getting a master's degree, and becoming a librarian. I loved books, and I was always at the library anyways, he pointed out. Of course, it should have been so obvious, but it wasn't, not until he said something. Plus, what else was I going to do with a Medieval history degree? It was a degree of indulgence, rather than practicality.

UCLA had a great library science program, and so I applied. It was the only program I tried for, and they took me. I was thrilled to move back to Los Angeles. I'd wanted another chance in LA, this time on my terms. I felt right at home in the city. I knew my way around, reconnected with my old metal friends, and enjoyed being a graduate student.

Librarianship was close enough to perfect in terms of a career. If I was lucky, I'd get a job that I enjoyed, with a good pension. I'd never get rich, but solid middle class was OK with me. My entire life had been spent struggling financially. Solid middle class, to me, was like winning the goddamn lottery.

And now I was getting ready to finish my master's degree—something that had, at one point, seemed impossible. Sometimes, it still felt foreign to me, like I was living in an alternate reality, or someone else's life. All of the things that had brought me to this point—books and heavy metal and adventure and rebellion and synchronicity and magical thinking—were things that I had trouble explaining to normal people.

Normal people, like my professors and classmates at UCLA, most of whom definitely weren't metalheads.

Somehow, I'd made it this far, and now I had to present a factual and original analysis and narrative of what I had learned at UCLA, and of what I could offer to the field of library and information science.

Everything I had worked for, every sacrifice I'd made and risk that I'd taken, every great concert I'd seen and rock star I'd met—and every shitty job I'd worked along the way—all of it came down to this One Thing.

So much was on the line. My hopes and dreams, all the effort of the past 6 years to get through school. *If I bomb this presentation I am really fucked*, I thought to myself.

18.1

The focus of the presentation was intellectual freedom, free speech, and censorship.

My heart flip-flopped in my chest. *Fuck. Here goes.* I took a deep breath and brought up my first PowerPoint slide on the overhead.

It was the album cover of Mötley Crüe's *Shout at The Devil*, complete with a pentagram and the inside spread showing the band members, looking demonic. Of the three academic advisors sitting in front of me, two of them leaned away and crossed their arms primly. But one, the younger guy from the UK, a PhD hipster with a beard and a lovely accent, leaned in toward me.

Is he a metalhead? I wondered to myself. He suddenly looked interested in what I had to say. With this tiny bit of positive body language acting as my only encouragement, I focused on him and dove straight into my material.

I explained some of the events in the mid-1980s that led to the creation of an organization called the Parent's Music Resource Center—the PMRC. Billed as a type of consumer protection agency, they sought to identify and label heavy metal and other "explicit" forms of music. Whether it be album art or graphic lyrics, sticker labels and categories were implemented to warn consumers—i.e. parents—about explicit content contained there within. Because it was the pet project of a senator's wife—our future Second Lady, Tipper Gore—it had some clout and funding behind it, and there were hearings in Washington about creating industry-standard ratings for music. It ignited a huge debate in the country about artistic freedom and the First Amendment.

My next slide was of Frank Zappa. My PhD Hipster Professor started nodding his head.

I was 14 years old when those hearings in Washington began in 1985. Zappa testified, as well as folk-music legend John Denver, and Dee Snider of heavy rock band, Twisted Sister. They were three musicians with entirely different styles of music, all speaking on behalf of artistic freedom and the First Amendment.

"This is where the seeds of my future career as a librarian were sown," I explained to the audience.

I told them that I had watched all the testimony and read news articles as the PMRC hearings unfolded in real time. Some of the testimony was really juicy, thought provoking, and hilariously funny—like when Tipper Gore stated that song *Under the Blade* by Twisted Sister was describing deviant sadomasochistic acts, while Dee Snider smugly rebutted that it was really a song about the fear of surgery, and that the only sadomasochism was in the mind of Mrs. Gore.

The PMRC sought to censor some of my favorite music, and because these musicians came together and fought back, actually testified to Congress—I was personally compelled to explore the concepts and boundaries of the First Amendment and what it actually meant.

It was the FIRST amendment because it was the most important thing, the thing upon which our republic was based. Without absolute freedom of speech, there was no freedom.

"The principles of free speech and intellectual freedom have been important to me ever since I learned what it meant from the PMRC hearings." I could see my audience processing my words.

There were a few more slides to show—album covers, including one of Guns N' Roses' *Appetite for Destruction*, Queensrÿche's *Operation Mindcrime*, and Megadeth's *Peace Sells...but Who's Buying?* albums—all best sellers, all my favorites, all showcasing these artists at their peak abilities.

I continued on, hoping I wasn't losing them. Heavy metal and librarianship? I wasn't sure anyone had ever made the connection, although just about every serious metalhead I knew was also a book-lover. Like the hipster professor on my panel.

"Each of these albums documented American culture in real time," I explained. "No different than literature." I described why each album was groundbreaking or controversial, and that, like books, this form of free speech ought to be protected and defended with much vigor.

My Hipster Professor friend was smiling and engaged as I worked my way through the point I was making, which was: that on a very personal level, my own love for marginalized, controversial music helped me understand what art was, what free intellectual inquiry meant, the parallels between art, music, literature, film and how only absolute free speech should be the standard for any healthy democracy. No Thought Police. Censorship was for dictators and despots. Libraries and librarians were an important part of defending the First

Amendment and ensuring access to ideas and information, to story and to history.

As for more controversy, I went on and mentioned the various lawsuits, such as those filed against Ozzy Osborne and Judas Priest regarding fans who had, or had attempted, to commit suicide. The lawsuits directly blamed the lyrics and artists for their content, saying that either hidden messages (known as backward masking) or the very words themselves, had caused people to take these suicidal actions.

It's no secret that some forms of heavy metal have strong occult or Satanic imagery—think Gene Simmons of KISS dressed as The Demon, spitting blood, or the song "Highway to Hell" by AC/DC—as well as a mixed bag of blatant sexual messaging, some misogyny, long-haired men either trying to dominate women with muscles and bravado, or trying to look like women, in spandex, lipstick, and scarves. Either way, promiscuity ruled.

Often, bands glorified open drug use and death. Newer artists pushed the envelope further with controversial stage shows that used imagery of violence and war in their stage shows. I showed them a slide of Marilyn Manson, and I mentioned how he had been targeted as partially responsible for the Columbine massacre because one of the shooters was, allegedly, a fan.

Being a fan heavy metal could be dangerous, too—the three kids known as the West Memphis Three were currently sitting on death row, and one of them, Damien Echols, happened to be a metalhead. The music he liked was used against him in trial, the prosecution implying that, by liking heavy metal music and wearing black clothing, he was a sadistic, child-killing Satanist. (Those three kids, the WM3, were eventually released.)

So, there was real controversy regarding heavy metal music, and widespread bias against it. It was outside the mainstream, and these bands and their fans were constantly questioned, made fun of, marginalized, and sometimes attacked in the press.

However, in all the cases I mentioned the artists weren't directly responsible in any way—in a court of law or otherwise. In a free society, each individual is responsible for their own behavior and choices.

So far, my audience was engaged and I wasn't losing them. I finally unclenched a little and took a sip of water.

Despite its bad reputation, my experiences as a metalhead had been good. I explained that, like libraries, heavy metal had been a very positive force in my life. Books were my escape, my babysitter while my mom worked, and rock and heavy metal music had been like the father I didn't have—a masculine force. It was the thing that gave me some backbone in the world—the courage to literally Shout at the Devil. It was a release for the aggression that I felt, but couldn't act on.

Like many who gravitate toward library work and books, I've always considered myself an introvert. Books were my gateway and guide, while heavy music encouraged my individuality and to take chances on my dreams. Heavy metal felt like a safe haven to me. It was the music of my generation, Generation X. Some of the finest musicians in the world were playing in heavy metal bands. It was music made by people like me, for people like me.

Metalheads were my tribe—the underdogs, the introverts, the marginalized, the misfits, the book lovers, the nerds, the feelers. The brothers and sisters I didn't have growing up as an only child.

I only mentioned it once, my belief in magic. That my specific love of heavy metal music and my life-long love of books had not only been my refuge as a young person, but had made me believe in the type of magical thinking—of possibility, overcoming the odds, of making my own luck—that had led me to Los Angeles as a teenager, and back here to UCLA as an adult to complete my education.

I was a welfare kid and a bad student and I had gone out and earned a master's degree. I wasn't supposed to be here, I told them, but I owed it all to heavy metal and books, and now, to student loans, I joked.

My audience chuckled.

This next part was the kicker. A deep breath. *Fuck. Here goes.* I was either going to blow it all or nail it with this section of the presentation.

My last slide was the album cover to Cannibal Corpse's *Butchered at Birth*. The illustration depicts a woman being eviscerated by two skinless ghouls, who are lifting a bloody fetus out of her corpse to add to the collection of lifeless babies hanging behind them. It's a graphic and shocking image, beyond decency. As a woman, it made me very uncomfortable.

The energy in the room shifted immediately, and I could tell people were uncomfortable with it, too, which is what I expected.

I explained to the room that shortly after I moved to Los Angeles when I was 18, I started working at the record company that had released this very album. I had worked with the band, had helped with publicity, and kept tabs on the controversy for my boss.

Although this album was banned in Germany, and its cover censored in various ways, Cannibal Corpse went on to become the biggest selling death metal band of all time up to this point, with over a million albums sold for Metal Blade Records. They were pioneers in the genre, and had spawned many, many copycat bands.

I told them the images were personally horrifying to me, that when I originally saw the art proofs for the album, I couldn't believe it. I couldn't believe any of it would be released. And then I heard the music, and I truly thought it was a joke. I was shocked that it could be called music.

But I guess that was the whole point of it. It was designed to push the boundaries and shock people.

My old boss, Brian Slagel, thought it was great. I mean, it was just an illustrated cartoon and really heavy riffs and gory lyrics, right? He was absolutely, 100%, pro artistic freedom. He'd walked away from deals—like the one at Warner Bros.—that had asked him or any of his label roster to censor themselves, and it was ultimately why he downsized the label.

He was willing to take the hit, and cut a few positions rather than voluntarily censor the content of the artists on his label for money. Brian Slagel had given platform to music and entertainment that wouldn't otherwise have made it to market—and he was immensely successful with this strategy

But, I confessed to my audience, I still felt weird about this particular album and the band, and that I had to make a choice as a younger person whether it was right, morally right, for me to even work at Metal Blade Records.

What I didn't tell them was that Cannibal Corpse was a negative, dark energy that weighed heavy on my heart. I believe that thoughts are things, that we attract what we put out, and I really didn't want this type of weird misogynistic death-energy around me, because I didn't understand it. I couldn't understand how people liked this music or the art. It commercialized and normalized torture and violence against women.

Even if they were cartoon zombie women. Not real women. Fictional women, extremely illustrated and lyricized.

I tried hard to rationalize these feelings away, and I never quite could. Misogyny lurked all throughout metal music, but as a whole it wasn't too bad or too extreme, and some of it was downright silly.

Mostly, I thought heavy metal celebrated and glorified women, and I was mostly OK with it all.

Then, there was Cannibal Corpse.

I told my audience that I had met this band, and they were seemingly normal people—but *Meathook Sodomy* and *Rancid Amputation* were actual titles of songs, I explained to them, hoping I wasn't horrifying my audience too much.

It's also really fucking funny, I thought to myself. *I just said 'meathook sodomy' to a room full of librarians with a straight face, God help me.*

The only redeeming thing about the band, I told them, was that they made money for the record label. People actually bought this stuff, on purpose.

We were, indeed, living in a free society.

The guys in the band were just dudes from Buffalo with girlfriend problems and car payments. They weren't monsters. They were pushing boundaries of entertainment and doing something different. The band explained that they were writing fictional short horror stories, set to music. I could relate to that one point alone, really. That this was fiction, all the violence and gore—it was not real.

But was it art? Even though I didn't like it, it didn't matter. It was still protected under the First Amendment, just like Larry Flynt's right to publish hardcore pornographic pictures in *Hustler*, or your right to read the *Satanic Bible* or *Mein Kampf*.

My former boss knew all this, he knew there would be controversy, and because of it, he knew there would be a market for Cannibal Corpse. He signed the band to a multi-album contract and placed a stake in their future, and they'd sold a lot of records by indie standards. It was entertainment, and it was OK either way: If you wanted to, you could buy it. And if you didn't want to, no one could force you. You had the freedom to choose.

There didn't need to be any kind of censorship and labeling: in this case the band's name, the artwork, and the album title actually served as the warning sticker. There was no ambiguity. You knew exactly what you were buying when you bought a Cannibal Corpse album: Brutal, heavy, guttural, scary music.

I also had to come to terms with my own personal feelings that two opposite things could be true at the same time. I had to reconcile that good people, like my old boss and the guys in this band, could create and promote ideas that were offensive to me. And that, even if I didn't like it, I had to defend it from government censorship.

I had to reconcile that in the United States, people have that right, the right to make art or publish pictures, to write books or to play music that pushes boundaries and offends people. This is what artists are *supposed* to do. This is true freedom, freedom of expression. This is rebellion against tyranny and groupthink. This is how cultures evolve—it seeps in from the margins. Free people can inform themselves and choose what they like and don't like. Artists can express themselves without fear.

And librarians, we protect access to all this, to ideas and culture, including heavy metal culture. We defend free speech—even if it isn't popular speech—from the Thought Police. We provide a level playing ground to marginalized people—whether it be from poverty, or because of race, or because of the music they like, or the God they worship, or other prejudices inherent in any society. We encourage freedom of thought and transparency and civil discussion about difficult topics. We help foster an informed citizenry for self-governance, the basis of democracy itself.

I understood all these principles in real life terms, as a young fan of heavy metal music, as an employee at Metal Blade Records, as a book lover and curious person, as an American, as the granddaughter of immigrants who fled fascism, grateful for the absolute freedom I had in choosing what to read and what to listen to and who to vote for.

"This is why I'm going to be an excellent librarian," I told the panel.

I understood because I had been a disadvantaged kid and I knew how important books and libraries had been to me. Because, despite its bad reputation, I loved heavy metal music, which gave me courage to believe in myself and to pursue my dreams. It helped me know that anything is possible if you take action toward it. And most of all, because I was actually living the American dream, right this very moment, rising above my circumstances and taking my education further than I ever thought possible.

And with all that laid before them, I was done with my presentation. I paused and took a deep breath.

I thanked the audience for their support and friendship throughout the program, and in true metalhead fashion, Ronnie James Dio style—although I had learned it from Mama, my Sicilian grandmother—I threw a set of devil horns to conclude my presentation.

The room exploded. My normally quiet librarian friends burst into applause and cheers, with a few rowdy woo-hoo's thrown in that jolted me straight into tears. No one held back. Waves of gratitude and relief as they clapped for me, for longer than I expected. I dabbed my eyes a bit, not believing it. I'd made it. I was alive. I was done. A friend had brought me a small bouquet of pretty flowers and I clutched them like a gracious diva.

I wasn't fucked after all. *Sweet baby Jesus*. In fact, I'd fucking nailed it.

The academic advisors were smiling at me. They went on to ask me a few questions about my work in the written portion of my portfolio. They enjoyed the way I had presented everything and had tied together my real-life experiences and interests with my coursework. They complimented me on the quality of the written papers and summaries I'd included in the portfolio and I took it all as a good sign.

As my time at the front of the room came to a close, the Hipster Professor told me he was impressed. He asked me the last questions, specifically about heavy metal—the bands I liked, and how I had ended up at Metal Blade Records in the first place. He was a Mötley Crüe fan, and wanted to know if I'd ever met them.

"Yeah, I did, I met Tommy Lee a few times," I told him. Hipster Professor was super impressed. He wanted to know more. More names. More stories. More dirt.

"Wow, it's all such a fantastic thing that I couldn't possibly explain it in just a few minutes," I said. I tried to deflect him from digging any deeper. "It was just a really, really fun time in my life and I was really lucky."

While I wished I could explain the whole of it, I knew I could tell him just a very small part of the story, and really only the very best of the good parts. This wasn't a cocktail party.

The things I saw, the things I did. Even some of my closest friends had no clue about my previous life in Los Angeles, or the hurt I felt as a child. But to go any deeper, beyond this polite small talk with my professor, wasn't something I could do in those moments after my presentation while standing in a classroom at UCLA.

Jesus. How could I ever tell this story? What Mötley Crüe had meant to me? How seeing Guns N' Roses changed my life? How Megadeth had affected me? How I grew up loving KISS, hoping Gene Simmons was my father? My affection for Lemmy? The real synchronicity of all the circumstances, and the experiences I had as a younger person in Los Angeles on the heavy metal scene, and how I survived—how could I begin to explain any of it?

How could I explain my transformation from there, to here?

I was still trying to figure it out and explain it to myself, more than a decade later.

Seeing my hesitation, Hipster Professor smiled at me and said in his charming British accent:

"Well, it all sounds like an epic adventure, moving to Los Angeles so young and having these experiences. You're certainly capable, so you'll just have to write a big, juicy book about it all someday, now won't you? I'll look forward to reading it. Congratulations on your master's degree, by the way. You're going to do great work."

19.0

[Hollywood Ending]

And so, I became a librarian, and I finally wrote the book.

It took me a few years of floundering around, and five full years of writing, to get this story out. During the middle of it, I was diagnosed and treated for breast cancer, which made finishing this book all the more important. I'm OK now, I think. I'm extremely grateful.

A lot of magic showed up as I wrote this book, signs, symbols, synchronicities. Even as much as I believe in the woo-woo and supernatural stuff, some of this Book Magic was downright surreal. I'd dream of something, and then it would show up. People appeared right when I needed them to—sources, old friends, friends-of-friends. Meditation and lucid dreaming revealed details that I had pushed aside. I felt guided by spirit the whole way, even when hopelessly stalled. I just knew that I couldn't abandon the story. It felt more important to tell, the older I got.

I worked for the premier heavy metal record label in Los Angeles, during a crucial time and place in history. I was witness to something—something meaningful and magical. My generation—GenX—we have many, many more stories to tell about our music, our journeys, our dreams. Our analog childhoods, our digital adulthoods. We're middle aged, now. We've all had to deal with a lot of shit. And we need to write that shit down. This is my testimony.

That time, the time I write about in this book, felt like a deep reckoning: For the country, for the City of Los Angeles, for the music business. We looked at things differently after AIDS, and after Operation Desert Storm. We looked at things differently after Grunge. We looked at things differently after Rodney King.

I looked at things differently, too. Who I was, who I wanted to be, and what I wanted to stand for. It was my own deep personal reckoning. The first of many, honestly.

***

Just as it did when I was a child, heavy metal and rock still soothe my soul, and this book was written on a steady diet of goodness: Everything from Chris Cornell to Willie Nelson to TOOL, Iron Maiden to the Travelling Wilbury's, U2 to Metallica to CSNY to Boston to Queensrÿche, Johnny Cash to Alice in Chains to Ozzy to Fleetwood Mac, Megadeth, Tom Petty, Heart, Guns N' Roses, Metallica. And of course, plenty of Mötley Crüe.

Ahh, Nikki Sixx. More than any other artist, he was my spirit animal—rags to riches, a rebellious, disadvantaged kid who followed his dreams to Los Angeles and made it big. He wrote great songs, had great vision, and lived a big huge life. He's a survivor. I recognized my kind. Underneath all of it, I knew there was a kid just like me, with abandonment issues and a big, fat daddy wound. He gave voice to my anger. He gave me courage in the world. To live life on my own terms. To take chances. I gambled it all, and I ended up happy. Not destitute. Not a statistic. Not dead.

I went to Los Angeles the first time looking for Nikki Sixx, and I never did quite find him.

I went to Los Angeles the second time and found something better—I found myself.

I found my future. I found my husband and family. I found my purpose.

I found my life.

I want to thank everyone along the way who was part of this story. Brian Slagel—it was such an honor to work for you. Tracy & Joey Vera—I love you guys, and thank you. Kathy Reble.—my dearest friend and high school partner in crime, thank you for the years of fun and the source material from all the letters and stories I wrote that you saved in your mom's basement. Aaron Pauley—thank you for the music and the good lovin' and all the support; Starlet Castle, Frank Chackler, Julie Foley Ellefson, Sam Iannarino, Sean Lewis, Robin Walker, Anne Fields, Doreen Fisher, Errol Gerson, Matt Avery, Ray Alder, Rick Sales, John Bush, Dave Mustaine, Bill Berrol, and Ron Laffitte—I learned important lessons from each of you along the way. Thanks to Evan Baisden, Julia Kogan, Alicia Maxwell, Jim Miller, Bill Metoyer, Layna McCallister, Julie Ruzicka, Ali Blau, and many others who offered their time, memories, clarifications and general cheerleading. And my dear old friend Kevin - thank you for everything, for being so enthusiastic, for showing up right when I needed you. I appreciate it more than you know.

Thank you to Lauren Sapala for being a kind and sympathetic ear—I could not have written this without your gentle support. And to my loving birthday-twin soul sister, Karen Pimental, thank you for the years of friendship and laughter.

Dr. Jonathan Furner at UCLA: Thank you for stating the obvious.

Thank you, Correne Henderson and family, for allowing me to share David's story a bit. I will never forget him. RIP, my friend.

Mario, Jr. passed away years ago, and I never had a chance to thank him or the Maglieri family for their hospitality during my first few months in Los Angeles. They were very kind to me. Thank you.

My old roommate and close friend, Aaron "Dale" Blevins, passed away as well, before I could reconnect with him, which makes me sad beyond words. I'll always miss him.

So many strangers rallied me as I struggled through the writing. To the wonderful people I've met through Facebook or Instagram—including Tom Trakas, Katherine Turman, Bryan Reesman, and to all of my current friends and coworkers at the Tempe Public Library—thank you for your support and for cheering me on. You made the process less lonely. And to Lonn Friend, your encouragement, generosity, and friendship has been pure magic to me. Thank you, Pilgrim.

***

My mom moved to Arizona after she retired, and became a full-time professional grandma. She and my step-dad, Dick are still married, and have provided so much support to me and my little family. They are adored by their grandchildren. It's come full circle in some ways—she wasn't around for a lot of my childhood, but she is here for my kids now, which seems like the greater reward. She raised me with a lot of love and independence, and I would not be who I am without her example of fearlessness and hard work. Special thanks to my step-dad for taking care of my mom all these years. I love you both.

My dad, Mike, passed away in 2012 at the age of 62 after his fourth divorce, having a mental breakdown and relapsing into alcohol after 18 years of sobriety. Vietnam killed him, 40+ years after he served. In many ways, I am lucky that I wasn't raised with my dad. His presence in my life surely would have been worse for me than his absence was. Still, I missed him my whole life. It affected me in many ways, for many years, and the truth is—I'll always miss him. See you in the woods, Dad. I love you.

My husband, Jim, deserves special mention and accolades. He's the man that never left me wondering. As of this writing, we've been together for 26 years. He's had more faith in me than I've ever had in myself. A long-term marriage takes a good amount of kindness and a lot of humor. It also takes a deep understanding, a knowing. And he knew. He's always known. He believed in me, he believed in us, he believed in marriage, he believed I could go to college and to graduate school, he believed I'd be a good mom, he believed I could beat breast cancer, and he believed that I could write this book. He knew.

This book is dedicated to my mom, Mary Ann, to my husband Jim, and to our children, Olivia and James. All of you have sacrificed in order for me to write this story. Thank you.

This book is also dedicated to all the Metalheads, misfits, bookworms, empaths, artists, dreamers, and writers who have ever struggled in this world. Find your tribes, follow your dreams, speak your truths, and tell your stories.

I'm with you.

THE END

About the author:

When she's not writing, Anna-Marie O'Brien is a mom, a wife, and a children's librarian. She has an affinity for the supernatural, alternative history, astrology and tarot, and a deep love for all things medieval. She's a little OCD+ADD+ESP with a good dash of rebelliousness thrown in. All fueled by coffee and rock n' roll.

Anna-Marie has an undergraduate degree in medieval history from Arizona State University, and an MLIS from UCLA. She's been a public librarian since 2003.

She lives in Arizona with her husband and children.

For updates and more information please visit:
www.annamarieobrien.com

Follow on Instagram at @metalheadlibrarian.

Facebook at @metalheadlibrarian

Twitter @annamarieobrien

www.ingramcontent.com/pod-product-compliance
Lightning Source LLC
Chambersburg PA
CBHW020351080526
44584CB00014B/974